LARRY BURKETT

BUSINESS BY THE BOOK

THE COMPLETE GUIDE OF BIBLICAL PRINCIPLES FOR THE WORKPLACE

A JANET THOMA BOOK

THOMAS NELSON PUBLISHERS
Nashville

A Division of Thomas Nelson, Inc.
www.ThomasNelson.com

Published in Nashville, Tennessee, by Thomas Nelson, Inc.

Edited by Adeline Griffith, Christian Financial Concepts.

Unless otherwise noted, Scripture is taken from the NEW AMERICAN STAN-DARD BIBLE ®, © Copyright The Lockman Foundation 1960, 1962, 1963, 1968, 1971, 1972, 1973, 1975, 1977. Used by permission.

Scripture quotations noted TLB are taken from THE LIVING BIBLE, copyright 1971 by Tyndale House Publishers, Wheaton, IL. Used by permission.

Library of Congress Cataloging-in-Publication Data

Burkett, Larry
    Business by the book : the complete guide of Biblical principles for the work-place / Larry Burkett. — An updated ed. of the bestselling classic.
        p.   cm.
    ISBN 0-7852-7141-4 (pb)
    1. Business ethics. 2. Business—Religious aspects—Christianity. I. Title.
HF5387.B855   1998   97-43793
658.4—dc21   CIP

Printed in the United States of America.
35 PHX 05 04 03

CONTENTS

PART 3
YOUR BUSINESS AND YOUR LIFE

Introduction

There never has been a time in recent history when such emphasis has been focused on business ethics and employee empowerment within the business community. Major U.S. businesses are spending megamillions of dollars for consultants to teach their managers how to better interact with their employees. Stiff foreign competition demands more production per work hour, and it recently has been rediscovered that happy employees are more productive.

When Edwards Deming went to Japan in the 1940s to teach modern industrial management techniques to the Japanese, he focused in large part on ethical management and employee involvement. These weren't new ideas in 1947; in fact, they had been taught in virtually all of the good business management schools through the early part of the twentieth century.

But America's prosperity and unique monopolistic position after Europe was devastated during World War I allowed American businesspeople to ignore the very principles that had made them great. Our business culture evolved into an elitist management style in which nonmanagement employees were on one tier (socially) and management on another, higher tier.

This system of "us versus them" fueled the union fires that eventually led to frequent strikes, higher overhead, and declining quality and productivity. By the late sixties, the door had been opened to more efficient competition; through which the Japanese and Europeans eagerly stepped. The Japanese in particular had adopted and applied what Dr. Deming had taught them.

By the late seventies American businesses were sending management teams to study Japanese management techniques in order to help recapture some of the market share we had lost. In the adage that "everything that goes around comes around," the cycle was being completed.

In this book you will learn the ageless principles that are the heart and blood of all successful businesses in America, Japan, and all the world.

Business by the Book is a step-by-step presentation of how businesses should be run according to the Creator of all management rules:

God. In the short run, you can violate these rules and continue to operate, but in the long run, profits will suffer as morale declines.

Decisions like hiring, firing, paying, and promotions will all be discussed from the perspective of what God's Word says. This isn't a book for the timid, Sunday-only Christians. God makes it clear that He wants Christians who are willing to follow the straight path, not those seeking the path of least resistance. If you're willing to follow God's Word, it lays out the straight and narrow.

We are instructed, *"Trust in the Lord with all your heart, and do not lean on your own understanding"* (Proverbs 3:5). The purpose of *Business by the Book* is to help you to trust in the Lord in your business life.

I want to thank Lee Ellis for his help with the information on leadership styles. Lee, the person most responsible for creating Life Pathways™, heads that department for CFC. He is an author, a speaker, a manager, and a friend. To date, Lee and his staff have helped more than 50,000 people with their career directions. Eventually, the testing tools they have developed will revolutionize how Americans choose their careers and how businesses choose their employees. Knowing who you are and knowing how the others around you fit in are critical to developing a successful management team.

Hopefully the tools given in this work will help you to develop a Christ-based management team in your organization.

Larry Burkett

Part 1
BUSINESS BY THE BOOK

1

A Radical Approach to Business Management

Early one morning, Will, the owner of a large manufacturing company, was greeted at his office door by his plant manager, John. Without comment, John was submitting his resignation, effective the following Friday. Will was devastated; for the past five years he had been grooming John to become president of the company.

When he questioned John about his reasons for leaving, John refused to discuss it. Will could not even begin to understand why John was leaving. He was paid more than anyone else in the company, including Will. But it was obvious that nothing was going to change John's mind. He had made the decision to leave.

Will asked John to stay long enough to hire and train a new plant manager, but he flatly refused and reacted angrily when Will asked. Since John had been such a good friend, Will held a company going-away party and gave John a substantial severance bonus.

Three months later, John's reasons for leaving became apparent when he opened his own company and copied Will's best-selling product. In time, John's company grew, and it became one of Will's leading competitors.

Nine years later Will heard that there was a design problem with one of John's new products and that several lawsuits were being filed against John's company. Will had forgiven John years before and regularly prayed for him.

He felt strongly that the Lord wanted him to reach out to John, so he bought one of John's products, tested it, and discovered what the problem was. Will then put his engineers to work to correct the problem. After he made the necessary modifications and tested it, he called John and told him how to solve his problem.

Radical Christianity! That's what some would say. Stupidity! That's what others would say.

Only time will tell how John will respond to this act of unconditional Christ-like love. The results are not Will's responsibility. His responsibility, like ours, is to do what the Lord tells him to do. Remember, God gave His Son to be crucified by the very people He had helped.

By now you may well be thinking, *What school of business did this guy attend?* I can tell you with certainty that the business school I attended taught the bottom line: If it doesn't make money, forget it. But since graduating from business school I have been studying another textbook: It's called the Bible and, compared to most business schools today, it takes a radically different approach—one more concerned with eternity than with profits.

BUSINESS THEN AND NOW

I am not the first person to discover the principles of business taught in God's Word. In America the use of the Bible as a business text goes back hundreds of years.

If you were to review a business school textbook from the nineteenth century, you would find that most companies were privately owned sole proprietorships. Businesses expanded through equity funding or selling an interest in the business, and taxes were so inconsequential as to be an incidental entry on year-end reports.

Business principles differed then too. Honesty, ethics, and moral values were taught in the classrooms of all major business schools. Professors placed strong emphasis on a company's responsibility toward its employees, customers, and creditors.

Why? Because prior to the twentieth century, business courses, and indeed business schools themselves, were based on biblical principles. In fact, it would be erroneous to label them "business schools." In reality, they were biblical schools that were training future business leaders.

Things began to change shortly after the Civil War. The federal government assumed a stronger position in the private sector.

Politicians, pressured by war-rich industrialists, passed laws that strangled competition. Monopolies sprang up in industries such as railroads, steel, oil, and utilities. The leaders of these industries, greedy for even more advantages, began to use their economic influence to promote laws that punished workers who were seeking minimum wages, shorter work weeks, safer working conditions, and child labor prohibitions. Although pretending to pass laws to protect labor, both Congress and the courts consistently used the law to protect business and control the growing organized labor movement.

Prior to World War I, America remained primarily an isolationist nation, although a few businesses managed to create huge profits in developing countries. By the end of that war, in 1918, the United States had become a global economic power—perhaps *the* global economic power. America was on a growth binge. The production of every other nation in the world was compared to that of the United States, and the U.S. dollar became the world's exchange currency.

But clouds hovered on the horizon. The Bible says that we reap what we sow, and America's business leaders were sowing distrust and animosity between management and labor. When circumstances changed and the unions gained political power, management began reaping the destructive harvest of unionism. Hourly workers and management began to develop an adversarial relationship, and government had to assume the role of regulator. That meant business had to pay. For the first time taxes began to take a significant bite out of profits.

Between 1930 and 1950, the government's share of business profits grew to more than 20 percent of gross profits. At the same time labor unions continued to gain strength and Congress began to reverse the labor laws it had passed in the previous several decades. Still, America retained its competitive edge in the world marketplace, primarily because we were the most industrialized and enterprising nation on earth. Even as late as the early sixties the stamp of value was the trademark: "Made in the U.S.A."

After World War II, however, a more ominous cloud began to form: debt. Prior to the Great Depression we had been an equity-funded nation: businesses had expanded primarily by selling a part of the ownership. But the Great Depression had caused a general lack of confidence in the stock market, and after World War II debt surpassed equity in business. Most companies simply found it cheaper and easier to borrow money than to raise it through equity funding. The decades from the fifties to the seventies saw the peak growth of debt in America. Borrowing became the accepted way to fund business expansion.

Not until the mid-seventies did we begin to see the cost of this debt expansion. Too much easy money eventually makes itself known by way of inflation, which is nothing more than a surplus of easy money in the hands of willing buyers who want to spend it. Such spending inevitably bids up the price of goods and services. Credit is like an opiate because it seems to numb the minds of those who use it.

THE BIBLICAL PERSPECTIVE ON GETTING AND SPENDING

I began a personal study on the biblical principles of how to operate a business shortly after becoming a Christian in 1970. The one principle that caught my attention most vividly was that God's people should be debt-free. Unfortunately most Christians weren't, and they didn't want to be. As one Christian friend who owned a car dealership told me, "Debt-free living makes no sense. Listen, I can finance my cars for 6 percent a year and then turn around and make 12 percent profit when I sell them."

My friend made a common error many Christians make. When the logic of what we're doing doesn't match God's Word, we assume it's a misinterpretation of the Word. A few years later, when interest rates climbed to nearly 22 percent, he began to see that God meant us to take Scripture literally. Too much debt makes the business vulnerable to the interest rate swings.

Between 1950 and 1970, the average cost of labor rose by 50 percent and government overhead increased to nearly 40 percent. This opened the way for major foreign competition as prices soared. Starting a new business and making it profitable became harder because capital, the key factor in business start-up, became the most costly overhead item. The combined cost of labor, government overhead, and credit sounded the death knell for many previously all-U.S. industries. Without government support, many of those that remained could not compete and make a profit.

During the next 10 years the cost of labor and government grew another 10 percent. Government became, quite literally, a partner in business. Through countless regulations, government made decisions for business and shared in its profits without doing any of the work. Government told farmers what they could grow, advertisers what they could sell, and schools what they could teach. To oversee this regulation, a massive government structure grew up, with nearly 20 percent of the American people on the government's payroll. Unwittingly, we had allowed a fascist form of government to develop—in the sense that fascism means privately owned but centrally controlled.

By the early 1980s, with interest rates climbing, the burden of debt made many industries structurally unprofitable. That trend has accelerated to the point that, according to one statistic, 60 percent of all American businesses are potentially unprofitable once the interest rates reach 15 percent. Our lack of fiscal discipline and our obsession with quick profits make U.S. industry vulnerable.

For nearly two decades we allowed countries like Japan and Germany to develop unrestrained while increasing the regulatory burden on our own businesses. As a result, we have lost major industries to our foreign competitors.

Japan is an interesting study in business development. At the conclusion of World War II, President Truman appointed General Douglas MacArthur to be the military governor of Japan. Capitalizing on the Japanese respect for authority, General MacArthur was able to establish many basic biblical doctrines as a part of their business ethic. This highly efficient system of labor/management cooperation, combined with a fierce national loyalty, propelled the Japanese beyond their teacher.

Unfortunately, General MacArthur established the correct principles but failed to share their source: the Lord. It remains to be seen whether unrestrained capitalism without the balancing influence of Christianity will succeed long term. Eventually, I fear, human nature will prevail.

U.S. industry has rebounded in the nineties—courtesy of Japan's financial collapse. The Japanese have also discovered that "everything that goes around comes around."

It's a shame that, instead of taking the relative prosperity of the nineties as an opportunity to pay down debt, American businesses, consumers, and their government have actually increased their borrowing. Once the economy cycles down again, as it inevitably always does, bankruptcies will set new records.

It's an interesting paradox that we taught the Japanese in the forties and fifties. They taught us in the eighties, and neither of us learned the real secret of success: biblical truth.

But God's principles of business are not offered "cafeteria style." In other words, you can't simply pick and choose those you like and ignore those you don't. God's Word sets up a whole structure by which a business is to operate: a foundation. You can build a business (or a house) without a sound foundation. But when the wind blows and the waves come, it will collapse. God's Word is the Rock upon which a business must be built.

Do the biblical principles of business work? Without question they do—over the long run. If you're looking just for quick profits, don't choose God's way; but, if you desire long-term growth and stability, God's way is the only way. As Jesus said in Matthew 7:24–25, *"Therefore everyone who hears these words of Mine, and acts upon them, may be compared to a wise man, who built his house upon the rock. And the rain descended, and the floods came, and the winds blew, and burst against that house; and yet it did not fall, for it had been founded upon the rock."*

I have seen these principles work in one-person businesses doing $50,000 a year gross volume and in 12,000-employee businesses making $800 million a year.

Our organization has grown from a budget of $40,000 a year in 1976 to more than *$12 million a year*—all without the use of debt. Even that figure is misleading, because we broadcast on 1,100 radio outlets daily—an outreach that would normally require an additional $10 to $12 million a year but costs us only a fraction of that. We have more than 15,000 counselors nationwide and receive nearly 100,000 telephone calls per month.

All of this is to say, God is looking for a few good men and women whom He can strongly support (see 2 Chronicles 16:9). Our great advantage today is that He doesn't have a lot of talent to work with right now, so if we are willing to be used God is willing to use us.

In the years that we have been teaching these principles to business owners and managers throughout the country, hundreds of businesses have been rejuvenated and thousands of lives have been changed. You'll read some of these stories as we discuss the different biblical principles. Although the names have been changed, the people are real.

THE OUTLOOK TODAY

What kind of an economic environment does a Christian business owner or manager face today? Certainly not a favorable one.

Anyone from past generations, looking at our economy today, would quickly assess that we have some potentially catastrophic financial problems facing us. When the success of an economy is determined by a 3 percent shift in interest rates at any given time, that economy is in deep trouble.

As the statistics demonstrate, the federal government is the catalyst behind most of our current debt. The United States government now owes nearly *$6 trillion and growing*. Most Americans work the first five months of each year just to pay their taxes, and it still isn't enough. In spite of taking in more than $1.5 trillion a year, the government must borrow another $150 billion each year—just about the interest on the debt. Basically, we borrow to pay the interest on what we have already borrowed.

God's Word is never wrong, and I believe this is a fulfillment of two principles the Lord gave His people nearly 3,000 years ago. He promised that if the people who were called by His name would obey His statutes and commandments, *"All the peoples of the earth shall see that you are called by the name of the Lord; and they shall be afraid of you. And the Lord will make you abound in prosperity, in the offspring of your body and in the offspring of your beast and in the produce of your ground, in the land which the Lord swore to your fathers to give you. The Lord will open for you His good storehouse, the heavens, to give rain to your land in its season and to bless all the work of your hand; and you shall lend to many nations, but you shall not borrow"* (Deuteronomy 28:10–12).

But He also warned that if His statutes and commandments were ignored, *"A people whom you do not know shall eat up the produce of your ground and all your labors, and you shall never be anything but oppressed and crushed continually. . . . The alien who is among you shall rise above you higher and higher, but you shall go down lower and lower"* (Deuteronomy 28:33, 43).

In other words, the foreigner would become the lender and they would become debtors. That is exactly where our nation is today. Nearly 35 percent of our total debt is now held by foreign lenders.

Is there hope? Can the cycle be reversed? Without a doubt, but only if God's people will turn to His way and be willing to be counted in His camp, without compromise. Throughout the remainder of this book I will try to outline God's plan for businesses. Some of you will be owners; others will be managers and employees.

Each of us at every level must be willing to live by the statutes and commandments of our Lord to make a difference. The bottom line is not "Are we able to make a difference?" It is "Are we *willing* to make a difference?"

2

Basic Biblical Minimums

Whenever most people think about the basic minimums of Christianity, they generally think of the Ten Commandments. Indeed, these are the minimums that God said would separate His people from those around them. In the business environment, the same commandments obviously apply, but there are some other minimums that set apart God's followers from others in the business world.

These are not lofty, obscure goals for us to fantasize about; they are outside indicators of whether we are serious about dedicating our businesses to the Lord. I myself find that applying these minimums is a continual challenge. They are particularly difficult to follow when those we encounter in business— even our peers—rarely attempt to do the same. Yet God's best is to do unto others as we want them to do unto us, not to do unto others as they do unto us.

SIX BASIC BUSINESS MINIMUMS

1. Reflect Christ in Your Business Practices

Let me say up front that I have no doubt that if you determine to adopt this one principle in your business it will cost you money. We live in a society that thrives on deception and tricky contracts. Anyone operating in a manner that glorifies Christ will be faced with many opportunities to suffer.

Take for example the practice of total honesty. Proverbs 3:32 says, *"For the crooked man is an abomination to the Lord; but He is intimate with the upright."* And Proverbs 4:24 says, *"Put away from you a deceitful mouth, and put devious lips far from you."* Both of these verses imply the same basic principle: Honesty is rewarded and dishonesty punished. If the issue were just to steal or not steal, most of God's people would have no problem in obeying. But in real-life situations, that principle gets a little sticky.

Sam owned a large health-care organization with more than 3,000 employees. During a routine check of Medicare billings, it was discovered that one of the traveling nurses had apparently delivered to a patient services that were not authorized for reimbursement by Medicare. Sam requested that an audit be done of all patient billings to Medicare for the past three years.

During the course of that process, it was discovered that Medicare had been billed for and had paid almost $300,000 worth of these unauthorized services. This was an internal audit and no one knew anything about it except my friend and the person who was conducting the audit. Without pausing to consider the economic impact it might have, Sam issued a credit memo to Medicare to remove the unjustified $300,000 that was received. Sam understood well that integrity was not for sale—not at $300,000 or $300 million. He believed the admonition, *"He who is faithful in a very little thing is faithful also in much; and he who is unrighteous in a very little thing is unrighteous also in much"* (Luke 16:10).

2. Be Accountable

Perhaps nothing in our society is more needed for those in positions of authority than accountability. Too often those with authority are able (and willing) to surround themselves with people who support their decisions without question. This may seem like an asset initially, but in the long run it becomes a liability. Why? Because without a system of checks and balances, anyone will eventually drift off course. If you don't believe this, just try to find an example of anyone who operated without accountability and stayed on his or her original course.

Even David, the king that God Himself chose, drifted off course when he listened to his generals, who told him he was too valuable to be risking his life in battle. Completely forgetting that God had brought him through many battles without difficulty, David believed their accolades. (Accolades are easy to believe when you want to hear them!) He stayed in town while his army fought. The result? That infamous episode with Bathsheba, which ultimately created strife within his household.

Many businesspeople think they are accountable because they operate with a board of directors or hold regular staff meetings. I have attended enough board meetings to know that most boards under the direction of a strong leader are simply rubber stamps. And only a rare staff member will confront the boss's directives once he or she has laid out a course, even if that course is in total contrast to the original goals and objectives of the company.

So what is the answer? I believe God's Word offers several. One is to seek the counsel of your spouse. This is important for any married person in a leadership position. Since more men run businesses than women, I'll direct my comments to them, but the principles apply equally to women in business.

Most husbands virtually ignore the counsel of their wives when it comes to making business decisions. And yet God's Word clearly says that He made husband and wife to become one person: *"For this cause a man shall leave his father and his mother, and shall cleave to his wife; and they shall become one flesh"* (Genesis 2:24). Is this relationship limited to a nonbusiness relationship only? If so, then find the reference in God's Word!

A valid argument can be made that often the wife doesn't know anything about the business. The solution is to start sharing the major decisions so that she will be familiar with the business when the need arises. Unfortunately, sometimes a wife doesn't want to know anything about the business. I would answer, "That isn't an option according to God's Word. When a wife takes on the responsibilities of a helpmate, she must be willing to learn enough to help."

I have been amazed at some of the insights wives bring to a discussion of subjects they supposedly know little or nothing about. For example, I was counseling with a Christian fabric manufacturer who was in a real quandary about selling his business. The whole industry was facing severe competition from the Chinese, and it appeared certain that many of the major manufacturers would move their operations to China or Mexico to reduce their overhead. This man's wife, who had been meeting with us at my insistence, stated during one meeting that she didn't think he should sell.

"Why not?" he snapped, his body language clearly indicating that he didn't value her opinion in business matters very highly. At first she retreated into her submissive-wife role and didn't say anything further.

"Come on, Jackie," I urged her, "if you have something to add, don't be bullied into silence. That's not meek; it's weak," I said. The husband sat in glaring silence, refusing to meet my eyes.

"Well," she said, "I just believe that God gave us this business and we have a responsibility to our employees." Glancing cautiously in her husband's direction, she continued, "If we don't stick it out, probably nobody will. I believe we should be able to compete with the Chinese. Maybe we can find a product that they can't make as well as we can."

"What do you mean?" I asked, watching as a shocked look spread across her husband's face.

"Maybe we should concentrate on developing our own line of denims," she suggested, really getting enthusiastic now. "I've noticed that the demand is growing in Europe for blue jeans and other such products. Maybe we can get the government to sponsor our export of these products, like they sponsor food products?"

I told her I thought the idea had some merit.

Her husband also perked up a little and said he had had a similar idea but had never explored it. Then his countenance fell again.

"What's wrong?" I asked.

"We don't have the capital to make the changeover or to survive until a good product can be found," he replied dejectedly. "And no banker is going to advance the money for such a speculative idea."

"Any ideas?" I asked his wife.

"Yes," she said excitedly. "I've been thinking about it, and I'll bet we could start an employees' cooperative and sell them an interest in the company. After all, it's their jobs that are on the line. Maybe we could sell out the company and the brand names we own and live comfortably for the rest of our lives, but they'll be out of work."

"You know, that's a possibility I hadn't considered before," Jackie's husband mused. "It's just possible that the employees might be willing to put up the money in return for a piece of the company. But if we do it and it fails, we'll have severely diluted our ownership."

"We started with nothing 20 years ago," Jackie responded gently. "I guess we could start the same way again if we had to. Besides, I'd rather try and fail than to fold our tents and fade away. There just aren't enough companies seeking to serve Christ in the garment industry. We can't afford to let this one go."

"Where in the world did you learn about the fabric business?" the husband asked. "And where did you hear about employee buyouts?"

Jackie replied, with just the slightest trace of a smile on her face, "You forget I was your only help when we began. And just because I stayed home to raise our children, it doesn't mean I let my brain atrophy."

Jackie and her husband did sell nearly half of the business to their employees and developed a thriving export business to the Eastern-bloc countries. They have since retired, and now they spend several months each year setting up jointly owned dealerships with Christians from the former Communist countries. This latest venture has been a tool for reaching a previously unreachable group of people.

Set up an accountability group. A businessperson can also set up an impartial group of Christian advisers. I know that it may be difficult in many areas of the country to find Christians who will agree to serve in this capacity. An alternative is to link up with one or two others in similar businesses in other parts of the country and communicate on major decisions by phone, fax, or e-mail.

Everyone needs to be accountable. I have helped to set up several accountability groups and would like to share some of the results that have come out of these sessions. The key phrase is *accountability* to other like-minded men or women. I recall one group of men who decided to hold each other accountable for their relationships with other people, including their own wives. For most businessmen, Christian or otherwise, it would be a sobering experience to be held accountable for how they treat their wives and families.

Essentially, it's easier to fake it with other people than it is with your family. And to be held accountable for those relationships is often very taxing. The question that most of us have to ask is, "What kind of a testimony would my spouse give about our relationship if she were speaking to my business group?" And, another question would be, "Am I working on correcting that relationship?"

Each of us has to ask penetrating questions about our relationships with other people, particularly our creditors. Are the bills being paid on time? Do employees consider us to be the kind of Christians we present ourselves to be? Do our customers see us truly practice what the apostle Paul told us to do in Philippians 2:15: Consider other people as more important than ourselves?

The fundamental questions are, "Would we feel comfortable if Jesus came into our business today? And are day-to-day decisions based upon the Word of God, or are they based more on what the world's system allows or does not allow?"

In this particular accountability group I led there were 11 men, and we met once a month from 9:00 in the morning until 7:00 at night. We had refreshments in the morning and we had lunch and dinner together. In all honesty, this group did not hold back on any comments. We rotated each month to a different location, meeting at each other's businesses.

I remember one occasion when we met at the manufacturing plant of one of the businessmen and looked over his financial statements. He explained how he was conducting business, and the group started to examine his relationship with other people around him: his customers, his family, and especially his spouse. They found that in his relationship with his customers that, as was typical with his particular industry, he promised anything it took to get the job or to get the contract, and then seldom, if ever, delivered on time. In fact, it was an accepted practice in his construction industry.

Typically, the customers would order several months before they needed his product, because they knew that he was going to lie to them about the delivery date, and they had to give themselves plenty of slack. The accountability group called him to task about this. His rationalization was very simple: "Well, that's just the way it operates in this kind of an industry, and that's the way we've always done business."

Immediately the other members of the group pointed out that that is not the way Jesus wants a Christian to operate. We encouraged this man to go to his customers and see if he could resolve the conflicts he was having with them. Obviously, most of the differences were caused by late deliveries, missed schedules, and false promises. As a group we urged him to be honest with his customers, ask them to be honest with him about what their true needs were, and begin the scheduling process that would allow on-time delivery.

Well, in all honesty, he was kind of taken back, because he had never operated that way in his entire business life. In this particular case, it took this Christian businessman several months to make the transition. But eventually he did, and he became the standard in his industry. Because once one manufacturer committed himself to delivering the product on time, the others were forced to do the same thing. Later, this Christian businessman was able to lead his own purchasing agent to the Lord, primarily as a result of his personal witness to the customers.

Another one of the men involved in this accountability group had a receptionist who dressed rather immodestly from time to time. He wasn't sure how to handle this situation. He was very embarrassed by it, and he knew it needed to be corrected. But he really didn't want to have to confront what could be termed a sexual harassment situation.

The group suggested that he ask his wife to come in, look at the situation herself, and then let her determine the best course of action. He decided to do as the group had suggested, and the next time we met he filled us in what had happened. His wife came in, assessed the situation, and then decided that she would deal with it herself.

This man's wife decided that her plan would not be to just confront the young receptionist and tell her, "If you don't stop wearing those immodest clothes, we're going to fire you." And she would not say, "Go home and cover yourself up." Instead, she would honestly take an interest in this young woman and care about her as a person—not try to beat her over the head with a Bible but really try to change the motivation that was causing the action.

Unfortunately, all too often today, particularly with business owners and their wives, we're not willing to do that, because it requires a humbling of self. It requires that we care more about other people than we do ourselves, because it's simply easier to tell them, "Do it, or don't come back to work."

Well, the long and short of this story is that within a few weeks, this young woman came to realize that what she was doing was embarrassing, both to herself and to her employer, and she began to dress more modestly. This business owner's wife involved her in her Bible study and, eventually, through that study with other women, this young woman came to know the Lord and has become a dynamic Christian.

As a result of a simple accountability group in which Christian businessmen were willing to make themselves vulnerable, two souls were brought into the kingdom of God. And during the subsequent years, hundreds more have been led to the Lord as a result of the lives of these Christian businesspeople. So accountability is a very important principle.

3. Provide a Quality Product at a Fair Price

The value of the products and services a company offers says more to the public about the real character of the company and its people than perhaps any other aspect of the company's life. *Value* can be defined as the effective return on a purchase. Low initial cost does not necessarily represent value. But when a Christian business accepts the standard for service and products that the Bible prescribes, the end result will be the best product at the best possible price.

I once read an article about a doctor who stopped charging fees and went to a set-your-own-fee policy. When a patient came in for a visit, the receptionist would give the person information on the payment policy, as well as an easily understood analysis of the costs of office overhead and insurance. Then the patient was asked to pay what he or she thought was fair.

To be sure, some patients paid less than their fair share because they thought this doctor was a sucker. But the doctor's overall income increased by approximately 10 percent after he switched from the fixed-fee structure. Apparently his patients felt they were receiving value for his services.

Another great example of this principle is Chick-fil-A, Inc., headquartered in Atlanta. This company's Christian leadership takes pride in the quality of their products. They are privately owned and internally financed, and yet they are one of the fastest growing fast-food chains in the United States.

Chick-fil-A closes its stores on Sunday, in contrast to the other fast-food businesses located in the same shopping malls, and they pay their employees well (even providing college scholarships). So how do they survive and even contrive to grow? They make a quality product at a fair price. Their customers are their best advertisement. The management knows that once chicken lovers taste the product, they will return with their friends.

The norm in our society today seems to be: Deliver the least possible at the highest price imaginable. But this works only during good times, when little or no competition exists. For Christians to follow the philosophy of providing high quality at fair prices says a lot about their spiritual commitment. When you truly love others more than yourself, you want them to get the best deal possible. In the process, you will also prosper.

4. Honor Your Creditors

Business creditors include those who have loaned you merchandise as well as those who have loaned you money. Too often in our modern business environment, suppliers are treated like a no-interest source of operating capital. When business is slow, it is considered normal to delay paying suppliers to offset the reduced cash flow.

If the situation is beyond your control and you can't pay on time, that's one thing. But if you are simply choosing a cheaper way to operate, you are violating a biblical principle: *"Do not withhold good from those to whom it is due, when it is in your power to do it. Do not say to your neighbor, 'Go, and come back, and tomorrow I will give it,' when you have it with you"* (Proverbs 3:27–28). That makes it pretty clear, doesn't it?

A Christian who continues to order materials and other supplies when there are already past-due bills is being deceitful. That may sound harsh, but just place yourself in the supplier's position. Would you want someone ordering your materials under an implied promise to pay when he or she knows that the business is losing money? Or would you want a customer to skip paying you, rather than borrowing the money at interest to pay for the needed materials?

I was teaching a seminar to a group of businesspeople, and I mentioned in passing that to delay paying suppliers because customers were slow in paying their bills was wrong. One of the participants stopped me and said, "Do you mean that if I don't pay my bills because I'm not getting paid it's a sin?"

"No, that's not what I mean," I replied. "It's only a sin if you know it's wrong and still persist in doing it."

"But what if paying all my bills would cause me to lose the business?" he asked, sounding very perturbed.

I used the standard response I always use in similar situations: "Are we discussing a real situation or a hypothetical one?"

"What do you mean?" he asked. I could see he was beginning to get the drift of what I was saying.

"Well, if paying your suppliers would really cost you your business when it might otherwise survive, I would suggest contacting the suppliers and allowing them to have a part in the decision. I'm sure most of them would be willing to work with you, rather than see the business fail."

"Well, it wouldn't really cause my business to fail," he admitted reluctantly. Then he added, "But it might for someone else."

"True," I agreed, "and if that's the case, then that person would need to face the issue at that time. God doesn't hold us responsible for what we can't do—only for what we can. But if the decision is purely economic—in other words, it's simply cheaper to finance the cash flow by owing a supplier than owing the bank—then it's wrong."

The businessman commented, "You have convinced me that I should borrow the funds and pay my suppliers what is due. My company can easily absorb the interest payments. I just delayed payment because my accountant encouraged me to ride the *float*" (a term for noninterest-bearing accounts).

Integrity is a rare commodity in our generation, especially when other people's money is concerned. A Christian who wants to have a credible witness needs to meet at least this minimum standard.

One Christmas I received a card from the chairman of one of the largest paper companies in America. It simply said, "Thank you for the integrity you have shown in paying your bills to our company."

I thought that was remarkable because our total purchases for the year were only a few thousand dollars—certainly only a fraction of their total sales. So I decided to call the chairman to ask why he wrote the note.

After a few tries I reached him and asked, "Why did you bother to write me the note?"

His reply speaks loads about business in America today. He said, "Your ministry is one of the few Christian organizations we deal with that pays its bills on time—every time. I'm a Christian also, but the delinquencies among churches and other ministries have become a source of consternation at some of our directors' meetings."

Think about it! The head of a major company being subjected to ridicule from his peers for the failure of Christian-run organizations to pay their bills on time! Is it any wonder that many people avoid doing business with Christians?

5. Treat Your Employees Fairly

Fairness is both a responsibility and an opportunity. Employers who practice fairness are able to share Christ with their employees because they "practice what they preach," as the old saying goes. To be sure, some employees will take offense against managers or employers, no matter what they do. But that's their problem. Those in positions of authority need to be concerned only with their own actions.

Fairness is usually related to issues of pay and benefits in the work environment, but that is not the total picture. Fairness also involves attitudes and relationships. For example, if the tendency is for managers to look down (socially or intellectually) on lower-strata workers, that attitude will be transmitted and received. Once the employees recognize that a social barrier has been erected, any effort to evangelize usually will be rejected.

The first step in establishing the principle of fairness is to recognize that all people are important, regardless of income or education. I first recognized this principle while in the Air Force. The barriers between the enlisted and commissioned personnel were real and absolute. The armed services deliberately create this separation in an attempt to make the ruling group (officers) seem infallible. They perceive this as a necessary ingredient in issuing life-and-death orders.

Unfortunately, that same mentality has been carried over into civilian business relationships. Perhaps this is a reflection of the master/slave mentality, even though we abandoned the actual practice of slavery more than 100 years ago. But Jesus did not establish any such artificial barriers between Himself and His disciples; nor did He ever allow them to do so between themselves and the people they desired to reach.

If you find that you can't give the same honor and regard to the lowest-ranked employee in your business, you need to stop right here and resolve this issue with the Lord. The second chapter of James covers this issue thoroughly, summing it up in one verse: *"But if you show partiality, you are committing sin and are convicted by the law as transgressors"* (James 2:9).

I saw a practical application of this principle as a young Christian. Our pastor was being reviewed for a salary increase. The board of deacons presented to the entire church its recommendation of an increase of several thousand dollars a year for the pastor, and the church body unanimously approved the increase. Then the board presented its recommendation for the custodian's salary, which was several thousand dollars a year less than the pastor's.

The pastor stopped the meeting and asked, "Why are we willing to pay me more than the janitor when he has more children and fewer benefits?"

The chairman of the deacon board was taken back by the question. The reason was obvious, although unspoken: You don't pay janitors what you pay senior pastors. That's called the Indian-chief principle. The chairman said, "Pastor, we can't afford that much of a pay increase."

"Then give him part of my increase," the pastor suggested. "I really don't need more money, and I'm sure he does."

The meeting ended that evening without any resolution. Eventually, however, the deacon board did recommend giving the custodian a substantial raise (though still not as much as the pastor's salary). And the events of that evening had a profound effect on the attitudes of the entire congregation. I was certainly challenged to examine everything I do on the basis of God's Word, not what is normal practice.

6. Treat Your Customers Fairly

If you truly want to be a faithful witness for the Lord, then one of your greatest opportunities will be to share with those closest to you. In business, this applies to your creditors, who will listen because you pay your bills on time and treat them fairly. It applies to your employees, who will listen because you treat them with honor and pay them fairly (we will discuss fair pay in Chapter 14). And it certainly applies to your customers, who will take you seriously because you give them a good product at a fair price and stand behind your word.

I saw this principle applied in a practical way in my own life several years ago when I was in the electronics business. I was calling on a potential customer for one of our products, a computerized circuit tester. This particular product was expensive for that time (about $25,000) but performed a function that would save a qualified user several times that amount each year.

However, this potential customer didn't seem to have a need for a $25,000 circuit tester. It was clear that he was a test equipment buff who wanted to own every new piece of test equipment made. He had already talked himself into buying the product even before I had finished explaining what it would do. Without a doubt our tester would have helped his operation, but he would not have been able to recover its cost in his application.

We needed the sale at the time, and he was a hot prospect. But even as I lifted the contract from my briefcase, I could hear the words of the apostle Paul ringing in my ears: *"Do nothing from selfishness or empty conceit, but with humility of mind let each of you regard one another as more important than himself"* (Philippians 2:3). I stopped and said, "I can't sell this equipment to you."

"Why not?" he asked with some indignation. "I can afford it. Do you need some money up front?"

"No," I replied, "the money is not the problem. It's just that I know you won't be able to recover the cost with your volume of work.

I think you'll regret it later, and I will feel like I've dumped our equipment on you."

His expression changed from indignation to surprise. Then he smiled and said that he appreciated my honesty but that he had already assessed the same thing. He planned to use the equipment to start a new line of business: repairing equipment for other small companies similar to his. At that point I readily agreed that our equipment would be perfectly suited for that function, and we closed the deal.

I had several opportunities to meet with this businessman over the next few years, and we became good friends. Later he became one of our investors and the source of a lot of business. I truly believe the process began when I felt the conviction to put his needs first and treat him fairly.

That $25,000 has been spent, and the equipment I sold him has long since worn out, but the one thing that still survives is our mutual love for the Lord. That sale will last for an eternity.

3

Business Bondage

I have never been in bondage to debt personally, even as a non-Christian. My temperament is such that I hate paying interest, so even if I borrowed money in business I always paid it back as quickly as possible. But I have been in financial bondage of a different sort.

I came from a poor background and from the start of my working career was driven by the need to succeed. As a result I dedicated virtually every waking hour to succeeding. I wasn't interested in the money as much as I was in the security it represented. I wasn't wasting money on foolish purchases, and I wasn't consumed by ego or pride but, nevertheless, I was in bondage. My pursuit of security robbed me of time with my family and, later, time with God.

Business bondage comes in many forms, from preoccupation with debt-related problems to overdedication to work. Perhaps it can be defined best as "anything that interferes with your relationship to God or your family and is out of balance according to God's Word."

Jesus Christ was very specific when He said, *"No servant can serve two masters; for either he will hate the one, and love the other, or else he will hold to one, and despise the other. You cannot serve God and mammon"* (Luke 16:13). If we serve a business, we cannot serve God. The sad truth is, I have yet to meet a successful businessperson who on his or her deathbed said, "I wish I had spent more time at work and had made just a little more money."

Bondage to anything is characterized by a lack of balance. Too much of anything (even good stuff) can wreck your life.

There was a great commercial in the eighties that demonstrated this principle very well. The first scene was that of a young man and a small boy talking. The boy asked if his father could take a little time off to go fishing.

The man looked up from his desk, piled with work, and said, "I really would like to, Son, but we just opened our new plant, and I just can't take the time off right now."

The next scene was of a teenage boy asking his father to take a little time off so they could go fishing together.

The man replied, "I would really like to, Son, but we just opened a new plant in Europe and I have to be there. But I promise I'll take some time off when I get back."

The last scene is of an older man asking a much younger man, "Son, do you think you could take a little time off to go fishing with me? Since your mom died it sure has been lonely around here."

"I wish I could, Dad, but you know we just opened the new plant in Japan and I just have to be there. But I promise I'll take some time off when I get back."

This father was in business bondage from the first conversation with his young son. Bondage is not limited just to those who find themselves unable to pay their bills; it is anything that robs you of your relationships with others or with the Lord.

Often I have had older people come up to me after a conference and say, "If only I had heard this 40 years ago, I would have lived my life differently." Perhaps so, but perhaps not. It's always easy to look back and see the mistakes. How much better it would be if we would look ahead and avoid mistakes! It's never too late to change bad habits and attitudes, but the sooner we start, the easier it is.

I have often heard Christians profess, "I promise to serve God in any way He chooses," but all too often that resolve breaks down when they sense that God wants them to do something that will cost more than they're prepared to pay.

We're a security conscious generation, and generally we precondition any commitment to follow God with the notion that we need a secure financial future first. We hedge by saying, "God, I'll serve You, *but* . . ." or "God, I'll serve You *when* . . ." or "God, I'll serve You *if.* . . ."

Jesus was confronted with this same rationalization when He was leaving Capernaum. A man wanted to go with Him but said, *"Permit me first to go and bury my father"* (Luke 9:59).

This comment was an obvious response to Jesus' challenge: *"Follow Me."* What is less obvious is that the man's father most likely wasn't dead. According to traditional Hebrew funeral customs, if the father had been dead, the son would certainly have been at home with the family, not alongside the roadway listening to Jesus. The young man was really saying that he needed to remain in his father's house until he received his share of the inheritance.

Jesus was not being callous when He replied, *"Allow the dead to bury their own dead"* (Luke 9:60). He was stating a simple truth that is still valid today: You have the choice to follow the world's way or God's.

If we base our decisions on our own security and comfort, we will have a hard time following the path God lays out. Rarely does God's calling coincide with our own human desires. As the prophet of old said, *"Decide this day whom you shall serve."*

Most Christians are more than content to live their lives surrounded by the trappings of our world, rather than to risk losing them by becoming a radical Christian. A radical Christian (by my definition) is one who will put God first in all decisions, regardless of the cost. In the business world, this means putting God first even when doing so costs you or your business. That is true freedom—spiritual freedom—as opposed to business bondage.

Let me share some observations about the symptoms of this spiritual illness. A symptom is merely the outer manifestation of what's going on inside a person. If one or more of the following describe you, you've caught the disease.

SYMPTOMS OF BUSINESS BONDAGE

Symptom 1: An Air of Superiority

Perhaps nothing epitomizes the sad state of our society more than the egotistical attitudes of many, if not most, self-made businesspeople. No one is self-made. Only the combined efforts of a great many people make anyone a success. And certainly it is the direct result of God's blessings.

I find it interesting that when we are experiencing severe problems (financial, marital, physical) we tend to be humble in spirit and appreciative of the help others provide. But take away the problems and substitute success and most of us will adopt an I-did-it-myself attitude.

Some years ago I met a very successful Christian who asked me to his home for an outreach dinner. He had invited several of the more prominent business and community leaders to his home also. After dinner he shared his testimony about his successes and properly gave the credit to the Lord.

At the time I questioned whether any of the people there would be particularly impressed by his testimony, since many of them had achieved a much higher level of success than he had. I thought to myself, *This dinner would be far more impressive if he had invited some of the poor in this city and presented a plan to share a portion of the riches God had provided to him.* Instead, he had invited a group of his peers to impress them with the fact that God was on his side.

Perhaps that's too harsh a judgment. Yet the principle is revealed clearly in a passage I mentioned earlier: *"But if you show partiality, you are committing sin and are convicted by the law as transgressors"* (James 2:9).

Unfortunately, the phenomenon of self-elevation also appears in Christian circles. Some Christians attempt to elevate themselves by spending time with successful Christians, particularly those who are well-known or in leadership roles, because it implies spirituality by association.

I sometimes find that community leaders who help sponsor a conference insist that I attend luncheons and other meetings set up for their friends. This in itself is not wrong unless the motivation is to show off a so-called Christian celebrity. In the first place, God doesn't need celebrities. And in the second place, I have never met anyone who is one in God's eyes.

Christian leaders who allow themselves to get caught in the "Christian celebrity" snare often find that God simply passes them by, and they end up living on past experiences. And those who seek to promote themselves by hanging onto the coattails of successful Christians miss the entire point of the message. There's no such thing as a self-made Christian!

I would have to admit to anyone that I am not very adept at maintaining the facade of a Christian leader. I am who I am, and I could just as well be a car mechanic. Instead, God has blessed me with an ability to write and teach. These abilities are truly God-given, and I have not had to work hard at either of them. However, don't let me mislead you. Putting conferences and books together involves effort, even if the inspiration comes from the Lord. And I cannot do it by myself!

I depend on many dedicated Christians around the country to help me reach people in their communities with God's message on finances, and I greatly appreciate these people.

Often when I go to a city to teach a conference, I find myself so engrossed with my teaching and counseling that I forget to properly thank the volunteers. I trust that God will properly thank them on my behalf.

Many of our volunteers have been helping for several years, and they truly expect nothing except the privilege of knowing they have served God and helped to change some lives. But I recall one businessman who helped to coordinate a conference in his city.

While I was there a difficult situation came up, involving a church leader who was divorcing his wife, and the pastor asked if I would meet with them. I agreed to do so but found that virtually all of my non-scheduled time during the conference was occupied by this situation.

As a result, I neglected to meet with the businessman who organized the conference (although my staff coordinator did). I also forgot to recognize the businessman from the platform (which, unfortunately, I am prone to do). I did find the time to have a snack with him after the last evening session, but we were joined by the pastor and his wife, so we had very little time together. Still, I tried to thank him and honestly express my appreciation for all his work.

Several weeks later I received a call from one of my board members who lives in that city. He said this businessman was very upset with me and had told a group of other businessmen that he was sorry he ever helped bring my teaching to his community. I immediately called to ask what had offended him so. In my teaching on finances, I've learned it's easy to alienate people who may misinterpret what I say or they might think I attacked them or their profession.

But that was not the case with this businessman. He was offended because I had not spent enough time with him while I was there. He had told several other prominent people that they could have lunch with us, and he had wanted to be recognized from the platform each evening. In other words, he needed to have his ego stroked and was merely using the conference to do so.

One day, I fear, that man will look back on this and other similar events and regret that he didn't strive for the greater reward God offers. *"If any man builds upon the foundation with gold, silver, precious stones, wood, hay, straw, each man's work will become evident; for the day will show it, because it is to be revealed with fire; and the fire itself will test the quality of each man's work. If any man's work which he has built upon it remains, he shall receive a reward"* (1 Corinthians 3:12–14).

Symptom 2: Overwork

Our lifestyles today demand more and more indulgences to keep us content. Often this necessitates two incomes and many extra hours on the part of either or both spouses. Compared to the dedicated businessman or businesswoman who is trying to build a small empire, the average worker is a sluggard.

It is not unusual for a person building a business to work 80-hour weeks regularly, and in some cases 100 hours or more. Unfortunately, many people think this is both necessary and normal. So, not only do they drive themselves to extremes, they also demand the same of everyone else.

It is true that a 40-hour work week will rarely, if ever, build a successful business. But a 100-hour work week reflects a gross imbalance of priorities, not dedication to being a good leader! I can state without hesitation that no one can maintain the correct balance between work, family, and God if he or she is working more than 60 hours per week. There may be occasional periods when an excess is necessary and unavoidable, but even then the relationships suffer.

I reflect on my college days when I worked 10- to 14-hour days at Cape Canaveral in Florida and carried a full school load as well. Those were some long days and weeks! But, I could see no other alternative at that time, since I knew no bankers who were crazy enough to lend me money to go to college.

It took me nearly six years to finish, and then I went into business with a friend who had started an electronics company. I simply substituted the hours in school for hours at work and continued the same pace. I actually believed this was the normal pattern for success, because it was the pattern of most of the successful businesspeople I knew.

What I didn't realize then was that most of them were working on their second or third marriages and were repeating the same patterns that had wrecked the previous relationships. To my knowledge, none were Christians, although some were professing church members (a membership they seldom took advantage of).

Then, in the midst of trying to achieve the world's idea of success, I found the Lord as my Savior and realized that my priorities were out of balance. I began taking half a day off on Sunday so that I could go to church, but then I started falling back into the old routine. I tried but could find no way to alter the habits of a lifetime.

When I had been a Christian approximately six months, I had an experience that really jolted me. I had been at the routine of working 20 hours a day and sleeping a little on the side. I came home about 2:00 one morning and crawled into bed. Then I awoke a few minutes later with one of those "revelations" from the Lord. I felt God was speaking to me through a passage of Scripture that was clear in my mind, and I spent the next two hours trying to locate the passage. (I knew so little about the Bible at that time I didn't realize there were concordances available to help locate elusive passages.)

I eventually found the Scripture and I will never forget it: *"It is vain for you to rise up early, to retire late, to eat the bread of painful labors; for He gives to His beloved even in his sleep"* (Psalm 127:2).

You can't say it clearer than that. I had promised God when I became a Christian that He would never again have to deal with my disobedience (ignorance perhaps, but not disobedience). I asked only that He would make His will for my life very clear so that I wouldn't misunderstand it. His Word said it for me: *"Just tell me what to do and I will do it, Lord. As long as I live I'll wholeheartedly obey. Make me walk along the right paths for I know how delightful they really are. Help me to prefer obedience to making money"* (Psalm 119:33–36 TLB).

From that point on I made a commitment to never again spend excessive hours pursuing success. I limited myself to a 48-hour work week maximum and have maintained that schedule (or even fewer hours) ever since. I find that I accomplish more and use my time better than when I worked twice as many hours. I also won't have to look back at 65 or 70 years of age and say, "I wish I had done that 20 years ago."

If you find you can't keep your time in the right priority, I would suggest a plan that a friend shared with me several years ago. Just ask God either to give you the wisdom to maintain the correct priorities or remove the temptation by shutting down the business!

Perhaps the worst offender I ever knew in this regard was a pastor. He shepherded a large evangelical church and spent almost every waking moment there. Even when he was at home his mind was at his office. And he felt justified because what he was doing was "for the Lord" (a common cop-out for someone who uses Christian work as an ego booster). Although this pastor had problems at home, in his marriage and family, he prided himself that he never allowed his personal problems to interfere with his ministry activities.

Then the local police chief called to say that his 16-year-old son had been arrested for drug possession—again. The previous day his wife had suffered an emotional breakdown and had been committed to the psychiatric ward at a local hospital. Initially, this made little impression on the pastor, and in fact he had prepared a sermon on suffering for that Sunday.

But as he prayed about his message that Sunday morning, he realized that his whole life was a lie; he was in bondage to his own ego and pride. He would have counseled any other church member to drop the business and get his life straightened out.

At church that day, he stood in the pulpit and told his congregation, "My life is a mess and I'm a phony. My wife is in a mental ward, my son is in jail for handling drugs, and I don't know if God still wants me in the ministry. So I'm resigning as your pastor. I'm going to try to salvage my relationship with God and with my family. If I'm successful I'll be back, if you still want me. Otherwise I will assume God has other plans for my life."

The silence hung thick as the pastor walked out of the auditorium. Then one of the deacons came to the podium and said, "I believe God is at work here—finally. My wife and I have been praying for something like this for a long time now. Let's pray for the pastor and his family."

The pastor was gone for nearly six months, during which time the church used several interim pastors and guest speakers. He spent his time ministering to his wife and working with his son in the detention home. After six months he felt that he had redirected his priorities, and he asked the deacon board to reconsider him for the pastorate.

But he set a condition for his return. Every deacon had to agree to a pact of total accountability with him and each other, including their finances, time, Bible study, and prayer. Second, they had to agree to a total survey of the church to determine how many of the members were actually Christians. Those who were not Christians would be asked to join a new members class, regardless of their social status or length of church membership.

After much debate the deacons agreed to the plan, and the pastor returned. His first official act was to post a sign above the entrance to the sanctuary: "Only sinners are welcome here."

That church was never the same again. The biggest change in the administration of the church was that the pastor required the deacons to assume the role of leaders and relieve him of the necessity to do all the counseling, development, and planning. This pastor had learned what many other Christians never learn until it's too late: God doesn't need us to burn out for Him. He would much rather have us wear out gracefully.

Symptom 3: Excessive Use of Credit

More than any other financial principle, credit has dominated the way we do business in our generation. In 1929 the entire country, and indeed the world, was shaken to its core by the collapse of our financial base. Millions of people were displaced as businesses failed and banks closed. At that time, it was thought that the Great Depression would make an everlasting impact on our society and that never again would ordinary people risk their homes and security by heavily indebting themselves. Now, nearly seven decades later, we are deeper in debt than ever!

Imagine the scenario: a 2 percent change in interest rates could determine whether the country has a growing economy or a recession. Now imagine that a shift of another 2 percent could destroy more than half of all the viable businesses and create unemployment for nearly 30 million people. Does that sound incredible? Well, we are poised on that precipice.

That tilt can happen at any time. One would think that business owners would be desperately paying off debts in an attempt to avoid the inevitable collapse. Instead, most of them are borrowing as if there will be no tomorrow. The newspapers are full of reports of takeovers and mergers, all done on heavily leveraged buyouts. Literally hundreds of billions of investment dollars are flowing into Wall Street, just waiting for the next economic downturn to explode.

We'll be discussing the subject of borrowing in some detail in Chapter 15, so I won't elaborate here, except to give an illustration of the bondage that misuse of debt can cause.

A real estate developer in the South became very successful developing and selling land syndications. This is a very fancy name for convincing a group of investors that property they paid too much for can be sold to another group at a higher price in the very near future. (This is known in some groups as the "greater sucker" theory.)

This syndicator had made a great deal of money selling land syndications within the Christian community. But each deal was more leveraged than the previous one. For instance, the developer would syndicate a piece of property with a group of investors and promise to pay the owner a certain amount. The syndication would usually make a small down payment and finance the rest, often through a promissory note with a local bank. Generally, the contract called for interest-only payments for a period of a few years and then a balloon payment for the total amount.

This strategy allowed an enterprising syndicator to tie up a lot of property with very little money. All that was needed was a group of willing (gullible) investors who would be able to make the interest payments until the property could be sold to another group of investors for a higher price. Often the syndicator would form the second group to rebuy the property from his first group. It was a little like musical chairs: when the music stops, someone is sure to be left without a chair.

When I first heard about this investment strategy, I thought it might be done by some unscrupulous men who were trying to cheat their clients. But I found that the majority of syndicators believed in what they were doing; in fact, many of them risked virtually all their profits to invest in their own deals.

The whole syndication area began to unravel when FDIC examiners audited one of the major banking chains involved. The examiners determined that most of the syndication loans were undercollateralized. Virtually the only collateral was the syndicated properties and personal endorsements from the syndicators themselves. The FDIC prohibited the bank and its affiliates from making any more syndication loans without alternate security from the investors.

At that point, the whole house of cards came tumbling down. The syndications began to dry up because such highly leveraged sales are totally dependent on increasing debt. The syndicators who had been reaping hundreds of thousands of dollars from these deals suddenly found themselves with no income and thousands of dollars a month in payments due.

For a while many of the investors, hoping for a reversal of the situation, borrowed against their homes and other assets to make the payments. But as investors saw their projected profits dissolve and found no buyers for the syndications, which required huge outlays each month, they became frightened. Many of them refused to make their payments, and thus the devaluation accelerated.

The whole scheme was like a downhill roller coaster with no track at the bottom. Many honest syndicators tried to hold the investments together by offering to take over the interest of any investor who wanted out. But the downhill slide continued until the standing joke was "You can tell the land syndicators by the bald tires on their leased Mercedes."

It was at this point that I met the pastor of a large metropolitan church, where the land syndication cycle started. He had invested some of his retirement funds in a few syndications and had made a substantial profit the first year. On the basis of this return he had convinced several of his close friends in the church to invest in the next few syndications with him. They also made substantial profits but, as with most of these leveraged investments, their profits were dependent on subsequent investors making payments to them.

The pastor was sold on the potential of the syndications. He openly praised them from the pulpit and convinced the deacon board that they should invest some church funds that were being held for a future church school building. The idea was that the funds could be multiplied in the syndications. By the time the cycle had run its course, the pastor had acquired his real estate license and was syndicating land himself, along with several of the businessmen in his church.

When the syndications collapsed, the church lost several hundred thousand dollars of building fund money, and many of the members lost their life savings. The pastor owed so much by then that he could no longer pay the multiple mortgages on his home. In a short period of time, he saw everything he had worked for dissolve. He left the pulpit disgraced and defeated. He and several thousand other people found out that they were in bondage to credit and didn't know it until it was too late to do anything about it.

Another example that comes to mind was a small building contractor I met several years ago. He'd become very successful building one spec home at a time. In other words, he would build a home, put it up for sale, sell it, and then build another. He made a nice profit on each home he sold. One of the reasons he was so successful was that he provided most of the labor himself and was actually on the job every day.

Before long, he decided to start building two houses at a time on adjacent lots to take advantage of quality discounts. So he went to see the banker that had been financing his previous homes to ask if he could borrow enough money to build two houses at a time. The banker, having seen his previous successes, agreed to lend him more money, because he'd been a very good client.

For another year or so, he was very successful at building two houses at a time and, as a result, he had accumulated more than $100,000 of working capital. Then a land developer approached him about coming to his area and starting a new community of houses. He had seen this young builder's work, thought it was quite good, and told him so. This young builder, kind of puffed up with himself by this time, unfortunately presumed that he was a lot more capable than he really was.

So he moved his construction business to the developer's area and started building more expensive homes. Prior to this time, he had been building primarily starter homes that ranged between $100,000 and $120,000. Now he stepped up to $200,000+ homes. Obviously, the potential was much greater. What he didn't realize is that the risk would be much greater as well.

Many people in the past have discovered that too much success can be a greater risk than too little. This young contractor began to build the homes; and, in fact, they were selling. So the land developer approached him about signing for more contracts for more lots and beginning more homes at one time. The young builder, with his successful track record now behind him, went to the bank, outlined the plan, and the banker agreed to lend him enough money to start construction on five or six houses at a time.

The banker didn't realize that this young contractor, not having any experience running a company before, had mistakenly credited the full amount on the sale of the home as a receivable. In other words, if he started the foundation of the house and somebody came along and bought the house, he took the contract amount of the house and recorded it as receivable, adding this to his net worth. Unfortunately, what he should have done was to show the potential profit as his portion of the net worth, because the remainder of the home was offset by a contingent liability: to the developer, to the provider of building materials, and to his laborers.

But, overall, the work was going well, houses were selling, and the contractor was ecstatic. He was able to buy some things that he had never been able to afford before. He bought himself a double-cab truck he'd always wanted. He rented some nice office space, hired an office manager, and set up a warehouse to store some of his materials in during the interim building period.

He and his wife moved into a new $200,000+ home, which he had built in this subdivision, and he thought everything was going well—that was until the economy dipped a little bit and the interest rates on his construction loans went from 7 percent to 10 percent. Along with the construction loan interest rates going up, permanent loan rates went up, and suddenly houses stopped selling.

Unfortunately, he had to keep building and borrowing in order to keep his company going. Within six months, he had six unsold, totally completed homes with a debt of nearly $1.2 million compounding interest at the bank. That meant he was losing an enormous amount of money every single month. He soon discovered that all the money he thought he had in the bank simply evaporated.

Vendors and suppliers started filing liens against the builder. The whole organization that he had built, believing that he had a large net worth and was an entrepreneur, all evaporated. He ended up losing his home and everything he had because he used credit to expand his business. He could have continued building one house at a time and been very successful at it.

His biggest mistake was thinking that good times would last forever and that credit was the way to build net worth. It may be. But as Proverbs 22:7 says, *"The rich rules over the poor, and the borrower becomes the lender's slave."*

Symptom 4: Disorganization

In Scripture this symptom is called slothfulness. Proverbs warns us about this attitude at least two dozen times. I particularly like the verse, *"Poor is he who works with a negligent hand, but the hand of the diligent makes rich"* (Proverbs 10:4). This in no way justifies overworking to the detriment of all else, but it does clearly state a biblical principle: Laziness is a sin.

We are all disorganized to some extent. Often the degree of disorganization depends on the project at hand. For example, before my left shoulder blade was removed due to cancer, I was an old car buff; I thoroughly enjoyed dismantling and rebuilding antique cars. When I did this work, I would try to be as meticulous as possible, because I know from bitter experience what can happen if even a single bolt works loose. On the other hand, I am quite content to patch my lawnmower with baling wire to get the job done as quickly as possible.

In business, organization is an absolute necessity, not an alternative. Some people, like accountants, are organizers by personality.

They are often attracted to the field of accounting because they enjoy detail and order. Rarely, however, will someone who likes detail work become an entrepreneur, unless the business is directly related to the accounting field. Why? Because most entrepreneurial types are free-wheelers who like to do a variety of things and don't enjoy routine tasks. But a smart entrepreneur will eventually learn that even though ideas start businesses, organization makes them successful.

That means an entrepreneur must either develop the necessary discipline or hire someone else to keep the company in order. Otherwise, when the business grows to the point that shooting-from-the-hip decisions no longer suffice, either the owner will have to sell out or the business will fail.

One entrepreneur I'll call Bob Gray was a businessman whose penchant for disorganization ultimately caused his downfall. He was a research chemist who had developed a unique formula for removing foreign particles from motor oil. His idea was to add his formula to an engine's oil and collect the unwanted foreign particles in a special electrostatic filter, which would replace the standard oil filter. The oil would stay clean indefinitely, and the filter would require cleaning through reverse flushing about every 10,000 miles, at a cost of less than $10. The invention was easily worth several millions of dollars to any automotive parts wholesaler.

Bob negotiated with a large trucking company to test his invention on their equipment. The company allowed him to modify 10 of their older vehicles for a trial period. During this time Bob paid special attention to the details and personally monitored the exchange of the filters and application of the additive. The results were spectacular. Not only did the oil stay free of dirt and other pollutants, the average gas mileage increased by more than 5 percent. The transport company ordered the units for every vehicle. Bob's company was off and running.

Unfortunately, as the company grew to meet this increased demand, quality began to decline. Bob learned a hard lesson about organization when, through the use of some defective additive his company shipped, some 30 semitrailers with blown engines were stranded all across the country. The company immediately removed the filters and additive from all their vehicles and sued Bob's company for $800,000 in damages.

Bob had neglected to increase his liability insurance to cover the increased liability and found that he had only $100,000 worth of coverage. He filed for bankruptcy protection but was denied that right because he was unable to prove he would have a viable company left after the lawsuit. His company was liquidated, and the patents were given to the trucking company as partial settlement of the damages.

Bob was only a step away from a lifetime of security when his company crashed. He had a test in the works with a large automobile company to use his product in all their new cars and trucks. They were days away from signing an agreement when word of the trucking company's disaster became public. The automobile company broke off negotiations and issued a company statement rejecting the concept. This ultimately spelled doom for Bob's company. A very good idea bit the dust because of Bob's inattention to detail, i.e., slothfulness.

Symptom 5: A Get-Rich-Quick Mentality

Some people view a business as a vehicle to make some quick money with a minimum amount of effort and then get out. The people who hold to this philosophy leave broken lives behind them and a distinct distaste for Christianity in the mouths of their employees, customers, and suppliers.

This get-rich-quick mentality can be seen throughout American enterprise today in the takeovers and sell-offs of thousands of companies. Employees are treated like so much chattel, and creditors often are left holding the bag when valuable assets are sold off and the proceeds are absorbed within the parent company. Then the shell of the original company is thrown into bankruptcy, with the creditors and employees getting virtually nothing for their efforts.

There is nothing unscriptural about becoming wealthy through the application of your God-given talents in business. But the point at which business does become unscriptural is when the lust for riches becomes the overriding drive behind virtually every decision.

What often separates the true Christians in business from the unsaved or even the carnal Christians is how they value the people with whom they interact. The apostle Paul said it as clearly as it can be said: *"Do nothing from selfishness or empty conceit, but with humility of mind let each of you regard one another as more important than himself"* (Philippians 2:3).

Are your real motives me-first or others first? All get-rich-quick schemes are based on greed, and all greed has me-first at its core.

I have often said that if I could convince most Christian businesspeople to save a small portion of what they earn and avoid all get-rich-quick schemes, they could cut the prices of their products and still end up with more money at the end of their careers.

How many doctors, dentists, or attorneys do you know who have made money doing anything other than what they were trained to do? A few, perhaps, but for every one that made money in a get-rich-quick scheme, 100 lost money.

Alex's case is a good example. Alex was a Christian businessman who had developed a thriving restaurant concern in his community. He ran a specialty fast-food service that catered to the lunch crowd during the week, then totally changed its cuisine to attract the dinner groups during the weekend. Each of his children had worked in the business as they were growing up, and most of them had stayed in it.

Then, in the midst of the franchise mania of the late seventies and early eighties, Alex decided to establish franchises. His driving motivation was a desire to build a national franchise business, sell out, and then become a venture capital entrepreneur. He had a brother who supposedly was making millions in the franchise business.

The first store Alex franchised in a nearby city did extremely well. Its success encouraged him to link up with a promoter to sell limited partnership shares in the parent company. This capital would allow Alex to develop the franchise business and, he was sure, acquire instant riches.

The promoter sold 20 franchises in several cities, but the project began to go sour even before the first stores opened. The legal fees to register the partnership offerings were nearly double what had been expected, and the law prohibited the offering of more shares. This forced Alex to borrow heavily from his local bank, using his operating restaurant as collateral.

Expenses continued to pile up as building costs escalated and store openings were delayed. Several of the franchisees had quit their jobs and borrowed heavily against their homes to get in on the ground floor of this new business. With each delay in the store openings, their chances of success dropped significantly.

After several months of delay, three of the franchisees sued to recover their investment, claiming fraud on the part of Alex and his company. The courts agreed: Alex was required to refund the franchisees' money, which he no longer had. The net result was that his business, home, and virtually all other assets had to be liquidated to pay his bills. For a time it even appeared that Alex would be prosecuted for criminal fraud, but his willingness to make total restitution helped convince the prosecutor not to file charges.

Alex could have continued to make a very comfortable living for himself and his family for the rest of his life, except that a get-rich-quick mentality caused him to take excessive risks.

Get-rich-quick thinking leads to three basic errors: (1) getting involved with things you do not understand; (2) risking money you cannot afford to lose (usually borrowed); and (3) making hasty decisions. Each of these actions violates one or more biblical principles that we will discuss in this book. Together they constitute a sin called greed. Remember, *"A faithful man will abound with blessings, but he who makes haste to be rich will not go unpunished"* (Proverbs 28:20).

One way to avoid the core problem of business bondage is to do realistic planning both in business and in personal life. We will consider personal financial planning in Chapter 4 and business planning in Chapter 5.

4

Personal Lifestyle Goals

The first question any Christian businessperson should ask about planning is not *why* plan but *how to* plan. The reason for keeping financial records and paying bills is clear; you must do these things or risk going out of business. But planning involves projecting months and even years into the future and setting some realistic goals.

I have heard many Christians ask sincerely, "Doesn't the Bible say to give no thought for tomorrow?" I can answer that question with an unequivocal "No."

The Lord said to His disciples, *"Do not be anxious for your life, as to what you shall eat; nor for your body, as to what you shall put on"* (Luke 12:22). This is not an instruction to ignore the future but, rather, to avoid being consumed by fear of the future. In the first place, you can't avoid most problems even if you want to. And in the second, faith becomes a part of our lives as we trust God to help us overcome unexpected, unplanned-for crises.

There is a very fine line between faith (*"Now faith is the assurance of things hoped for, the conviction of things not seen"* [Hebrews 11:1]) and assumption (*"For which one of you, when he wants to build a tower, does not first sit down and calculate the cost, to see if he has enough to complete it?"* [Luke 14:28]). I have often observed Christians who stepped over the line in one direction or the other, and I have done so myself because of confusion about what I should do and what I should trust God to do.

For example, suppose you're running a real estate sales company and realize that your income is both seasonal and highly volatile. If you have an exceptionally good sales period and still have a substantial surplus on hand after paying all the outstanding bills, would it be better to give all the surplus away to various charities and then trust God to provide the additional income needed for the next month? Or should you retain some portion of the excess in anticipation of lower sales? If so, how much should be retained?

Giving everything away may not be so much an exercise in faith as the lack of good planning. God's Word describes how we are to observe one of God's smallest creatures, the ant, and follow her example of laying up during good times so that there will be enough during lean times (see Proverbs 6:6–9). Obviously God can convict someone to give away all his or her surplus and trust Him for provision, but that is the exception, scripturally speaking.

Usually, the decisions in real life aren't always as clear as they are in a Sunday school class. To respond to life's challenges and attain some reasonable balance between trusting God and being a prudent steward requires more than a cursory knowledge of God's principles. "Pure faith" demands disposing of all surpluses each month. "Pure logic," on the other hand, requires retaining all the surplus to ride out the downturns. Biblically, a case can be made for either position if you just focus on a single verse or two.

Jesus said, *"So therefore, no one of you can be My disciple who does not give up all his own possessions"* (Luke 14:33). Certainly no one could interpret this as anything other than an instruction to divest ourselves of all worldly trappings. But Luke records a dialogue between the Lord and His disciples that suggests a different emphasis: *"He said to them, 'When I sent you out without purse and bag and sandals, you did not lack anything, did you?' And they said, 'No, nothing.' And He said to them, 'But now, let him who has a purse take it along, likewise also a bag, and let him who has no sword sell his robe and buy one'"* (Luke 22:35–36).

This passage seems to indicate that the problem is not so much with retaining resources as with depending on them more than on God. In other words, when considering the question of the surplus, you would need to ask yourself, "Am I able to trust God while holding some resources? Or do I need to divest myself of everything in order to trust God totally?"

The majority of Scripture leans heavily toward retaining modest surpluses because of the dangers associated with materialism. Yet, since it is difficult to operate a business in our society without available capital, the alternatives are to (1) get out of business, (2) borrow what is needed when necessary, or (3) retain some surplus for the lean times.

As I said before, the passage that seems to best balance this question is, *"Go to the ant, O sluggard, observe her ways and be wise, which, having no chief, officer or ruler, prepares her food in the summer, and gathers her provision in the harvest. How long will thou lie down, O sluggard? When will you arise from your sleep?"* (Proverbs 6:6–9).

Ants don't hoard; they store only what will be needed to carry them through the winter. If an ant colony is moved to a climate where the provision is available virtually all year long, the ants will close off food storage chambers until the ready reserves again match the need.

The bottom line on planning is that it is both biblical and necessary to be a good steward, and this usually involves looking ahead — with caution. Too much planning can lead to self-reliance and too little can lead to unnecessary crises. But through studying the Word and seeking the Lord's guidance, you can strike the right balance.

PERSONAL GOALS

Before you can work toward effective business planning, you must have some personal financial goals, which can easily be determined by taking two major steps.

1. Set up and maintain a personal budget. During the Carter administration the director of budgets, Bert Lance, found himself in trouble over some ill-advised loans from banks where he served as director. His defense in several instances was that he never balanced his personal account and had no way to know how much he owed at any given time. I wondered at the time, "Is it too much to expect for the government's budget director to live on a budget?"

The way people handle their personal finances is usually the way they will handle their company's finances. The principle is simple: Someone who is faithful in the small things will be faithful in the greater. But someone who is slothful in the small things will be slothful in the greater (see Luke 16:10).

J. C. Penney once said, "A man who is too rich to pick up a penny is too rich." The inference in a biblical sense is, *"Better is he who is lightly esteemed and has a servant, than he who honors himself and lacks bread"* (Proverbs 12:9).

More often than not, someone who operates a business delegates these trivial tasks to someone else. In the case of a married couple, the husband often delegates the responsibility of finances to his wife and gives her little or no input. But God's Word says that two working together are better than one (see Ecclesiastes 4:9), and it also says that a husband and wife are to function as one (see Genesis 2:24).

That means that personal budgeting, and sticking to the budget, is the responsibility of both husband and wife. If you're too busy to be bothered with things like home budgets, you are simply too busy.

I won't discuss the particulars of budgeting here; that topic has been covered thoroughly in my other books. But I would like to emphasize that when a husband and wife work together on their personal budget, they will learn more about each other than through any other single thing they will ever do. God puts opposites together so that one can offset the imbalances of the other. If a husband and wife are not communicating about finances, the probability is they're not communicating about anything.

2. Establish some short-range and long-range personal goals.
Every Christian has a responsibility to establish some fundamental personal financial goals. Those who have the ability to earn more have an even greater responsibility according to the Lord's admonition: *"For whoever has, to him shall more be given, and he shall have an abundance; but whoever does not have, even what he has shall be taken away from him"* (Matthew 13:12).

Establishing goals involves weighing values as well as just setting objectives. It also involves lifestyle issues, such as how much financial success is enough. I firmly believe that many Christians are trading their inheritance in eternity for a few temporary indulgences in this world.

Few Christians understand the concept of eternal rewards, even though the Lord dedicated a great deal of His precious time on earth to teaching about them. The one certainty is that our position in the Lord's kingdom will be inversely proportional to how we indulge ourselves in this lifetime. *"Whoever exalts himself shall be humbled; and whoever humbles himself shall be exalted"* (Matthew 23:12).

There is not a lot of balanced teaching on this subject today because so few people understand it. The stoics believe that to follow Jesus, a Christian must sell everything and become a pauper. The scriptural justification they normally cite is the Lord's statement to the rich young ruler in Luke.

I believe such teaching is totally out of context. The Lord was addressing a specific problem in the life of one man. Nevertheless, His warning to this young ruler about the dangers of wealth is meant to be a universal principle for all of us: *"How hard it is for those who are wealthy to enter the kingdom of God!"* (Luke 18:24).

On the other side today are the prosperity peddlers who bring a message of health, wealth, and success. This group comes and goes with the changing economy. It's easy to teach the prosperity message when people are making lots of money, because such a message helps them justify the indulgences. It's hard to sell the prosperity message when people are having their homes repossessed in spite of all their giving to keep God on their side. God does give to those who trust Him but not if they give in an attempt to bribe God.

Somewhere in the middle of these two extremes is the proper balance. The words of an ancient prophet express it best: *"Two things I asked of Thee, do not refuse me before I die: keep deception and lies far from me, give me neither poverty nor riches; feed me with the food that is my portion, lest I be full and deny Thee and say, 'Who is the Lord?' or lest I be in want and steal, and profane the name of my God"* (Proverbs 30:7–9).

If you can accept the truth from God's Word that we are merely stewards (managers) of God's resources, the task of determining how much is enough is made much simpler. Since God owns everything and it is all being recycled through each generation, we just have to determine how much we need in order to accomplish the task God has assigned us during our cycle on Earth.

Indulgence can be defined as buying things that have little or no real utility to us. Examples of this can be found in the backyards of many families in America in the form of boats, campers, and motor homes. We can extend the list to include sports cars for teenagers, condos in Aspen, summer homes, winter homes, and so on.

But price alone does not determine an item's indulgence or utility value. I have a friend who bought an airplane for nearly $50 million. I don't believe that purchase was an indulgence. Why? Because he owns an airline, and the plane is a tool for earning a living. Value, not price, is the key element.

I also believe God wants His people to prosper, but not so that we (or our children) can indulge in every trinket our society can produce. John Wesley once pointed out, "You cannot keep a devoted Christian poor. For by the very nature of God within him his frugalness will eventually make him successful."

We have lost some of that frugality in our generation. Some Christian leaders in business and ministry seem bent on demonstrating how indulgent they can be. But I find that very few unsaved people are impressed by a Christian's affluence. Most businesspeople have seen enough affluence in the world around them to be convinced that godly people don't usually accumulate the most money.

What attracts successful people are the dedication and commitment of those rare individuals who have learned to control their lifestyles and use the abundance they have to help others.

It really doesn't take all that much talent to make money today. It's usually a matter of being in the right place at the right time with the right product. The real test is learning how to manage success.

I have listed a few basic goals that require the input of both husband and wife and a great deal of prayer. Remember, your goals must grow from your understanding of God's plan for your lives, not my plans or anyone else's.

Debt

One goal every believer should establish is to become totally debt-free. That means your home and business as well as cars, clothes, and appliances. In an economy that cycles like ours does, this is simply common sense. At some point, your economy is bound to hit a severe downturn. Those who are in debt at that time risk the possibility of financial ruin.

If you need any additional motivation, just consider this verse: *"The rich rules over the poor, and the borrower becomes the lender's slave"* (Proverbs 22:7). Ask anyone who was in the farming business in the late seventies or the oil business in the early eighties if that principle still holds true.

Lifestyle

It is not mere coincidence that the biggest homes, fanciest cars, and costliest toys belong to the most affluent group of Americans. Many well-known Christians in the business world openly state that if you aren't one of the affluent you probably missed God's bus.

Are the Christians living in 1,500-square-foot homes and driving four-year-old cars being deprived of God's best? Many must obviously think so, because they will buy a bigger, more expensive home and a new car as soon as they can afford it.

Let me propose a radical idea from God's Word: Determine God's best for your life and be satisfied with it, even if it means moving down in lifestyle. In Luke the Lord said, *"Whoever has, to him shall more be given; and whoever does not have, even what he thinks he has shall be taken away from him"* (Luke 8:18). And He promised, *"There is no one who has left house or wife or brothers or parents or children, for the sake of the kingdom of God, who shall not receive many times as much at this time and in the age to come, eternal life"* (Luke 18:29–30).

God obviously has a different plan for each of us and a different lifestyle that will bring us the greatest freedom to serve Him. Some Christians may well need a 5,000-square-foot home to accomplish what God calls them to do in their community. But the majority of affluent Christians today have never honestly applied their faith to the question: How much is enough? Instead, they have instinctively responded as financier Bernard Baruch did when asked that same question. "How much is enough? Just a little more."

Automobiles

Clearly many American Christians (mostly men) display their value systems in their automobiles. For many this attitude probably started in high school, when a teenager's popularity is partly determined by the car he or she drives. Someone driving by a Christian (or public) high school today would have no difficulty determining which is the student parking lot and which is the teachers'. The student lot is filled with Z-cars, S-cars, Corvettes, and on and on. The cars in the teachers' lot look like castoffs from a bargain-basement auto sale.

I'm not judging anyone. The kind of car you drive is between you and the Lord. But I would be remiss as a teacher of God's Word if I didn't caution that unless your giving to God's work matches your car in quality, you may need to reassess where your heart is. *"For where your treasure is, there will your heart be also"* (Luke 12:34).

I personally love machines, especially cars. And I appreciate the higher-priced cars because of their performance, but I won't buy a new car because of the lost value the minute you drive it off the lot. A few years ago, my wife, Judy, and I were going to buy a new car, since the one we were driving was on its last legs. I had decided to buy a Honda, based on the *Consumer Reports* magazine analysis of new cars and the fact that I had a friend in the Honda business.

Judy's primary requirement in a car is an electrically adjusted driver's seat, an option which Honda didn't offer in the models we were considering. So she began to pray that the Lord would provide a car with an adjustable front seat, and I countered that prayer by asking the Lord to make her contented with a Honda. Our friend the Honda dealer told her that the Acura, a car made by Honda, offered the option she wanted. However, the price of an Acura was nearly double that of the smaller Honda, and I said, "No way."

Apparently the Lord was not as concerned about the cost as I was! A few weeks later, a member of our board of directors asked if there were something he could do for Judy, since she has been such a faithful helpmate to me all these years. "Is there any one thing she would like to have that you are not willing to buy for her?" he asked.

What could I say? "Yes, there is," I answered him, "but I don't think it's worth the difference in price."

"That's okay," he replied. "You let me be the judge of that."

So I shared Judy's desire for a car with adjustable seats, my commitment to value, and our resulting stalemate.

Three weeks later Judy took possession of a new Acura. As I said, I guess the Lord is not as concerned with cost as I am. It helps if we keep in perspective the fact that He owns it all, and He may want us to have some of it, but we must be willing to allow Him to decide how much and when.

A PERSPECTIVE FOR SETTING LIFESTYLE GOALS

As a Christian in the business world, you have an opportunity to represent what you really believe in, for good or bad. What you do with the resources that have been entrusted to you will reflect what you hold most precious. I believe Christianity is in dire need of some affluent Christians who know how to exercise self-discipline. With rare exception, once a Christian reaches a position of importance in the business world (or other sphere of influence) that Christian becomes hard to distinguish from other successful people. Affluence is an easy habit to adjust to, and indulgence is easy to rationalize. What we need today are some radical Christians who will live for the Lord first and the world last.

Perhaps one of the greatest examples of this principle was John Wesley. During his lifetime, John Wesley was one of the wealthiest men in England. At a time when the average income for most British citizens was around 20 pounds per year, Wesley was earning more than a million pounds per year. The fact that he made so much money did not, in his opinion, give him the right to spend it all. In his diary, just before his death, John Wesley wrote, "If you find in my possession, upon my death, more than 20 pounds total, then you'll know that I lived a lie."

Upon his death they found, outside of the home he owned, Wesley's total worth was 20 pounds sterling. The rest of the money God had provided to Dr. Wesley was used for the furtherance of the kingdom of God. John Wesley's life still stands as a testimony of God's faithfulness today.

I'm sure there were wealthier in the world, and many who lived in and around London where Dr. Wesley grew up, but they're gone and buried, and their wealth has been dispersed to other people. What they've accomplished in this world is irrelevant. Now the only thing that will be important is what they did for the Lord for eternity.

The big cars, lavish homes, expensive vacations, and overstuffed bank accounts will not matter a whit one second after your heart stops beating. The only thing that will be of any importance for all eternity is what was done in the Lord's name and in the Lord's way.

Our Lord spent much of His ministry on Earth warning us about the dangers of service to the world rather than to God. I want to close this chapter by sharing some of the warnings that have most affected my life over the years that I have been a Christian. After all, the principles of operating a Christian business are important, but without the heart attitude that "Jesus is Lord," they are just so many rules.

Please take a few moments now to read and pray about the following Scriptures.

"Do not lay up for yourselves treasures upon earth, where moth and rust destroy, and where thieves break in and steal. But lay up for yourselves treasures in heaven, where neither moth nor rust destroys, and where thieves do not break in or steal; for where your treasure is, there will your heart be also" (Matthew 6:19–21). Where we spend our money reflects our heart attitudes.

"But seek first His kingdom and His righteousness; and all these things shall be added to you" (Matthew 6:33). Seek God and prosper.

"And everyone who hears these words of Mine, and does not act upon them, will be like a foolish man, who built his house upon the sand" (Matthew 7:26). Sand and money make poor foundations.

"For what will a man be profited, if he gains the whole world, and forfeits his soul? Or what will a man give in exchange for his soul?" (Matthew 16:26). He who dies with the most toys loses!

"And everyone who has left houses or brothers or sisters or father or mother or children or farms for My name's sake, shall receive many times as much, and shall inherit eternal life. But many who are first will be last; and the last, first" (Matthew 19:29–30). A man is no fool who gives up what he cannot keep to gain what he cannot lose.

"But the greatest among you shall be your servant. And whoever exalts himself shall be humbled; and whoever humbles himself shall be exalted" (Matthew 23:11–12). Rule now, serve later. Serve now, rule later.

5

Biblical Business Goals

Planning and *goal setting* are synonymous terms. In order to do good planning you must first establish some realistic goals, both short- and long-term, and in order to accomplish your goals you must do some planning. It's amazing how many businesspeople lope along without establishing any specific goals and end up with financial troubles in a business that could have been successful. Perhaps the prime example of this principle in our generation is what happened in the farming community.

Since the late forties farmers have been able to grow more than the available market could absorb. This often created market conditions in which prices would fluctuate wildly, depending on how much of a particular crop farmers cultivated. If soybeans sold well one season, farmers would produce twice as much the next season and prices would plummet, often to well below production costs. This created havoc within the industry, and unfortunately our Washington politicians decided to come up with a fix.

The crop allocation system was a government-sponsored program designed to stabilize prices by encouraging farmers to grow less. To do this, the government came up with a tried-and-proven political system: pay the farmers not to grow certain crops. Of course the farmers loved this system, since they made money for doing nothing.

By the mid-seventies farming was considered the ideal business to invest in. The more land you owned, the more money you could make for not farming it. So the idea was to own as much land as possible. Many new-generation farmers came out of agricultural schools that taught the way to succeed was to take the old family farm and leverage it to buy more land.

At first this new breed of farmers had a hard time convincing the older generation that borrowing on debt-free land was logical. But armed with allocation contracts from the government, they were able to borrow huge amounts of capital to buy additional acreage. As the demand for land went up, the price of farmland went up with it. By the late seventies farmland prices had grown totally out of proportion with real value. Farmland was selling at prices that made farming it without the subsidies economically impossible. But that mattered little because those who bought the land weren't planning to farm it anyway.

A strategic error made by most farmers, Christian farmers included, was that they never set any realistic short- or long-term goals to take their increases and pay off even a portion of their land. Instead they continued to leverage even more as land values spiraled. They didn't seem to really need the government contracts; the land itself had become the speculative commodity.

Eventually all such cycles must come to an end. This one crashed when the government decided it could no longer afford the subsidy programs; they reduced the allocation program during the early years of the Reagan administration. Land prices plummeted and bankers found themselves greatly overextended, with loans often totaling several times the market value of the farms and equipment. As a result they foreclosed on thousands of farmers, forcing them out of business. Land that had been in families for generations was sold at auction for a fraction of its former value.

It would be easy to point to many biblical principles that were violated during the farming fiasco, but chief among them has to be the lack of discipline on the part of Christian farmers, which caused them to follow the lead of the unsaved farmers. Following simple biblical principles would have allowed them to avoid the get-rich-quick mentality that overwhelmed the farming community, and the Christians would have been buying the surplus farmland when the system collapsed.

LONG-TERM GOALS FOR A CHRISTIAN IN BUSINESS

When I discuss business planning with an owner, I begin by establishing the long-term goal or purpose for a Christian's business. In reality there is one primary purpose for a Christian's business: to glorify God. But there are various ways to glorify Him. *"Whether, then, you eat or drink or whatever you do, do all to the glory of God"* (1 Corinthians 10:31).

These become the functions of business—literally, the service provided by the business. So, the purpose of a business is to glorify God. Its functions are as follows.

1. Fund the Gospel

An important function of a Christian's business should be to help spread God's Word. The Bible says that we are to honor the Lord from the first fruits of all our produce (see Proverbs 3:9). For Christians who have the authority to do so, this means giving a portion of a company's earnings to Christian ministries.

The funding function is an important one, but it is only one element of a business truly dedicated to the service of God.

2. Meet Needs

Another important function for a Christian business is to supply the physical needs of those who depend on it: your own family and your employees. God's Word puts it this way: *"But if anyone does not provide for his own, and especially for those of his household, he has denied the faith, and is worse than an unbeliever"* (1 Timothy 5:8). I believe this Scripture applies not only to providing for our own families, but also to a businessperson providing for his or her employees.

In later chapters we'll discuss how much to pay employees and what constitutes a need. But a good rule of thumb is to consider whether you would be willing and able to live on what you're paying the people under your authority. If not, and you are able to pay more, you need to consider James 5:4: *"Behold, the pay of the laborers who mowed your fields, and which has been withheld by you, cries out against you; and the outcry of those who did the harvesting has reached the ears of the Lord of Sabaoth."* This verse indicates that God holds us responsible for providing for those under our authority.

3. Be a Disciple

The apostle Paul wrote, *"The things which you have heard from me in the presence of many witnesses, these entrust to faithful men, who will be able to teach others also"* (2 Timothy 2:2). On several occasions I have encountered Christian businesspeople who spend thousands of dollars a year to share their faith with people in other countries; yet, often their employees have never heard the Gospel in a meaningful way.

One Christian businessman I'll call Alfred shared his concerns with me after going through our business seminar. He said, "I really thought I was a sound Christian businessman, but I'm not doing even a third of the things presented here. How do I get started?"

My response was, "Please don't go back and tell your employees how *they* should apply these principles. You just focus on the principles that apply to *you* and demonstrate to your employees that you care about them."

Alfred went back and called a company meeting. His employees thought, *Oh no, he's been to another one of those religious seminars. Now he's going to tell us what we need to be doing to serve God.* I've seen this happen many times. A businessperson becomes enthusiastic about something he or she learned at a seminar and decides, *I've got to go back and get this started in my business.* Usually the employees dread it, thinking, *It's going to be three weeks of misery again until this works out of the boss's system and we get back to normal.*

But Alfred took a different approach. He told his employees, "I attended a seminar that changed my life, and I'd like to try to share with you what God is teaching me. So once a week I'm going to shut down our plant for an hour, and I'm going to share what God's Word says I should be doing for you. The meetings are voluntary, but everyone is welcome. From this point on, I want you to hold me responsible to be the kind of Christian employer that God expects me to be."

The next Monday, when the plant stopped for the meeting, every one of Alfred's employees was there. He began to share what he should be doing as a Christian businessman. Sometimes he would say, "I can't implement this immediately or it would ruin our company, but eventually I am going to do this to the best of my ability." One of the programs Alfred wanted to implement was a benevolence program to help employees with special financial needs, such as medical bills, family crises, or special education expenses by providing company-sponsored grants.

To do this would first require reeducating the employees so that those who didn't receive this benefit would not resent those who did. It also would require establishing an employee committee to oversee the fund and evaluate the candidates. But Alfred was determined to get it started.

About a year after the meetings began, Alfred asked me to speak to his employees. At one point in my talk I asked, "How many in this room have personally accepted Jesus Christ as your Savior?" Out of more than 100 employees, about 25 hands went up.

A year later I went back. This time I asked, "During the last year, how many of you have personally accepted Jesus Christ as a result of the influence of your boss?" Hands went up throughout the room. In one year, more than 60 people had come to the Lord through Alfred's influence, and he didn't even know it. Evangelizing his employees hadn't been his goal. His goal had simply been to become more Christ-like in his business.

The apostle Paul tells us we reap in the measure that we sow (see 2 Corinthians 9:6). Alfred learned that truth when he ran into some business and financial difficulties. During an economic downturn, business got so bad he needed a large infusion of money in order to continue operating. The high interest rates at that time made borrowing out of the question. Word of the company's financial problems spread to Alfred's employees, several of whom got the idea of banding together to lend Alfred the money (almost $300,000) themselves. They raised the needed funds from among the other employees and provided Alfred with an interest-free loan.

Alfred was simply reaping what he had sown. When he began following God's principles, he didn't know that more than half of his employees would accept Christ as their Savior through his witness or that his employees would decide to lend him $300,000 interest free. He had simply sown biblical principles such as "Do unto others as you would have others do unto you," and he reaped the benefits of those principles.

Employees, especially unsaved employees, have the tendency to believe what they see rather than what they hear. If what we do doesn't match up with what we say, they will usually discount our words. This principle is acknowledged in the following: *"But prove yourselves doers of the word, and not merely hearers who delude themselves"* (James 1:22).

4. Make a Profit

Contrary to the opinion of some, there is no biblical admonition against making a profit. Profits are the normal by-product of a well-run business and should be considered as both normal and honorable. If a business cannot generate profits, it will fail, and its ministry to employees and customers will cease.

Profits are the economic rewards of good service and products (normally). No business can succeed without them—not even General Motors or IBM. Prior to the eighties, many General Motors and IBM employees seemed to think that their companies printed their own money, like the government. But the time came when both GM and IBM could no longer make a profit, and the companies were forced to eliminate jobs and employees, many of them permanently. Suddenly GM and IBM employees started to wake up and realize that company profits were important to them.

Every Christian in business, employer and employee alike, should work to maximize profits, but not to the exclusion of other key elements of a biblically based business. For an employer to maximize profits by underpaying employees, for instance, is a violation of the second function of a Christian business: meeting needs.

Christian employers also must acknowledge that, since God really owns the business, all of the profits cannot accrue to them alone. Profit sharing is thought to be an innovation of the late twentieth century. Not so. *"There is one who scatters, yet increases all the more, and there is one who withholds what is justly due, but it results only in want"* (Proverbs 11:24).

For the first time in several decades Christian businesspeople have the opportunity to show individual employees that they care. Organized labor got started because management demonstrated an uncaring attitude by treating workers like tools: to be used and discarded as necessary. As a result employees organized, and adversarial relationships developed. Today, with the power of organized labor on a downhill slide, Christian managers and owners have the opportunity to sow good seed. If Christian-run businesses can rekindle the lost sense of work ethic in their employees by establishing an atmosphere of caring and responsibility, perhaps industry as a whole will study their methods.

SHORT-TERM OPERATIONAL GOALS FOR A CHRISTIAN BUSINESS

Once the long-range goals for a business have been established, the next step is to set specific, short-term operational goals. Here are some of the most important categories to consider in short-term business planning.

Set Priorities for the Use of Money

Good planning must involve setting priorities and working on the most important ones first. In the area of money this is called budgeting, and everyone must budget in one fashion or another. Budgeting is the process of allocating available resources among the variety of possible expenditures. If you have a company that sells a product or service, you must have a plan to bill the customers or you involuntarily become a nonprofit organization. Don't laugh! There are lots of potentially profitable businesses losing money because of sloppy billing practices.

Pam, for instance, operated an interstate trucking company she had inherited from her father. She had worked in the business for several years before her father's death, so she understood it well. She even had several good ideas for expanding the operation, including leasing trailers to other companies during peak load periods, a system that has now been adopted by many transporters.

Pam had inherited not only her father's mechanical aptitude but also his system of budgeting, which consisted of several boxes of bills and receipts thrown in together during the course of a month. At the end of the month a local bookkeeper would come in, sort through the boxes to determine the income, deposit the checks, and pay the outstanding bills. This system had been barely adequate when the company was small.

Now, with the operation beginning to grow, it quickly became disastrous. The bookkeeper fell further and further behind without telling anyone, and many bills went unpaid. Even worse, many accounts receivable went uncollected. Since the trailer leasing operation depended on billing the users each month, the revenues dropped off drastically, and the expenses for advertising and maintenance increased.

Within a year, Pam had several lawsuits filed against the company for past-due bills, and her fuel supply was cut off for delinquent payments. She confronted the bookkeeper, who confessed that she was unable to reconcile the billings and receipts. By the time she called to ask for help she was seriously considering filing for bankruptcy protection because creditors were threatening to attach all of her operating vehicles. If this happened, she would have been left with no cash flow.

When I saw Pam's accounting system, I suggested that we call in an outside accounting firm to reconcile the records. She protested that she had no money to pay an accountant. But we located a firm that was willing to take the job on a contingency basis; their pay would depend on their ability to locate the needed cash. Pam agreed and spent the next week working with the accountant, reconstructing the leases, and determining where all the leased trailers were.

In the final analysis we found that four of Pam's most irritated creditors were also her most delinquent leasees; they owed Pam nearly $20,000 more in lease payments (that had never been billed) than she owed them. They quietly withdrew their lawsuits and agreed to pay their bills. When all the accounts were reconciled, Pam had made a net profit of nearly $180,000 over the previous 10 months! Once a regular system of billing was established, she went on to operate a business that was sold a few years later for several million dollars.

How we use our money is the clearest outside indicator of what we really believe. The Lord said, *"No servant can serve two masters; for either he will hate the one, and love the other, or else he will hold to one, and despise the other. You cannot serve God and mammon"* (Luke 16:13).

The priorities we establish for the use of our money can give us good insight into where we are spiritually. Just as a thermometer doesn't make a room hot or cold but measures the temperature, so money doesn't make us spiritual or carnal; it reflects who we are.

I have felt that way many times. I doubt there is a believer who hasn't questioned his or her salvation at one time or the other; I know I have. I am a very pragmatic person and I have asked myself, "Is salvation a real experience?" I have long since concluded that salvation is based on the Lord's promise, not on how I feel.

I have always been comforted by the apostle Paul's confession: *"For I know that nothing good dwells in me, that is, in my flesh; for the wishing is present in me, but the doing of the good is not. For the good that I wish I do not do; but I practice the very evil that I do not wish. But if I am doing the very thing I do not wish, I am no longer the one doing it, but sin which dwells in me"* (Romans 7:18–20). I believe Paul was saying that he couldn't always depend on his feelings or reactions, only on the promises of God.

If someone is a true disciple of Jesus Christ, the evidence will be visible in that person's everyday life, including his or her use of money. I find it difficult to believe that a follower of Christ can deliberately cheat, steal, and lie in the normal course of business. I also find it hard to believe that a person who refuses to share in the needs of others has the spirit of Christ within. The measure of true giving is to share with someone who has no platform from which to speak and may never benefit us in any way. After all, isn't that what true love is all about?

As the Lord said, *"And the King will answer and say to them, 'Truly I say to you, to the extent that you did it to one of these brothers of Mine, even the least of them, you did it to Me'"* (Matthew 25:40).

Financial Priorities

I believe Scripture supports a priority system for paying creditors, employees, and owners. Basically it comes down to who gets paid first when things get tight.

Priority 1: Pay suppliers. Without a doubt those who provide materials on credit have the first right to any available income from a business. I realize this runs contrary to current business logic, which says, "When money is tight, string out your accounts payable." But consider this verse: *"Lying lips are an abomination to the Lord, but those who deal faithfully are His delight"* (Proverbs 12:22). When you order materials, there is an implied promise to pay. A Christian's promise is his or her bond (word).

Jesse was in the wholesale shoe business on a large scale. He would often order $100,000 to $200,000 worth of athletic shoes to be sold to various discount stores around the country. As competition increased, Jesse found that he had to give deeper and deeper discounts to get business.

Ultimately he found himself offering the shoes at less than cost many times. Initially he justified this practice as a necessity to maintain his customer base until the prices rose again. But as time went by and he continued to order more and more shoes he couldn't pay for, he got further behind. Only the oldest bills got paid, and then only when the suppliers refused to ship him any more merchandise until he paid.

Jesse's priority of paying was simple. He took what he needed to ·pay his personal bills (which was not excessive); then he paid the basic overhead costs, such as lights and rent, to keep the door open. Then he paid a small portion to his church. Last, he paid the suppliers what was left from his sales, which was often less than 50 percent of the cost of the shoes.

I met Jesse through a mutual friend who had helped to finance his business initially. Jesse had gone back to him twice in the previous year to ask for additional capital. The lender realized the third time that something was wrong and agreed to help only on the condition that Jesse seek counsel, which is how I became involved.

When I saw Jesse's progressive accumulation of debt, I asked him to describe his business plan. He replied, "Just trying to stay alive." He went on to explain that because of competition from the shoe manufacturers' own sales staffs he had been forced to discount his merchandise below actual cost.

"How do you intend to get out of this cycle?" I asked him.

"I don't know right now," he replied. "But if I shut down the business, I won't ever be able to repay what I owe. I keep hoping the situation will turn around."

Jesse went on to say something I have heard countless Christians say under similar circumstances: "I know God put me in this business, and I believe He will work a miracle if I just have faith."

I believe in faith and I believe in miracles, but the line between faith and presumption is very thin. For Jesse to trust the Lord is faith. But to put the burden of debt on his suppliers was presumption. It was the suppliers who needed faith. Jesse willfully violated God's principles and then expected God to bail him out.

I told Jesse this and got a defiant reaction. "Job's friends accused him falsely too," Jesse retorted. "I believe God is capable of anything we ask, if we just have faith."

There's that word again: *faith.*

"Jesse," I said after he calmed down a little, "your current business plan requires your creditors to have faith. They're taking the risks, not you. The Scriptures clearly teach that Job suffered because of false accusations by Satan, not because of any disobedience on his part."

I then asked Jesse to prioritize his payment system in conformity with God's Word. According to Proverbs 3:27 we are not to *"withhold good* [payment] *from those to whom it is due."* Since the suppliers have provided the materials, they have already invested their time and money, and they hold the position of highest honor, financially speaking. "So," I said, "make a commitment to pay your suppliers first out of any cash that comes into the business."

"But if I do that I won't have enough money to keep the business going," he protested.

"That's what real faith is all about, Jesse. Hebrews 11:1 says that faith is the conviction of things not seen. Do you honestly believe that if the Lord were operating your business He would order merchandise without a reasonable expectation that He could pay the suppliers?"

Jesse sank back into his chair, thinking about what I had said. Finally he replied, "God told me to start this business, and nobody will talk me into quitting unless God tells me to." And with that, he left.

It's unfortunate that many well-meaning Christians stubbornly refuse to follow the principles in God's Word. Instead, they adopt the same attitude the Jews displayed in the desert when they complained about everything Moses told them to do. Ultimately God passed them by and waited for others who would obey Him.

God's Word says, *"If I regard wickedness in my heart, the Lord will not hear"* (Psalm 66:18). If you know something you are doing is wrong and persist in it, God will not listen.

The sad conclusion to Jesse's story is that, ultimately, he filed for bankruptcy protection, and his business was dissolved. Instead of being a potential witness for the Lord, he became one more stumbling block in the path of several unsaved people with whom he had done business.

Priority 2: Pay employees. Once the creditors are paid, the next priority is to pay the employees what is due them. This also runs contrary to common business practice. After all, the owner has a right to get paid first, since he or she owns the business, right? Wrong. Remember, *"Do nothing from selfishness or empty conceit, but with humility of mind let each of you regard one another as more important than himself"* (Philippians 2:3).

More often than not, the owner/manager of a business can better afford to lose a paycheck than the employees can. In addition, scripturally speaking, Christian leaders are admonished to humble themselves. In other words, put others first.

Priority 3: Meet owner's needs. Once you are sure that the creditors have been paid and the employees have received their due compensation, then you should draw your portion. (We'll discuss how to determine this amount in a later chapter.)

It is not unusual for people who start businesses to feel that they sacrificed to build the companies, so they have the right to any and all proceeds. Clearly, that is not what God's Word teaches.

The critical decision in this and other matters becomes whether to obey God's Word or to adopt the common practices of our society. That choice is what separates Christian businesspeople from all others. That's why we can be called "followers of Christ"; we follow His principles, regardless of the costs. We know that God is watching even when others are not.

One of the greatest inhibiting factors in God's using Christian businesspeople today is that so many lack that absolute commitment to follow God's path even when no one is watching. We can all learn from the example of Daniel, who refused to compromise what he knew to be God's best even to benefit himself and who suffered the consequences without the "woe is me" attitude of a reluctant disciple.

When King Darius signed a decree forbidding the worship of any god or man other than the king for a period of 30 days, Daniel continued to worship God in view of his open window. When challenged he readily admitted his disobedience and submitted to the punishment: being sealed in a lions' den. True, God intervened on Daniel's behalf, but it was only after Daniel had shown obedience and the willingness to follow God's path unswervingly. *"As an example, brethren, of suffering and patience, take the prophets who spoke in the name of the Lord. Behold, we count those blessed who endured. . . . The Lord is full of compassion and is merciful"* (James 5:10–11).

Set Priorities for Use of Time

There is no biblical principle that sets normal business hours at 40, 60, or 80 hours a week. The preponderance of evidence in Scripture seems to indicate, however, that a six-day work week is not excessive.

We seem to have developed two opposing perspectives in business today. Employees tend to think that anything beyond 40 hours should be a bonus (overtime), and owners think that anything less than 80 hours is being lazy. Both sides have adopted extremes.

When a business owner adopts an excessively long work day that seldom provides any time for relaxation and other outside activities, he or she establishes an unwritten policy: "If you don't work long hours, you won't get ahead in this company." This puts the employees (particularly managers) under great stress and eventually makes them less productive.

The attitude in such companies is known as the burnout mentality. Owners work their best people until they drop, then find someone else to replace them. The turnover in such companies is usually enormous, with high salaries the necessary enticement to attract more workers.

Often owners who adopt this style in their own lives think that if they pay the good people enough, they will be able to keep them. I have found that money is only a temporary motivator. It is true that too little pay will usually force good people out, but too much pay will not keep them on a job that totally dominates their lives. In fact, as soon as they have accumulated enough money to live on a lesser salary, they will leave and trade dollars for time.

Set Ethical Priorities

Once you have established money and time priorities in your business you need to establish some ethical priorities. A few of the more common areas of business ethics violations are taxes, fraud, and misuse of company assets. We will examine each of these areas before outlining the biblical principle for dealing with unethical conduct.

Taxes. Perhaps nothing represents a Christian businessperson's spiritual values more clearly than that person's attitude toward paying taxes. No one likes to pay taxes; even the people who recognize the necessity of collecting taxes for roads, schools, and defense rarely count taxpaying as a privilege. But to actually cheat on income taxes or any other tax is a sin, and sin separates us from God.

Unless you believe that your relationship with God is the most important asset you have in this world, sin will easily ensnare you. I personally believe that cheating on income taxes is the most common sin among Christians in business. Much, if not most, of it is so well concealed that even the best auditors cannot detect it. But God already knows.

Over the years I have probably heard just about every possible way to cheat on taxes. I have met professing Christians who never paid their apportioned amount and rarely, if ever, thought of their evasion as a sin. Many of these people were generous givers to God's causes. Many did wonderful jobs of speaking out for the Lord and working to spread the Gospel. Yet all of them had one characteristic in common: a lack of peace and fulfillment in their spiritual lives.

These people might fake being dynamic Christians when they are out among others who feed their theatrical abilities, but when they are alone they realize that something is missing from their relationship with Jesus.

A few years ago, while teaching a conference in a western city, I reaffirmed that cheating on income taxes is one of the most common sins among Christian businesspeople. I also expressed my belief that people who cheat on income taxes, or in any other aspect of business, are no longer useful to God's plan. Until they confess and repent from their sin, I said, God will simply pass them by.

As soon as I said this, I noticed a man in the second row of the auditorium; he closed his notebook and sat with a scowl on his face for the next 30 minutes, until I announced a break. Then he headed directly for the platform. He pushed his way rudely past the people ahead of him and stormed up to where I was standing.

"I don't see how you can call yourself a Christian and teach something that is so totally unscriptural," he said angrily.

"Tell me about it," I said as nicely as I could. I recognized him to be caught up in the sin he so angrily denied. I've learned that most angry people have had their toes stepped on, spiritually speaking. I also have learned not to take their anger personally. They're not really mad at me; they're mad at what I said.

By this time a large group had gathered to hear the discussion. Apparently this man's anti-tax teaching had become well known in the town, where he pastored a church. He also owned a large construction company and, therefore, had no need of income from the church, so he volunteered his services.

I asked him if he ever paid income taxes.

"I used to pay income tax until I heard some enlightened teaching on the fact that the Sixteenth Amendment was never legally ratified, and therefore it is unconstitutional," he replied defensively.

"But how does that relate to Scripture?" I asked him. I was very familiar with the argument that the income tax laws are illegal. But since the Supreme Court had consistently sided with the tax laws, I had to assume that they are legal, whether or not they are fair.

"God would not have us support a heathen government," he shouted in his best preaching voice. "This government stands against God, and therefore we must stand against it too."

"Are you familiar with the instructions the apostle Paul gives in the Romans, chapter 13?" I asked. By this time the group surrounding us had grown to include some of his followers, who nodded their heads in agreement with everything he said.

"But what about the tax the Lord discussed in Matthew 22 when he was questioned by the Pharisees?" I asked. "Wasn't that the temple tax?"

He stopped for a minute, thrown off track because he had his arguments prepared to counter Paul's instructions to the Romans. But then he recovered. "That doesn't matter," he replied sternly. "The tax we're asked to pay is illegal and is therefore totally voluntary. If you don't want to pay it, the government can't make you."

"So would you say the issue is more constitutional than biblical?" I asked.

He thought for a moment. "Well yes, probably so. It is unconstitutional for the government to order a tax on wages. And besides that," he continued, now confident that he was in control, "the money we're using is counterfeit, since only gold is legal tender."

"Well, I would say two things in response to that argument. First, just pay the taxes in the same counterfeit money the government issues. They won't quarrel with that. Second, if you really believe that income taxes are unconstitutional, you should place your apportioned tax money in an escrow account, so that no one can say your motives are selfish, then file suit against the government to challenge the income tax system. If you're right, use the same legal system that created this tax to remove it."

Then I told him what I still believe: "The motive behind this issue is one of greed, not conviction. If so, you're leading God's people into sin."

The man fumed off the platform, muttering something about my being stupid and part of Satan's plan to confuse true Americans. I learned that scores of well-intentioned Christians had been following his advice and had stopped filing their income tax returns. Later I also heard that this same man had been discovered having affairs with several of the women in his church. Once someone decides to live in sin, the opportunities to increase the sin will multiply.

Fraud. I am constantly amazed by the degree of dishonesty in our society that the average American accepts as normal. We often see clear evidence of politicians' dishonesty, and yet we reelect them to public office. We hear of athletes who break the rules, and yet fans organize campaigns to keep them in sports. One area in which most Americans will not tolerate dishonesty is in the business world. It's not that Americans demand more of their business leaders; it's that they see themselves as the victims of business fraud.

Many studies over the last several years have attempted to measure the honesty index of the average American, both consumers and merchants, and the results are saddening. Consistently, the most acceptable kind of fraud is practiced against insurance companies. Many businessmen surveyed felt they had the right to collect from an insurance company once they had paid into a policy for several years. They saw insurance policies as something like annuities, from which a person who pays a certain amount in has the right to draw a certain amount out.

One common area of fraud is medical fraud. Even well-meaning Christian doctors sometimes conspire to cheat an insurance company on behalf of their patients. The procedure is simple: increase the bill based on the patient's deductible amount. Then discount the bill and the entire amount is paid. Many Christians who call into our daily radio program are concerned about this practice but are fearful of confronting the doctors. When someone cheats, even with the best of intentions, everyone loses.

Fraud is also prevalent in many other sectors of the business community.

Lamar, a friend of mine, recently bought into a new-car dealership. His partner in this venture was a Christian who owned several other dealerships. What Lamar saw when he took over management of the dealership appalled him. The salespeople were deceiving customers by inflating the prices of new cars, then offering discounts to bring the prices down to "dealer cost," when in truth no car sold for anything approaching cost.

In the service center, customers were being charged for service work that was never actually performed; that way the warranty fees available through the manufacturer could be used to boost the dealer's profit margin. Little noncritical problems, such as problems with trim or finish, were simply ignored. Everyone knew the average customer did not have the time to keep bringing the car back for service on such minor items. The established procedure in the service center was, don't fix any noncritical problem unless the customer gets really upset and then only after the third appointment!

Lamar also discovered that the dealership had a recourse agreement with a local finance company that would rebate up to $200 on an installment contract. Many unsuspecting customers were sent to this finance company, where they often paid interest rates and fees several percentage points higher than they would have paid if they financed through a local bank.

As soon as Lamar realized what was going on, he put a stop to unethical practices and fired the sales and service managers. Within three months the dealership's profits had fallen by 25 percent, and the partner wanted to know why. When he heard about the changes, he was furious.

"Don't be stupid!" he shouted at Lamar. "You don't know anything about running a dealership. You just do what I tell you, and we'll be all right."

"But what about the customers? Don't they matter?" Lamar asked in amazement. He had known his new partner for several years, but he now realized he hardly knew him at all. The man had professed to be a Christian and had always treated Lamar well, so he just assumed they would get along in business.

He replied, "Listen, what the customers don't know won't hurt them. If they think they're getting a good deal, they'll be satisfied. Besides, they think they're cheating us, so what's the difference?"

"I guess it's something called integrity," Lamar replied as he walked out of the dealership. He ultimately sold his interest to his partner, who held legal control over the company.

Clearly God's Word says that a deception will always be found out: *"He who walks in integrity walks securely, but he who perverts his ways will be found out"* (Proverbs 10:9). Total honesty is the minimum acceptable standard for a Christian. If a business cannot survive in total honesty, then it's time to do something else.

Charles had been in the furniture manufacturing business for years. He started out sweeping the floors and had worked his way up through the organization, becoming the plant manager in one of the three family-owned plants. However, he felt he should leave the company and get some experience working in another company.

He had been attending a large church in North Carolina and knew the owners of several fine manufacturing companies. One was owned by a man he had admired for years: a strong Christian who gave generously and supported many worthy causes. Charles went to him and shared his ambitions: to become more familiar with different types of manufacturing. He asked if he would allow him to work in his plant in some capacity.

"Yes," he said, "by coincidence I've just had a plant manager leave and I would love to have you run it for me."

After Charles became the plant manager he studied every aspect of the business. He quickly realized the company was sending out literature advertising one type and weight of upholstery fabric but actually using one that was far inferior. Further investigation showed they had been doing this for many years. He called the company owner and asked to see him.

When confronted by the evidence the Christian owner, whom he had admired so much, just stared out into space as if he were totally unconcerned. If Charles expected anything, it was not what happened next. The owner was angry that this young man had the audacity to challenge his business practices. The conversation broke down into a shouting session between boss and employee.

The owner dismissed Charles and accused him of being a back-biter. Charles left the business and ultimately went on to run the family business. He is known for his honesty, ethics, and the growth of his business.

Misuse of company property. I could have included this topic under the area of income taxes, since they are related. But since the use (or misuse) of company property by Christian owners is so widespread, I thought it was worth a separate heading.

Most business owners go to great lengths to reduce and eliminate employee misuse of company property. It is estimated that employee theft accounts for the loss of nearly $160 billion in American businesses each year. But I wonder what owner theft of company property amounts to each year. In total numbers it is probably less than the employee theft but, on a per capita basis, I imagine it is considerably higher.

Owners of businesses tend to believe they can treat company assets as their own personal property. Since the current laws don't agree with that perspective, to do so constitutes sin (missing the mark). Following are some of the more common ways owners tend to misuse company property.

1. Company vehicles. With rare exception most company-supplied vehicles are also used for activities not related to business. When that is the case, the proper procedure is to keep track of these uses and reimburse the company from personal funds. An alternative is to declare the value of this personal use in your income and pay taxes on it. This choice is normally specified by company policy.

2. Telephone use. I would venture to say that the majority of business owners don't hesitate to make personal long-distance calls on the company telephone. The correct procedure is the same as with the company car: either reimburse the company from personal funds or claim the value of the calls in your income.

3. Copy machines, pens, pencils, and paper. These items are normally viewed as perks of ownership. In reality they can be snares set by Satan, who knows that if someone cheats a little bit the next step will be easier. Business owners need to set their guard against the little acts of dishonesty, so that bigger ones won't end up being a problem later. *"Do not enter the path of the wicked, and do not proceed in the way of evil men"* (Proverbs 4:14).

Confession and restitution. It's usually far easier to avoid the temptation to lie or steal from your company than it is to confess and make restitution, because confession and restitution almost always involve some unpleasant consequences. Many times Christians think that all God requires of us is to give up the sin, but that isn't true. God asks that we give up the sin, confess it, and then offer to make restitution whenever possible.

The Bible contains hundreds of examples of confession and restitution. One that often comes to mind when I think of this principle is that of Zaccheus: *"Zaccheus stopped and said to the Lord, 'Behold, Lord, half of my possessions I will give to the poor, and if I have defrauded anyone of anything, I will give back four times as much'"* (Luke 19:8). When he came face-to-face with the truth, he repented of his sins of cheating people, confessed, and offered to make restitution above what Jewish law required, which was double the amount.

Some years ago I met with a Christian businessman who could have profited by following Zaccheus's example. This man, who operated a large cosmetics packaging company, was having some financial problems because of investments in several unsuccessful businesses. It was clear that his financial problems would clear up if he would just stop investing in these side ventures. The packaging company itself was profitable and had the potential of growing much larger. So my recommendation to him was simple: Stop wasting good money in the side ventures.

A few months later I received an urgent call from this man. Another business he had started was in trouble to the tune of nearly $1 million. Over the next several days we talked many times by phone. After looking through the financial statements on the new business, I determined that it was hopelessly in debt and that, although a very good idea, it was doomed to failure.

I asked, "Why in the world would you risk over a million dollars on a venture like this? If you'll just concentrate on making the packaging company as efficient as possible, you'll make all the money you'll ever need."

In all honesty I thought it was the case of another small business-man who wanted to become a conglomerate. What puzzled me was that this man didn't seem to have the huge ego that normally accompanies someone with this motivation. He seemed to be subdued and humble—in other words, a nice guy.

A few days later he called me at home to ask if he and his wife could fly to Atlanta the next morning for a personal meeting. Sensing urgency in his voice, I agreed. Then I called my secretary and asked her to adjust my schedule.

In my office the next morning, this Christian businessman related one of the most remarkable stories of dishonesty in business that I had ever heard.

"I inherited the business from my father," he told me, looking down at the table. "Dad had run it for 20 years and was well respected in the industry, but the business never seemed to reach its potential. So I started a shipping company to transport raw materials and finished products to and from the distributors. But we lacked the capital to develop a large enough fleet, so I had to borrow against the business.

"The costs associated with the transport business were much higher than I anticipated, and since we already had so much invested I borrowed even more against the business. Within a year I found myself in financial trouble, and it looked like I could lose the business and, with it, my mother's livelihood.

"The company we package for has never been able to break into the discount store market because its products are too costly. I could see a sizable potential for increase in our packaging business if their products could be sold there. So I hired a chemist to analyze their formulas, and we began to manufacture their cosmetics, using less costly ingredients. We then mixed the new formulas half-and-half with the old and marketed them to this new outlet. They were an instant success, and our volume doubled.

"We did this for over a year and got totally out of debt. Then I began to really feel guilty about what we were doing and stopped."

"Didn't the company have any idea what you were doing?" I asked.

"I'm sure they did," he replied, looking at his wife who nodded her head in agreement. "Since we mixed the product half-and-half, our orders for their products increased substantially, and yet our sales to their normal outlets didn't change proportionately. I think they knew what we were doing but turned their heads. After all, it was new business for them too, and they didn't have to pay the royalties that made them noncompetitive in this market.

"Unfortunately, with the oil price increases, the trucking company again became unprofitable, and we had to restart the old mixing practice again to bail it out. Now we find that the business is dependent on that source of income and we can't stop."

I asked if he realized the practice he was engaged in was not only unethical but probably illegal as well.

"I know it is," he replied uncomfortably, "but we're so far into it now, I just don't see a way to get out. Over a hundred employees and their families depend on our business."

The man was presenting the needs of others as justification for continuing an unethical practice, often called "offering a red herring," which means it is supposed to divert attention from the primary problem. I realized the decision had to come from him, not from me. But I did recommend that he go to the parent company, confess what he had been doing, and take the consequences whatever they were.

"Eventually something will happen to bring this to light, and you won't have the chance to confess it first," I said. "Take the opportunity to do so now." With that our session broke up, and they returned home.

A few weeks later I received a frantic call from the husband, saying that one of the employees involved in the illegal mixing process had been dismissed and, out of anger, had gone to the parent company and revealed the entire operation. He also submitted a written report to the board of directors, who initiated a mandatory audit of the packaging company.

At the conclusion of the audit, the directors of the parent company withdrew its contract with this so-called Christian businessman, demanding that he sell off all his company's assets and send them the proceeds. They contended that his profits had been made at their expense and that they were the true owners of the assets.

Ultimately, the packaging company survived, because the parent company was shown to have made substantial profits from the illegal business. They refused to prosecute because they wanted to avoid the adverse publicity that a public trial would have generated. But the real loss in this process was the loss of credibility on the part of an outspoken Christian businessman.

Remember, *"He who walks in integrity walks securely, but he who perverts his ways will be found out"* (Proverbs 10:9).

6

Keeping Vows

A *vow* is defined in *Merriam Webster's Collegiate Dictionary* as "a solemn promise or assertion; one by which a person is bound to an act, service, or condition; to bind or consecrate."

The term appears many places in the Bible to refer to a promise or pledge, and the emphasis is that such promises are binding. *"You shall be careful to perform what goes out from your lips, just as you have voluntarily vowed to the Lord your God, what you have promised"* (Deuteronomy 23:23). That means that when we give our word to do something, we are obligated to do it!

Unfortunately this is not the typical attitude today. Sometimes we think that fulfillment of a vow is conditional: "I'll do it if it profits me" or "I'll do it if the judge forces me." In other words, we keep the vows that are to our advantage and break those that are not.

This mentality is clearly visible in professional athletics today. An athlete who receives a multimillion-dollar contract to play a sport is thrilled with it until he or she hears that another athlete received an even better deal. Then the athlete becomes disgruntled and refuses to play until the contract is renegotiated.

Clearly value is not the issue. Who can realistically believe that any athlete is worth millions when compared to other professions? The issue is integrity and values—commodities often found lacking in our society. The same basic issue is at stake when a building contractor refuses to complete a job because the work was underbid, when a Christian speaker cancels an engagement because he or she received a better offer, or when a teenager fails to show up for work at the local McDonald's on Saturday because he or she is "too tired" after the Friday-night party.

A FAITHLESS SOCIETY

The breaking of vows is so common in our generation that airlines overbook approximately 30 percent of their seats to compensate for the expected no-shows. Such a practice doesn't sound all that ominous until we realize it is symptomatic of a society built on the expectation that few people actually will keep their word. Those who do keep promises without compromise often find themselves branded as suckers. Other people assume that almost anyone can take advantage of these honest folks because of their personality flaw.

Yet, only a generation ago keeping a vow was the norm in our society. Those who didn't keep their word were shunned by those around them, and few people would do business with them. I doubt that most of our grandparents knew anyone who had gone bankrupt or even defaulted on a loan to a local merchant. Debtors' prisons were still in operation as late as the 1920s in America, and divorce lawyers would have had a hard time earning a living in our grandparents' day.

Marriage and parenting are the two strongest vows anyone will ever make. When you see these commitments being carelessly discarded, you can be certain that the ethics of that generation have been abandoned. Today people seem to fall in and out of marriage relationships as easily as we did boy-girl friendships when I was a teenager. Approximately one-half of today's marriages dissolve. With the commitment level so low, is it any wonder that it is so hard to get people to finish jobs if they don't think they are profitable?

Just look at the number of babies abandoned by their mothers in hospitals today and you'll get a good indication of how vows are viewed in our society. Parents of all social and economic levels have been known to walk off and leave babies who are less than perfect. Not long ago, for instance, I read of a couple who refused to take their baby home from the hospital because she had a disabling genetic deficiency.

What our society needs is a good dose of biblical ethics from God's people—the kind of ethic that requires us to keep our word no matter what the costs. Situational ethics have so shaped our society that even God's people have lost the concept of absolutes when it comes to keeping our word.

In the mid-eighties some of the players in the National Football League went on strike for more money and better contracts. Other players resisted joining them in the strike. Feelings ran so intense on this issue that there were reports of offensive linemen who allowed the opposing team free shots at their own running backs—just because the backs didn't support the strike. Other players refused to ride to practice with friends with whom they had shared rides for years.

During this time I received a call from a Christian player who was in the middle of the controversy. He wanted to decide his position on the strike according to scriptural principles, but he felt he needed some advice to define what those principles were. He felt a personal loyalty to his teammates but a contractual duty to the team owners. Up to that point, he had continued to go to practice, but many of the other players were accusing him of being a strike breaker.

He said, "Larry, I need to know whether I should stand with the majority of my teammates in support of the strike or with the owners."

"What's the feeling among the players?" I asked.

"No doubt about where they stand," he answered. "They feel like those who won't support the strike are just out to get what they can for themselves. But what I can't figure out is this: Should my loyalties be to the players' union or to the team's owners?"

"Who did you sign a contract with?"

"Obviously, I signed with the owners. But I also signed an agreement with the players' union that they could represent me in contract disputes."

"Do you have a contract dispute?" I asked.

"Not really," he responded. "But that's what the union is saying in support of the strike. Their contract with the NFL is running out, and they want the players' support to renegotiate."

"Well, you certainly can't have two authorities in this issue. Who pays your salary?"

"The team owners do," he replied. "But I know what the guys are going to say—that I've already got my money and that's why I won't strike. I don't think that's my motive, but how do I convince them? I'm doing okay financially, but many of them do have bad contracts, and I know they should probably get more money."

"But that really is not your problem," I counseled. "Your responsibility is to follow your convictions on the basis of God's Word. Remember Ecclesiastes 5:4–5: *'When you make a vow to God, do not be late in paying it, for He takes no delight in fools. Pay what you vow! It is better that you should not vow than that you should vow and not pay.'*"

"That's what I believe too, but if I follow it I won't be very popular on the team!" the player predicted.

"God never said it would be easy to follow in His steps! In fact, Jesus warned in Matthew 16:24: *'If anyone wishes to come after Me, let him deny himself, and take up his cross, and follow Me.'*"

"Well, you're right about it not being easy!" he said. "But would you be willing to talk to some of the other Christians on the team? So far, they don't agree with my decisions, either."

I told him I would be glad to. "If you can get them together, I'll be there."

Unfortunately, the meeting quickly fell apart. The other 14 Christian players had brought a local pastor, who supported their position on the strike. I questioned him about his scriptural basis for supporting the strike, and his defense was that the team owners were callous and cheap. "And," he said, "the real authority for the players is the union."

"But who pays the salaries, and who signed the contracts with the players?" I asked.

"That doesn't matter," he replied heatedly. "They were forced to sign contracts that don't even guarantee them a job if they're hurt."

"I don't disagree that a typical NFL contract primarily benefits the team owners," I replied, "but that is not the issue here. In fact, that's not even the issue behind the strike. The players aren't disputing the contracts they have; they simply want more money attached to the existing contracts. I rather doubt that the issue here is fundamentally one of conviction or principle."

The rest of the abbreviated meeting was truly a shouting match, with the most vocal players winning. But one additional player, a quarterback, did say that he was convicted not to strike. He said he had signed a contract and had given his word to play and would do so unless the owners told him not to show up. This didn't set well with his teammates, and eventually the stand this fine athlete took that evening cost him a brilliant career. The negative feelings of the other players greatly influenced his trade to another team.

As the strike continued, both the player who had originally called me and the one who made his decision at the meeting went daily to the park to practice. Initially several other players joined them, but the ill will from the striking players soon coerced the others into joining the picket lines.

Eventually the owners told the two nonstriking athletes to stay home and refused to pay them the salaries due according to their contracts. The quarterback was later benched and then traded. But the player who called me went on to become a Hall of Fame player. He never doubted his decision to do what God's Word commands, and he would have done so even if he had been dropped from the team.

WHAT IS YOUR WORD WORTH?

In my father's generation when a man gave his word to do a job he did it! If he didn't, no one would do business with him again. Today, if you reach an agreement on almost anything, you need several attorneys to review the contract to make sure it contains no legal loopholes that could allow the other parties to escape fulfilling their part of the bargain. In fact, the highest-paid, most successful attorneys are often those who can weave the most ambiguous language into a contract so that the actual intent is assumed but not mandated.

I recall a time when my father, who was an electrician, agreed to rewire a neighbor's house for about $2,000. In the midst of the job he found that he had underbid by several hundred dollars and, at the same time, the cost of materials jumped because of a copper shortage. On a $2,000 job, my father stood to lose nearly $1,200, a sizable sum in the early fifties.

Today, under similar circumstances, a contractor would just look for some real or imagined reason to raise the price or quit the job. My dad never considered either option. He simply went down to his bank and procured a loan against our home to complete the job. The customer didn't thank him because he never knew. My dad just did what any honest, ethical businessperson would have done under similar circumstances.

A PROMISE IS A PROMISE

A man I'll call Roy was an antique dealer who operated a monthly auction. On a buying trip he purchased a desk that he thought might be a valuable early American antique: a Jefferson desk. Upon closer inspection, however, he decided that the piece was just a very good reproduction. So he decided to include it in his next auction with the intention of at least recovering his initial investment.

The day of the auction a woman came into Roy's store, spotted the desk, and fell in love with it.

"How much is that lovely old desk?" she asked.

"Ma'am, it's really not an antique. It's just a real good reproduction," Roy said with a sigh. He knew that she couldn't possibly know the difference, but he couldn't sell her something as an antique that he knew was not.

"Oh, I don't care about that," she said. "I just love it. How much is it?"

Roy quoted her the price, explaining, "I'll sell it for what I have in it."

"Oh, that's a good price," she responded enthusiastically. "I'll leave a deposit and return with the rest of the money later."

"That's not necessary, Ma'am," Roy responded. "If you'll just give me your name and phone number, I'll hold the desk for you until you return."

"That's very nice of you," she said, writing the needed information on a pad. "I'll be back tomorrow morning with a van to pick it up."

Roy was happy just to recover his money. "It really is a good copy," he mused as he looked it over once more. "It would fool almost anybody if it weren't for the dovetailing on the drawers. But that style of work wasn't even available in the eighteenth century."

Just before Roy's auction that evening the bidders began to browse through the merchandise. One dealer Roy knew well stopped at the desk with the "Hold" tag on it and examined it thoroughly. Roy chuckled as he saw the dealer on his hands and knees looking under the desk and inside the drawers. *It really is a good reproduction*, he thought.

The dealer walked over to where Roy was seated. "I see you have a hold on that desk, Roy. I guess you got a good price for it?"

"Not really, Tom. I just got back what I had in it, or at least I will tomorrow."

The dealer exclaimed, "Why, I'll give you twice what you paid right now!"

Roy responded, "You're crazy, Tom. That's not a real Jeffersonian. It's just a copy—a good one, I'll grant you, but still a copy."

"It's not a copy, Roy. Only the insides of the drawers have been replaced. The chestnut is eighteenth century, and the craftsmanship is definitely original."

Suddenly Roy realized that what his friend said could be true. He hadn't considered that someone might have reworked the drawers. He had just assumed that no one would be ignorant enough to alter an original.

"I'll tell you something else, Roy," the dealer said softly. "I think this is one of the desks that was in the Jefferson mansion until the War between the States. This may well be the missing Jefferson desk."

"What?" Roy exclaimed. "You must be wrong. That desk has been missing for more than 100 years now. It would be worth $100,000 or more!"

"More like $200,000," his friend replied. "If you haven't actually sold that desk, I would suggest you put it away somewhere."

"But I have sold it," Roy said. "The buyer's coming back to get it tomorrow."

"Have you actually accepted the money?"

"No, but I gave her my word she could have it."

"Listen, just make some excuse or substitute another piece. Who knows what it might actually be worth. It's probably a one-of-a-kind that Jefferson made himself. You might get a collector to give you a quarter of a million for it."

The rest of that evening Roy wrestled with his conscience. He knew he had agreed to sell the desk. But since no money had actually changed hands, he knew there was some doubt about his promise's being legally binding.

After lying awake for several hours, Roy got up with the thought of calling an attorney friend to ask him about the legalities of refusing the sale. But he changed his mind when he glanced at the clock and saw it was nearly 2:00 A.M. "Besides," he told himself, "it's really not a legal issue anyway."

The next morning, when the woman returned to claim the desk, she couldn't find it. "Where's my desk?" she asked. "You didn't sell it to someone else after you promised it to me, did you?"

"No," Roy answered. "It's still here. I put it in the back for safe-keeping." He then went on to explain what he had learned about the desk and its value.

"Then you won't sell it?" she asked dejectedly.

"Yes, I'll sell it," Roy replied. "I have to admit that I struggled with this most of the night. But this morning as I was praying the Lord led me to Proverbs 11:3: *'The integrity of the upright will guide them, but the falseness of the treacherous will destroy them.'* I gave my word, and I have to keep it. Just don't let anyone talk you out of that desk, Ma'am. It's one of a kind."

"Well, I don't think I can accept it. If it's really valuable, I would always be worried that something would happen to it. You keep it and be sure it goes someplace where people can see it."

"But, Ma'am, it's worth maybe $200,000. And it's rightfully yours."

"Then why don't you sell it and buy me a good reproduction to use in my study?" she said as she headed toward the door. "Just give me a call when you find what I'm looking for, will you?"

Roy later sold the desk to a Washington museum. He used a portion of the money to purchase a beautiful Jefferson copy made to his specifications and presented it as a gift to the woman buyer, along with a check for $100,000. Roy realized that his integrity was worth more than a short-term profit.

GUIDELINES FOR MAKING VOWS YOU CAN KEEP

All of us, at one time or the other, have promised something we later wished we hadn't. With me it's usually a matter of committing to speaking engagements I later regret. Ordinarily, when I make the commitments, they don't seem too pressing; often they are a couple of years away. Then the time passes and the engagement is at hand. As a rule, by then I have too many commitments and I end up wishing that I could think of a convenient way to get out of speaking.

I have made it a policy to do whatever I say, so when this happens I go, if it is humanly possible. Knowing that a commitment is a vow, however, I make it practice not to commit to anything without praying about it first and considering all the problems that can arise later.

Since as Christians we are bound by the words of our mouths, we need to be very careful about what we promise. I have developed five simple rules that help me to avoid making commitments I might later regret.

1. When in Doubt, Say No

I often tell my staff not to ask for a decision on a critical subject when I am working on a book. I tend to concentrate so completely on the project at hand that I can respond to a question and later not even remember the conversation!

Since I know I have this tendency, I have devised a system to keep me out of trouble. First, my secretary controls access to my time while I'm writing. Second, I schedule regular times to deal with other subjects when I am at logical breakpoints in my writing and can relax. Third, if someone asks me for an answer at any time other than these scheduled periods, I will always answer no. If staff members don't want a "no" answer, they learn to wait until I am free to concentrate on their issues. (Being able to follow this particular rule requires that I have a good administrator who can take charge of the day-to-day operations in the company. That way the wheels of business can continue to roll and interruptions can be kept at a minimum.)

2. Keep a "Year at a Glance" Calendar

Personal friends sometimes call me at home to ask for a special favor, such as speaking at their church or at a business meeting. I have learned over the years to maintain a single schedule calendar at my office. That way, I can honestly tell anyone who calls me at home that I will need to check my schedule and call back.

I use a "Year at a Glance" calendar that covers at least two years so that I can see all my previous commitments at once. Why? Because although the particular week in question might be free, I may need that open week to recharge my batteries after a rough week or to prepare for one to come. I have learned the hard way that I need to preserve some down time to keep from running down myself.

3. Prioritize the Day

I find I make the worst decisions when I work myself into a time bind because of bad scheduling. As most people do, I run into unscheduled interruptions over which I have little or no control. These will include visits from my grandchildren and calls from friends with urgent needs (an ex-president even called to have lunch one day).

Interruptions like these perplexed me for a long time. I didn't want to eliminate them entirely, but I also didn't want them to run my life. Then an obstetrician friend shared his solution with me. Since delivering babies is seldom a scheduled process, he would often have his workday disrupted by patients who needed immediate attention.

Finally he recognized that although the disruptions weren't the same every day, they were fairly regular. So he had his receptionist pencil in unscheduled appointments every day and not book patients during those time periods. If no one showed up during his unscheduled periods, he had an extra hour or so to handle paperwork, read his Bible, or do whatever he wanted. When someone showed up with an emergency, he would fit that person into the unscheduled time.

I decided the same principle would work for me, and I began to use a time management system and it works great in prioritizing my working day and scheduling in even the unscheduled interruptions.

4. Don't Book Too Far Ahead

In the Bible we are gently chided, *"Come now, you who say, 'Today or tomorrow, we shall go to such and such a city, and spend a year there and engage in business and make a profit.' Yet you do not know what your life will be like tomorrow. . . . Instead, you ought to say, 'If the Lord wills, we shall live and also do this or that'"* (James 4:13–15).

That is sound logic from a business perspective also. Who knows what may occur in a year or two? If you schedule your time too far into the future, you may limit God's ability to change your direction without some rather severe "tree shaking" in your life.

Each person must decide where to draw the line. For me it is about two years. I simply will not schedule any events beyond this period. I know some people who schedule as far out as five years. Usually they do this because they are unable to say no to anyone. And the vast majority will admit that policy has come back to haunt them at times.

5. Use a Written Contract

The probability of a misunderstanding in a written agreement has been calculated at 20 percent, more or less. The probability of a misunderstanding in a verbal agreement is nearly 100 percent!

I always advise, "Write it down." Anyone who would be offended that you want a written agreement would be even more offended by misunderstandings over a verbal one! Plus, interestingly enough, I am a visual, rather than a verbal, person. I remember what I read far better than what I hear. The very process of writing something down does two things for me: it slows me down and it triggers my visual memory. For me, writing down any and all commitments is essential.

I have arbitrated many disputes between Christians, in which both parties were certain they were right, but each held opposite perspectives. Most of their disagreements could have been avoided by committing them to writing first. Often the two parties didn't do so because they didn't want the other person to think there was a lack of trust. It isn't a matter of trust. It's a matter of understanding what you are committing to.

My advice is to *keep your word.* If you aren't willing to perform what you vow, even at the cost of all your material assets, then you need to realize that you don't have a material problem. You have a spiritual problem that is being reflected through your finances.

In a world permeated by half-truths and legal compromise, God is looking for diligent stewards to bless. *"For the eyes of the Lord move to and fro throughout the earth that He may strongly support those whose heart is completely His"* (2 Chronicles 16:9).

There is little doubt that a totally honest businessperson will experience some losses and will be misused by others, at least in the short run. But I believe God will compensate for any losses in many ways, not the least of which are rewards in the kingdom of God.

The apostle Paul expressed it eloquently: *"I count all things to be loss in view of the surpassing value of knowing Christ Jesus my Lord, for whom I have suffered the loss of all things, and count them but rubbish in order that I may gain Christ. . . . And the peace of God, which surpasses all comprehension, shall guard your hearts and your minds in Christ Jesus"* (Philippians 3:8; 4:7).

7

The Benefits of Counsel

"Without consultation, plans are frustrated, but with many counselors they succeed" (Proverbs 15:22). This is a clear admonition for us to seek the counsel of others. But what about the problem with bad counsel? (There certainly is a lot of that in Christian circles!)

The Bible offers some advice in that regard: *"The naive believes everything, but the prudent man considers his steps"* (Proverbs 14:15). In other words, a wise person seeks many counselors, and a fool listens to most of them.

The standard against which all counsel should be weighed is God's Word. If the counsel you hear doesn't measure up to what the Word says, ignore it. I recall a story I heard once about a tourist who, upon viewing the *Mona Lisa* in the Louvre in Paris, shook his head and commented, "That's not a very good painting." A guard standing nearby leaned over and said, "Sir, that painting is no longer on trial." That's how Christians are to view God's Word: It is no longer on trial.

CONSIDERATIONS IN ASKING ADVICE

I have been asked for advice and counsel many times, so I believe I can speak with at least some degree of authority on this subject. There are some useful questions to ask yourself when asking advice.

1. Am I Looking for Someone Else to Make My Decisions for Me?

Unfortunately, no one can really know God's plan for your life except you and your spouse. A good counselor will refuse to be put in the position of making someone else's choices. The role of a counselor is to act as an objective observer in a situation and point out alternatives the counselee might have overlooked. Because a counselor usually has had the experience of dealing with many different situations, he or she should be able to draw from greater experience. But no counselor has the right or the responsibility of making decisions for someone else.

Cal had come to my office seeking advice about selling his company. He had been offered a deal that would ensure his future financially, but he didn't have a firm direction about it.

"What's your primary reason for selling?" I asked Cal.

"They offered me nearly $12 million for the business," he answered.

"Okay, I understand the offer, but what is your reason for selling? What will you do if you sell the company?"

"I don't really know," Cal replied. "I never thought seriously about selling before. I just assumed I'd be running the company the rest of my life."

"What will you do with the money if you do sell?"

"I'm not really sure of that, either. I guess I would give a lot of it to the Lord's work and put some away in a retirement plan. Then I'd probably start another business with the rest."

"Could you go back into the same kind of business?"

"No," he replied. "I would have to sign a noncompetitive agreement for at least ten years."

"Do you believe the Lord has originated this offer and wants you to sell the company?"

"I honestly don't know. My wife doesn't want us to sell, but she says she will go along with whatever I want to do."

"Do you believe God put you in your business?"

"Absolutely," Cal replied. "I have seen the Lord's hand in it many times. In the first place, I don't have the brains to put all this together! I went in competition with a large national company and have actually outproduced them over the last five years. That's why they want to buy the company."

"Why did you start this kind of company?" I asked. "I know the company you're negotiating with, and they had been doing business for a long time before you started."

"Yes. In fact, I used to work for them," Cal replied with a grimace. "I didn't like the way they treated their employees. They would constantly change the way they paid commissions so that the salespeople would never be able to earn more than the management. That's why I left, and that's why I have been able to grow so quickly. I was able to hire some of their best people."

"So let me get the facts straight, then. First, the primary reason for selling is $12 million. Right?"

"That's right," Cal answered. "It's probably twice what I could get for the company anywhere else."

"Second, you don't have a need or a real plan for the money. Right?"

"That's true, although I would use a lot of it for the Lord's work."

"Third, you wouldn't stay home and count your money. You probably would start another business."

"Yes. But I really don't know what the business would be right now. This is all I have done for the past 20 years."

"Fourth, you would be turning your employees, whom I assume you care about and have been witnessing to, over to a company you didn't like and couldn't work for. Right?"

"I guess it seems pretty stupid when you put it that way," Cal admitted.

"If someone had come to you for counsel with the same list of reasons, what would you have said?" I asked.

"I probably would say the same thing my wife originally said," Cal responded. "She asked me, 'How can you take what God gave into your care and sell it to someone who will undermine all you have accomplished?'"

Cal probably knew the right decision from the beginning, but he got blinded by the dazzle of the world: in his case a $12 million dazzle. The decisions become clearer when viewed from the apostle Paul's perspective: *"And whatever you do in word or deed, do all in the name of the Lord Jesus, giving thanks through Him to God the Father"* (Colossians 3:17).

2. Am I Just Shopping for Rationalizations?

It seems to be human nature for those who are doing something they know is wrong to seek the approval of others to justify it. And this is true of many Christians, particularly when the counsel is from someone in full-time ministry. Apparently it is assumed that the word of a professional minister carries more spiritual weight than the word of an ordinary Christian. I find little difference in wisdom between the counsel given by those in ministry and what is given by those who are not ministers. The critical factor is the degree of a person's commitment to the Lord's direction, not his or her vocation.

Perhaps one of the worst legacies of ministries like the PTL Club in recent years was the very bad counsel they offered in the name of the Lord. I have personally witnessed Christians who were violating basic biblical principles and rationalizing it because they heard a television evangelist (or other leader) say it was okay. Jim Bakker, former head of PTL, has detailed this well in his book, *I Was Wrong* (Thomas Nelson).

I have counseled with Christians who borrowed tens of thousands of dollars with no visible way to repay it and rationalized this deceit because they had heard a TV evangelist promise that if they just gave more to God's work He would never let them fail. In truth they were violating basic biblical admonitions against surety, get-rich-quick schemes, greed, and materialism, because of their poor application of the Word.

Remember, God is under no obligation to bail us out of every tight spot we get ourselves into just because we promise Him a "tip"! The counselor who says, "Give, and God will bail you out," is usually hoping for a sizable gift to his organization on the basis of that advice. And the counselee is usually hoping to continue his or her indulgence and slothfulness while covering them with a bribe to God. Anyone who actually believes that our giving obligates God to prosper us just needs to review the verse: *"For who has known the mind of the Lord, or who became His counselor? Or who has first given to Him that it might be paid back to him again?"* (Romans 11:34–35).

God is not impressed by the volume of counsel for or against a particular subject. There is just one source of truth, God's Word. When the counsel you receive runs contrary to Scripture, walk away from the counsel. Remember, *"He who walks with wise men will be wise, but the companion of fools will suffer harm"* (Proverbs 13:20).

3. Am I Looking for a Miracle or a Handout?

I had a meeting with a Christian woman who ran a trucking business. She was frantically looking for a way to save her business, but I concluded it could not survive. Her current need for additional capital and her existing debt load were just too much! I tried my best to help her come to the same conclusion, but she refused to even consider such a possibility. She wanted me to recommend some "rich Christians" she could approach for the money she needed.

"I can't do that," I responded. "In the first place, I don't believe your business can repay any additional loans. And, second, arranging loans is not a part of what I do."

"Well, what good are you then?" she snapped. "Why bother to apply biblical principles if they don't help when you really need it?"

What she really meant was, if she agreed to using these principles in her business would they ensure her success, including giving her the money she needed?

"No," I assured her. "They probably won't work for you the way you want them to."

"Why not?" she asked. "I'm a Christian. Other Christians should be willing to help me."

"Well," I replied, "I can think of several reasons why you should not have gone into business and several principles that would suggest that you should shut down the business and trim your losses while you can. A Christian is not automatically obligated to invest in another Christian's business. Sometimes it is discipline that is needed, not more money."

"Well, I personally think your counsel stinks," she retorted. "I have someone who is willing to cosign a note for me, but only if you will agree that he should. So if you don't help me, and my business fails, it will be your fault."

"I won't accept that responsibility," I replied. "In the first place, I would never act as a go-between for you and a lender. And in the second place, I would discourage anyone from cosigning on the basis of God's Word."

She stormed out of my office, shouting some colorful obscenities about what I should do with my advice. Within a few weeks her business was shut down by the creditors. She owed nearly $500,000 on a business that had only $20,000 in total assets, including the car she was driving. As a counselor, I could offer her neither a miracle nor a handout.

A Christian friend called one of our counselors and said that his father-in-law had invested a great deal of money in his son-in-law's business venture. The business was not doing well and they wanted someone to look at it and determine what the situation was.

The father-in-law said, "I want to do whatever it takes. If my son-in-law is capable of running the business, I'm willing to sell my home and invest the money to salvage what I already have in the business."

The counselor agreed to evaluate the business. After spending several days analyzing the business and talking to the employees and to the son-in-law, the counselor determined that the business probably couldn't be salvaged and, in fact, the son-in-law most likely could not run any business; he should be working for someone else!

The business had accumulated a lot of debt, and unless it could be sold the investors were going to lose everything.

When the counselor told the son-in-law his conclusions, he became angry. He assumed the counselor had been brought in to help turn the business around and make it profitable. The bottom line was that the business did eventually fail and all of the investors lost their money.

If the family had received some honest, objective counsel early on, the father-in-law could have saved nearly $500,000. The counsel he had received previously was kind and supportive but very costly.

4. Do I Genuinely Want Honest Counsel Before Making a Decision?

Over the years I've done counseling, I have sincerely appreciated those who understood and used the counsel they received as it was intended—as a source of perspective and a chance to examine as many alternatives as possible.

I regularly get calls from Christians in business who have a good grasp on their finances and often know as much as I do (or more) about the biblical principles of operating a business. They normally ask if I can see any biblical principle they are violating in the pursuit of their profession. Whenever an unusual circumstance arises, I search the Scriptures with them to see if there is an appropriate application.

One example I recall was a friend who wanted to turn the ownership of his company over to his employees while maintaining management of it. He had chosen to form a limited partnership, in which the employees would acquire the majority ownership, while he would remain as the general partner in control of the company.

This certainly was a unique arrangement, and I was not qualified to comment on the legalities of the agreement or the tax consequences. Fortunately he didn't require either of those from me. What he wanted was input on the advisability of transferring ownership to the employees. He wondered if he would be violating any biblical principle by doing so.

My first question was, "Why do you want to do this?"

He replied, "I want to show my employees that I really care about them and I want to build a Christian company that will perpetuate itself. From this point on the employees will realize that they are really working for themselves, so I hope they will put 100 percent of their efforts into their work."

"What if they don't see this like you do?" I asked. "I have been around people long enough to realize that others don't always appreciate our good intentions; nor do they always change their bad habits just because it's their lives they're messing up."

"I think I can get them to understand," he replied. "I'm doing what I believe the Lord wants me to do. I just hope I'm not trying to buy loyalty at the cost of a company."

"I'm continually amazed that what we expect out of people is not what they give," I replied frankly. "I remember one of the first couples I ever counseled. The husband was out of a job and out of money. He had a job offer that required him to have a reliable car. But he had no money and no credit to buy the car he needed since he didn't have a job (a classic catch-22). After praying about the situation, I decided to give him one of our cars—a five-year-old automobile that I had cared for meticulously as long as I had owned it. I felt good about being able to help someone in need.

"The next time I saw the couple, they were driving a brand-new car. Shocked, I asked what had happened to the car I had given them.

"'I used that old clunker as the down payment on a good one!' the husband explained.

"It was all I could do to keep from throwing him out of my office. Then I realized my error. I had played God with that couple and decided on my own to provide what I thought they needed. All I had done was allow them to go deeper into debt. I should have placed some restrictions on the gift or made it a temporary loan instead.

"I also realized that I had expected a certain pattern of response from that couple, and when they hadn't done what I expected, I felt resentful. Therefore, my gift had not really been a gift; it had been the benevolent act of an overlord. After that experience, I committed both my attitude and the car to the Lord and set about trying to help the couple rather than to coddle them."

My friend discovered this same hard lesson in his business. He went ahead with his plan, but his employees didn't respond to his benevolence. The ones who worked hard before still do, and the complainers continue to complain.

Perhaps the project was not really for their benefit ultimately, but it may well have been designed for him to be able to "let go and let God." He left the company two years later and it failed. The lesson learned? Sometimes what we "feel" isn't God speaking.

USE OF PROFESSIONAL COUNSEL

Should a Christian in business seek the advice of professional counselors, particularly non-Christian counselors? This is a difficult and controversial question. Many Christians are fed up with the low caliber of counsel they have received from many attorneys, accountants, and planners who call themselves Christians. As a result, they tend to seek the help they need from the secular world.

Without question, there are many knowledgeable non-Christians in many of the technical disciplines. But to answer this question satisfactorily, we have to return to our ultimate source of counsel: God's Word.

We are told, *"How blessed is the man who does not walk in the counsel of the wicked, nor stand in the path of sinners, nor sit in the seat of scoffers! But his delight is in the law of the Lord, and in His law he meditates day and night. And he will be like a tree firmly planted by streams of water, which yields its fruit in its season, and its leaf does not wither; and in whatever he does, he prospers"* (Psalm 1:1–3).

Does this mean we should never listen to any non-Christian advice? I don't think so. But I do believe it is an admonition not to seek out unbelievers as primary counselors. In other words, those who advise you day by day.

The difficulty isn't the advice they give; it's the advice they don't give, specifically, the lack of spiritual insight.

How, for instance, can a non-Christian attorney understand and accept the premise that one Christian should not sue another? I have heard some very persuasive arguments presented by secular attorneys to their Christian clients on the merits of suing everyone equally, without discrimination. If it had not been for my acceptance of the Word as the ultimate source of counsel, I could have been swayed myself.

Try to convince a secular attorney of the logic of not defending a legal action by countersuit. The attorney probably will think you're crazy and refuse to defend you for fear of being sued for malpractice.

The same could be said of trying to convince the average secular accountant of the logic of not charging interest to other Christians. Or try to show the same accountant the logic of becoming totally debt-free when he or she knows the multiplication factor of leveraged money in today's economy.

The excuse often given by Christians for using secular advisors is that good Christian advisors aren't available. That simply is *not* true. If God's Word requires it, God provides it. Many highly competent professionals who also are committed Christians can be found in every field. You just have to expend energy to locate the good Christian counselors. They may not be the most visible; nor will they necessarily use the term *Christian* in their logos.

The best way to find a good counselor is to ask other committed Christians for referrals. If you still have difficulty locating one, contact some of the national associations such as the Christian Legal Association in Washington, D.C.

8

Your Business and Your Spouse

Gordon was doing very well in the computer service business. His company, which specialized in repairing and maintaining business computers, boasted 12 employees and nearly $1 million a year in sales. Gordon had procured authorized service agreements with the top 10 business/computer companies and made a tidy profit servicing their warranted equipment sold in his area.

In the process of doing his repair work, Gordon saw the potential for a new area of business. He noted that customers often had problems integrating hardware and software. Typically the customer would discover a glitch that the software firm would say was a hardware problem, but the hardware supplier would claim it was a software problem. Sometimes the discussions would go for several days, while the customer would sit with a critical system that was unusable and business was being lost.

Gordon's idea was to provide his customers with an integrated service. If they had a problem, they could call a service center, which would analyze the problem and determine its source. Gordon sounded out his customers and found them more than willing to contract for this service on an as-needed basis.

To carry out his idea, Gordon knew he needed funds to hire experienced systems analysts who could diagnose software errors quickly and efficiently and coordinate their work with the hardware technicians. He borrowed $75,000 on his home to raise the needed capital and to start the integrated service business.

Almost immediately, however, Gordon began to see the error of his decision. The computer companies whose equipment he serviced began to see him as a competitor, whereas before they had regarded him as a subcontractor. Two of his largest clients insisted that if he continued with his software service business, they would withdraw their contracts and develop their own service divisions. Reluctantly Gordon agreed to shut down his integrated service.

When he shared with his wife what had happened, she reminded him that he had promised to consult her on any decision to borrow additional money, especially on their home.

"Why didn't you at least tell me what you were going to do?" she asked.

"I figured you'd object, and I just knew this idea was a good one," he said.

"If I'm to be your helpmate, Gordon, you're going to have to allow me the privilege of expressing my views too," she told him. "I don't know a lot about the business any more, but I was your only help when you began. And you know I have never objected to anything you've done when I was a part of the decision process. After all, if I'm expected to share in the consequences of your decisions, it seems only fair that I should share in the decisions as well."

"You have a point," he admitted. "All I can say is that I'm sorry. And I guess I'll remember this lesson for a long time while I'm trying to repay the $75,000 I lost."

Ultimately Gordon's business loss forced the sale of their home because it strapped the business of too much cash. Gordon was fortunate that he had an understanding wife and that they had good communications before this happened. I have encountered situations in which one spouse felt so estranged from the other's business decisions that such an event might have wrecked the marriage.

Ned was doing extremely well in the construction business. He had been building spec homes for about seven years with a consistent profit. He and his wife and three children had a nice home and he had time to be with his family on the weekends; life had settled into a nice pace. But, Ned knew that a recession was coming soon and that he had no real provisions for a long dry spell in the construction business. Without discussing it with his wife, he decided to build two spec homes at a time, rather than just one.

To do so, Ned went to the bank and borrowed an additional $200,000. He realized that if the market would hold for a few more months he would have the nest egg he needed to ride out the downturn. Unfortunately, he guessed wrong and the housing market slowed dramatically.

To make a long story short, Ned couldn't sell either of the spec houses he had completed and was paying interest on over $450,000 in loans. He eventually lost the two houses and the bank foreclosed on his own home. His wife was hurt and resentful that he had risked their home without discussing it with her. Since their pastor referred them to me for financial counseling, I had a chance to hear the "rest of the story" (as Paul Harvey would say).

I asked Ned to tell his wife why he borrowed the money that ultimately cost them their home.

"Well, I did it for her and the kids," he said defensively.

"Don't you think you should have told me what you were going to do, Ned?" she asked.

"There was no need to worry you about it," he said. "You might not have agreed with what I wanted to do."

"I am your wife, Ned. You're going to have to learn to trust me again," she told him. "Remember when I was your only help? When you began?"

Fortunately Ned was blessed with a spouse who stuck by him. Once she realized he hadn't tried to ignore her, she was willing to do whatever it took to recover their losses.

"After all," she said before they left my office, "it's just a house."

The shocked look on Ned's face told me that he had totally underestimated the caliber of his helpmate.

A footnote to this story is that Ned and his wife moved into an apartment and Ned started over, working for another contractor. He worked his way back and is building one spec house at a time. In a couple more years they expect to own their home free and clear. Ned no longer uses their home as collateral for bank loans.

THE NEED FOR ACCOUNTABILITY

If I were to ask the majority of Christian businessmen what role their wives should play in their business careers, most would stammer a bit and try to evade the question. In truth, most wives play little or no role in their husbands' careers once they have passed the start-up phase. Likewise, in our era of more professional women, husbands occupy a diminishing role in the careers of businesswomen. However,

I would say honestly that of the hundreds of couples I have counseled far more often it was the men who excluded their spouses from their business lives.

Sometimes wives are excluded because they don't want to be involved in the business. Many women feel inadequate to help make major business decisions, and some simply don't want the bother. These are excuses, not legitimate reasons.

The relationship between a husband and wife is unique and is critical to good decision making. If a husband and wife are willing to communicate, they will make better decisions together than either can individually. Why? Because one helps offset the other's extremes. If a husband and wife are too similar, one of them is unnecessary.

As well as I can determine, God puts opposites together to help balance our decisions. The majority of really bad decisions I have seen businesspeople make probably could have been totally avoided, or at least lessened, by the counsel of their spouses. The problem is that the typical entrepreneur is independent in nature and not prone to take anybody's counsel, including a spouse's, unless the situation gets really bad and he or she has no choice.

For the sake of simplicity, I will address the remainder of this study to businessmen, since they represent about 94 percent of all business owners at the time of this writing. However, since most entrepreneurs are High D personalities (*Directing* decision makers), and there are as many *Directing* women as there are men, this counsel is equally applicable. (See Chapter 10 for more about personality types.)

As a general observation I have found that the men who were not willing to be accountable to their wives also were not accountable to anyone else. In our society we have developed this wimp image of any man who regards his wife's counsel as important. That is nonsense—a lie promoted by Satan. The unwillingness to be accountable to a spouse makes most men, and now women, vulnerable to their weaknesses.

Consider what God's Word says: *"You husbands likewise, live with your wives in an understanding way, as with a weaker vessel, since she is a woman; and grant her honor as a fellow heir of the grace of life, so that your prayers may not be hindered"* (1 Peter 3:7). In other words, a husband who does not treat his wife as his "fellow heir" (true partner) cannot expect to have an effective prayer life. I don't know about you, but that is a stern warning to me!

How can a wife who has no training in business and never has run a company have a vital role in the decisions? Because she may have a discernment about people that her husband doesn't possess and never will. I tend to believe what people say until I find out they have deceived me; then I tend to never believe what they say again. This black-or-white mentality serves me well in many areas of business or ministry.

However, that same tendency often will get me in trouble when it comes to dealing with people. This has been especially true in hiring people. In the past I have hired people I thought to be good potential employees, only to discover they had some significant personality flaws. My wife, Judy, is far better with intuitive judgments about people than I am. For someone like me, who deals in facts, intuition plays little part in decisions, at least where people are concerned.

Early in the ministry, I hired a fellow I'll call Dave. I was counseling with Dave and his wife and was moved by their hard-luck story. Dave, a commercial artist, had been in business with another Christian. They had worked together developing an advertising company for nearly four years. Then, just as the company was beginning to do well, Dave's partner kicked him out. Subsequently, Dave and his wife, Michelle, lost everything, including their clothes, when the apartment manager locked them out of their apartment for failing to pay the rent.

After listening to Dave's tale of woe, I decided to help. First I called the ex-partner and was told that he would not talk about Dave with anyone. "He's a liar and took me for several thousand dollars," the voice on the other end of the phone said. "He's just fortunate that I don't sue him." With that he hung up the phone and refused to talk with me again.

"That's just like him," Dave and Michelle both said. "He thinks he can intimidate us with threats. We have been advised to sue him, but we know the Bible says not to sue a Christian, so we decided not to."

This impressed me because if only one-tenth of what they had told me was true they had an airtight case against this man. After learning that they had no place to stay, I asked Judy if they could stay with us for a couple of days. Dave said he could get a loan from his father who was a successful attorney in Miami. Since I had done similar things before, including opening our home to a pregnant young girl who set fire to the bed in our guest room before she left, Judy was a little skeptical, but she agreed.

The two days stretched into a month, and still no money came from Dave's father, even after passionate pleas from both of them each evening on the phone. Finally I offered Dave a temporary job doing some layouts for our company, a make-work type project.

Just before Dave was to start the project, he was offered a job managing the film development department in a photographic store. Michelle offered to do typing in my office until Dave's first paycheck came in. She turned out to be an excellent typist, but she talked too much and bossed other people around.

All this time Judy was telling me that something was amiss with those two. I asked for facts, which she couldn't provide. So I discounted her counsel as unfair toward two people who were having a string of bad luck.

For another month Dave and Michelle lived with us while he worked long hours at the photographic lab, tying up one of our family cars. When I mentioned to him that I needed the car back, he asked if I knew anyone in the car business who would finance a car for him. One of our board members had a good used car for sale and I arranged for Dave to meet him. On the basis of my recommendation, he sold Dave the car on time, with no money down.

At this point Dave started coming up with some wild stories, such as being robbed of his pay on the way home from work and being asked to play in a professional golf tournament in Atlanta. (This was after discovering that my stepfather was an avid golf fan.) Finally, even I became suspicious, so I decided to do some more detailed checking and asked Dave for his father's name and telephone number in Miami.

"Why do you need my father's name and number?" he asked in a hurt tone of voice.

"Because I just want to find out why he won't help his son when you're obviously having so much trouble."

"But what I didn't tell you is that I'm his illegitimate son," Dave said with tears in his eyes. "My father doesn't want his wife to know, and she might find out if you called."

Red flags went up in my mind as I considered the counsel Judy had been giving me about this couple. I said, "Dave, I feel that something is wrong here. I'd like the name and number of your employer too. I'm going to do some background checking."

Dave provided me with a list of numbers, and then he and Michelle went to their bedroom. The next day when we got up they were already gone. We didn't hear anything for several days, during which time I learned that all the numbers Dave had given me were phonies. He never had been in business; he never had worked at a photo lab; and he never had lived in Miami. To top the whole thing off, they had disappeared with my friend's car.

From that point on, I vowed to listen to my wife's advice, at least where people are concerned. That doesn't mean she is always right, but it does mean her track record beats mine by a factor of 100 to one.

I find that the same principle is basically true in all our lives. No one person is equipped with the ability to correctly evaluate all situations. When it comes to areas like morality and ethics, the input of both husband and wife is essential.

Let me make it clear that such accountability to each other doesn't happen overnight. It requires a strong commitment to each other and a lowering of the basic ego level of the average Christian businessperson.

The need to communicate and share decisions can be viewed from a totally different perspective as well. In more than 80 percent of all marriages, the wife is going to survive her husband. (The average age of a new widow in America is 52.) Thus the majority of wives will be left to make all the decisions after their husbands die. The more a husband communicates while they are together, the better decisions a wife will make later. It's worth the effort.

SET ASIDE TIME TO TALK

The best way to start communicating is to set aside some time regularly to discuss important business decisions. That's important whether you're the owner of a business or not.

Since a husband and wife tend to be opposites, one of you will probably want to talk late in the evening, when the other is totally wiped out and ready for bed. A good compromise is to set aside some time for devotions and prayer together and to use a part of that time to discuss the business events of the day.

To extend this idea further you will need to block out some regular time to discuss long-term goals, such as business growth, retirement, or sale of a business. This is best done by setting an entire weekend aside. If necessary, trade off child care with another couple or even hire a sitter to free yourselves. You will find the sacrifice of doing this about once every year or so is well worth it.

If you have never done this, a good way to start is by planning your family budget. This can be helpful to break the ice and begin the process of communications so necessary for a good, accountable marriage. I have a measure of understanding for those who have never done this; I was guilty of neglecting my wife's counsel for many years myself. But now I can honestly say that the time we spend together is some of the most productive time I have outside of my time with the Lord.

I don't mean to imply that Judy's and my communications are perfect. They're a long way from that and probably always will be. I'm a person who feels very comfortable making decisions—even bad ones. I surround myself with excellent employees and comfortably turn over much of the daily routine to them, and I regularly listen to their counsel. But input from employees or even board members is not the same as input from your spouse. Nobody knows us like our spouses, and therefore nobody can provide the input that a spouse can.

Many women wonder why their successful husbands end up leaving them when their businesses flourish. Sometimes a man becomes involved in sexual relationships in the middle years, but I also think there is a deeper reason. Too often wives have failed to become companions and partners, and the husband feels his wife doesn't really care about what he does in business. He has poured his life into his work, but to her it's just a source of income.

More than a few wives have told me in later years that they wish they had given their husbands the kind of time and attention they gave their children. Obviously children require a lot of attention, but the marriage relationship will last longer (or should) than the parent-child relationship. If a relationship is important, both partners must invest some time in it.

The Lord gave us an interesting principle: *"Where your treasure is, there will your heart be also"* (Matthew 6:21). This principle extends beyond money itself to everything we do. It means, in effect, that you will invest your time and energy in those things that are important to you. Make your spouse one of them.

Working Together in Business

When you and your spouse work together in the business, it is important that you start out by discussing the relationship honestly. There can be only one leader, and attempting any other arrangement will usually frustrate the employees and often lead to some heated discussions between the husband and wife.

I have found over the years that when spouses work together clearly defining the roles is more difficult in the short run but absolutely essential in the long run. If you find that you cannot comfortably work in the same office or even the same company, it's better to face this issue honestly from the outset.

Clearly defined roles are essential to good communications. If you can't discuss this together without arguing, a good counselor may be able to help you resolve the differences.

Carlton was an insurance agent who had recently opened his own office. Paula, his wife, was his secretary, bookkeeper, and receptionist. Soon after the business opened, the two of them found that personality differences and poor communication were wreaking havoc in the business and in their relationship.

Paula was a perfectionist who demanded absolute conformance to all rules. Carlton was a somewhat typical salesman who generalized much of his advice and treated rules as guidelines, not absolutes. Paula saw Carlton's exaggerations as lies and went to extremes to correct him, often in the presence of clients. As a result, some of their clients got the impression that there was friction between Carlton and Paula and that she was the one trying to protect their interests.

For instance, when Carlton would bid a client's policy, the client would call and ask Paula to review the estimate to be sure there were no "exaggerations." Paula was flattered that the clients wanted her input although she was steadily undermining Carlton's authority. Carlton was at a loss about how to handle Paula's obvious disrespect for his authority and expertise.

A client to whom Carlton had sold a commercial insurance policy suffered a large fire and then found out the insurer would not pay because of some flammable materials that had been stored on his premises. He claimed that Carlton should have told him the exclusions in the policy. Carlton's position was that the policy was very clear on that subject. He also pointed out that he could not have known about the chemicals stored in their building since it was a new operation, begun after the policy was purchased.

The owner sued Carlton's company for negligence and, in court, produced several other of Carlton's clients, who testified that they also considered him negligent as an insurance agent. As part of their arguments, they asserted that Carlton's own wife often disputed his assertions to clients.

Sitting in court, Paula was shocked to realize that the men she thought were just seeking her advice thought her husband was totally incompetent in his profession. She knew that he was a very knowledgeable agent and had taught her everything she knew about the business. Her only difficulties with Carlton had been with what she thought to be exaggerations, not incompetence.

Carlton lost the case and was assigned the damages for the fire. As a result, his underwriter canceled their relationship and effectively put Carlton out of the insurance business. Paula knew she had seriously undermined her husband's integrity and, in the process, ruined their business. Her perfectionist personality could have been a good balance to Carlton's sales personality. Instead it had become a source of dissension.

Paula also learned a great deal about her husband's true integrity when he never once accused her of disloyalty, even though he knew what she had done. Carlton soon was hired as an agent for a former competitor who realized his value. Paula became a wiser wife and a secretary for a local telephone company.

Part 2
CRITICAL POLICY DECISIONS

9

Leadership:
The Foundation for All
Your Decisions

The key to the success of any organization is found in two key elements: the leadership and the people and, of course, these two are intimately related. Leaders must show the way, provide the resources to reach the goal, and provide accountability — to be sure that things stay on track. People bring enthusiasm, energy, talents, ideas, motivation, and, yes, problems. Your attitudes and outlook as a leader and toward your people will frame every policy decision you make. So, before getting into specific policy issues, let me share some thoughts about the responsibilities of a leader.

KNOW YOUR PERSONAL(ITY) ASSETS
AND LIABILITIES

So often we make the mistake of comparing ourselves to others, but the Bible teaches very clearly that we are each a unique design and we have different talents. There really is no one else exactly like you. (See Psalm 139:13–14 and Romans 12:1–8.) That's why I believe it's so important for you to have a realistic appraisal of how God has made you. Then you exercise your leadership based on your own style and not someone else's.

I believe He has gifted each of us to do certain things better than anyone else. The questions you need to answer are: "What is my design?" and "What talents do I bring to the mix in my organization?"

By having a clear picture of who you are, you are able to lead from your strengths and minimize the negative impact of your weaknesses. A realistic appraisal of your pluses and minuses can be critical to your long-term success. Let me illustrate.

Eddie is a natural entrepreneur. He's a visionary who's good at seeing a need and then coming up with ideas for new products and services to meet that need. This type of creativity is definitely his strength. He has an uncanny ability to see the big picture—all the way to the end results. Likewise, he is able to see how all the pieces can fit together to make a project successful, and he has the drive to push things along to get results. Eddie loves adventure, he's drawn to a challenge, and most of all he likes doing something different every day.

Like the rest of us, though, Eddie has some limitations to go with his strengths. He is not very good at projecting the actual amount of work and resources required to make his projects become a reality. Also, since he naturally thinks in terms of the finished product, it's easy for him to assume away most of the detailed work (which he hates anyway) that is required to make his ideas successful. This contributes to his impatience with others who are working for him.

Like most entrepreneurs, Eddie is not one who flourishes at running the day-to-day activities of an established organization. Keeping focused on the details is not his strength. He's much better at pioneering something new, rather than operating the old and established.

Eddie's contributions are important to the success of his business. Yet there are several essential functions that he lacks. He needs good management help to make his vision a reality.

Mannie, on the other hand, is a good manager. He may lack the visionary strengths of someone like Eddie, but he has other talents that are just as important to success. Mannie likes to focus on the process of getting things done on a day-to-day basis. He enjoys tracking the details to ensure that tasks are accomplished and schedules are kept, all the while keeping within budget.

Good managers like Mannie tend to be consistent, time sensitive, scheduled, and good listeners—strengths that are not typical for entrepreneurs. As you can see, good managers are usually different from entrepreneurs in their talents and temperament; yet, both people are equally important to an organization.

Of course there are many other roles in a business besides entrepreneurs and managers. More relevant questions you need to be able to answer are: "Who am I?" and "Does the majority of my work match my strengths?" These can be key questions to ensure you are making the best use of your talents. If you don't have an accurate picture, then you may want to get some feedback from your spouse and friends; and even a personal assessment can be a big help.

Over the years in doing financial counseling, it became obvious to me that most people don't know their strengths and weaknesses. It was out of this concern that we began a program at CFC in 1990 just to help people get this type of information. Our *Career Direct*^{TM} assessment has now served over 50,000 people by helping them understand the unique talents God has given them. We have developed applications of this product for use in the workplace specifically to help businessmen and businesswomen identify their own key talents and for use in matching people to positions in their organizations.

With the intense competition in business today, I believe it's essential that companies know how to match individual talents to tasks (a process we call *RightPathing*^{TM}). To maximize your effectiveness, you'll want to "rightpath" yourself by making sure that your leadership capitalizes on your personality strengths and your best natural talents.

PROMOTE RESPECT AND DEVELOP TRUST

One of the best things you can do to ensure a good working environment and even improve the bottom line is to display and encourage respect for others. Although this sounds simplistic, especially for Christians, it's not always easy to practice. We are human and are affected by our fallen nature. Thus, we can suffer from pride and fear, which can motivate us to react in ways that are not uplifting to others.

Just as we have committed our organization to certain goals, I have adopted a personal goal of truly caring about and respecting everyone in our organization and, for that matter, everyone with whom I come in contact. I know this is the attitude that honors Christ and I continually remind myself that I am serving Him and this is His way. When pride rears its ugly head, I remember that all that I have comes from our Lord. Period!

Respect is the foundation for good relationships. Likewise, it is the key ingredient for trust, and trust is essential to any smooth-running operation. I know this sounds obvious, so let me share some insights on how respect can enhance the teamwork in your organization.

I have already emphasized how important it is to know yourself, but it also is important for people to know each other in the workplace.

The more that people are able to discuss openly their strengths and weaknesses, the more they will be willing to be transparent, and transparency is a powerful tool to promote respect and trust.

We use our *ViewPoint Profile*™ personality survey as a means of helping people understand themselves and the ones they work with. This tool has paid tremendous dividends by facilitating open discussions of strengths and weaknesses. Most important, it has helped people see that being different does not mean being wrong.

Our employees know that when people respond differently than they would have, our employees can accept and respect them as operating from another viewpoint. We have come to recognize these differences in personality (operating style) as assets to our teams.

I have used this tool in counseling couples for many years. It is critical for a husband and wife to understand why the other person reacts the way he or she does. Often the very thing that motivates and excites one person is what strikes fear in the heart of his or her spouse.

This same understanding is essential to developing a smooth-running business. Every good business needs the marketers *and* the accountants, even though both look at the same situation differently.

Owen and Winston, two managers, are about as opposite in personality as any two people you will ever meet; yet, they work together very well. Owen tends to be outspoken, assertive, change oriented, and somewhat entrepreneurial. Winston is his mirror opposite. He measures what he says and makes it count. Winston also tends to keep his opinions to himself, prefers stability, and is more of a focused manager.

For several years Winston worked for Owen but, because of some restructuring within the organization, now Owen works for Winston; yet, in both arrangements they have had a very effective relationship. The key is that they have a great respect for each other. They understand their differences well enough to laugh about them, and each looks to the other for wisdom on key decisions. They recognize the value that the different viewpoint of the other brings to decision making and problem solving. Not only do they work well as a team, they are good friends.

By demonstrating respect for others, especially those who are different, you set the example and empower those around you to do the same. This attitude is contagious and can promote strong relationships that will enable your organization to keep individual talents harnessed together and headed down the same path (toward your vision) even when the inevitable storms and stresses of business occur.

COMMUNICATE, COMMUNICATE, COMMUNICATE

I know I've already mentioned communications numerous times but there is no way I could overemphasize this subject. Keeping good communications is the most difficult challenge in any organization; yet, it is the lifeblood that enables the various parts to function together as a whole.

Some of the best illustrations I've heard on the role of communications have come from one of our staff members who spent more than five years as a POW in Vietnam. He says that the Communists went to great effort to isolate the men from each other in order to limit communications. The North Vietnamese understood well the theory of divide and conquer, and they sought to prevent Americans from supporting or encouraging each other.

The POWs knew they couldn't let their captors succeed and took incredible risks just to keep in contact. They devised a variety of methods, including tap codes, visual codes, and secret note systems to keep everyone in the loop. Communications were used to encourage those in solitary confinement and pass along resistance policies and intelligence on the camp activities; but, most of all, this kept everyone on the same wavelength in their thinking. The unity promoted through communications was a major factor in the success of our men in resisting the enemy's tactics and returning with honor at the end of the war.

Most organizations don't need a Communist camp commander to foil their communications; it just seems to happen, unless everyone makes it a high priority. Without good communications, people begin to function in isolation. When this happens they are likely to make bad assumptions, which eventually result in a harvest of problems that affect relationships and profits.

I recommend you regularly review how policies are coordinated among various departments. Too often one area will be working in isolation, not stopping to think about the impact their action will have on another department.

Like any organization, we have had our headaches from a lack of coordination among departments over the years. I can remember a time or two when we mentioned a CFC resource on our radio program, only to find out later that no one had coordinated with those who were answering the phones on our materials line. Those situations happen in every business and will require constant adjustment.

My advice is to work through this problem every day. Ask yourself, "How well is information flowing in my organization or department?" "Where are the roadblocks?" "Who is not passing the word?" Make a special effort to see that the information necessary for good decisions is getting to the right people.

In line with that, you'll have to make a conscious effort to be sure you are getting good feedback. Too often, people don't tell the boss what he or she needs to know. Sometimes it's because they are afraid it will make them look bad. Depending on how you handle bad news, your employees may just be afraid of telling you what you don't want to hear. Probably a more common situation is that they are just too busy to stop and think that this is something you'll need or want to know. It takes time to provide input through the proper channels to the boss, and busy employees may fear that providing some information will only generate more questions that will slow them down even more.

I recommend both formal and informal feedback systems. Regularly scheduled reports and briefings can help the key staff stay current on the information needed for decision making. At other times, you would do well just to stop by and show an interest and find out firsthand what is happening. Generally you can expect that the ease with which feedback flows to you is directly related to your willingness to be an open and interested listener. If people think they can share things with you without fear that you'll step in and micromanage, then information probably will be free flowing.

INVEST IN TRAINING

One thing I've noticed is that this information age requires highly trained people. The new technologies that are available offer some opportunities for real breakthroughs in productivity—but only if employees are fully trained to use them. Unfortunately, with the changes in technology coming so fast, our schools can't keep up, so the young people are going to need more training, and older workers who weren't trained in technology will need to be brought up to date.

The practical truth is, most of the training is going to have to come from the employer. This means you'll need to include training in your budget and find the people who can do high quality training on an ongoing basis. If you've done much reading in business magazines, you know that one of the key indicators of the top companies on the Fortune 500 is that they invest heavily in training. I believe this will continue to be a key component of successful businesses, and I would encourage you to take a good look at your training programs.

Recently, we upgraded our computers and software. From past experience, I knew that people would be slow to adapt to this new capability, so I decided to put out a decree that we were going to a paperless workplace as fast as possible. The learning curve was difficult at first but, anticipating this, we had hired some excellent information specialists who were gifted in training. We put everyone in the organization through training courses in the new software programs. In short order, our people were using computers in a way they never thought possible.

Our use of a computerized information system has significantly improved communications in our organization. This investment in training seemed time consuming and expensive on the front end, but looking back it has very quickly paid big dividends in productivity.

HAVE A CLEAR VISION FOR YOUR BUSINESS

Although the need for a focused vision seems obvious, it's amazing how easy it is to get off track. Consider that an aircraft flying only 10 degrees off its planned course would be 10 miles off at 60 miles but more than 1,000 miles off after flying from New York to Hawaii.

A clearly defined vision or mission statement can keep you on course and serve as a benchmark to help you evaluate all the opportunities that pop up. At CFC hardly a day goes by that I'm not presented with some "good deal" or new slant on how what we do can be used both for ministry and for profit. Knowing what the Lord has called me to do has enabled us to stay on course, remain focused on what we do best, and avoid getting sidetracked. I believe this is one of the key reasons we've been so blessed in carrying out our mission over the past 20 plus years.

On the other hand, your vision may need to change direction or expand from time to time. Our first major shift was when we began the vocational testing program in 1990. That was a major decision and involved much prayer and discussion by our board of directors. Initially, some board members weren't sure how developing a career test could fit in with our mission of biblical stewardship. As we discussed the issue, it was clear that management of our God-given talents was certainly a factor in both overall stewardship and even financial stewardship.

The value of a clear vision statement is that it provides a standard for evaluating any potential changes in direction. Although at times you may feel like a written vision statement is too restrictive, if you have the normal entrepreneurial tendencies, you'll always have to fight the tendency to change things; it just comes with the territory. But a clearly articulated vision statement, shared with your employees, can be just the discipline you need to stay on course for the long haul.

Remember, it's not enough that it is just your vision; you want it to be the vision of the people in your organization. In the best situation, everyone on the team sees the company vision as their own and sees how it fits their personal values and goals. As the leader, one of your key responsibilities is to continually communicate the vision so that everyone, down to the newest person on the payroll, has a clear picture of what you stand for and what you want to accomplish.

Everything I read points to the fact that the American workforce is now seeking employment from companies whose values match their own. By providing a corporate vision and environment that will allow individuals to realize their personal goals and fulfill part of their own missions, you will increase your potential to attract and retain quality people. If you are running your organization based on biblical principles, the values that most people are wanting will be stated in your vision and built into your corporate culture.

Ultimately, I believe that a business operated on biblical principles can be so attractive that it will be a shining light in the community. And isn't that what we are supposed to be about? *"Let your light shine before men in such a way that they may see your good works, and glorify your Father who is in heaven"* (Matthew 5:16).

10

Hiring Decisions

"You know, it seems like I never make the right decisions in hiring people," Stan said, gesturing with a piece of toast. He was talking to Brandon Barnes, one of our counselors, over breakfast. "I get people who are quickly dissatisfied, and they end up leaving within a year or two. What's my problem?"

"Let me ask you a question first," Brandon replied. "What are your criteria for hiring people in the first place?"

"I'm not sure I know what you mean," Stan replied. "I usually advertise in the local paper and choose from the people who apply."

"No, I don't mean how you find them. I mean, what are the criteria by which you decide whom you will hire out of those who apply?"

Stan then began to describe a fairly typical system of hiring. "I know what kind of experience is necessary to perform our tasks, which primarily involve assembly and repair of test equipment. We try to find people with at least two years' experience in a related industry that can live with our hourly rate of pay."

"What other criteria do you require?"

"I don't understand what you mean."

"What about work history, personal references, skill evaluation, and personality type?"

"We do check with an applicant's present or previous employers if the applicant says it's all right. But the law prohibits us from doing much beyond that."

"Absolutely not true," Brandon replied to this comment, which as a business consultant he had heard many times before. "The law prohibits an employer from discriminating on the basis of race, religion, sex, or national origin. It does not prohibit an employer from discerning whether someone has been a capable and reliable employee."

"Well, most of those things cost too much, anyway," Stan said defensively. "Only big companies can afford to do them."

"Not so," Brandon replied again. "The large companies do these things because they have found it is considerably cheaper to hire the right people than it is to replace the wrong ones. It takes a little time to get started, but the dividends will last a long time too. Let me tell you some of the things we teach in our business seminars." And he went on to outline the essential steps an employer should take in establishing a reasonable hiring policy.

STEPS IN HIRING EMPLOYEES

1. Define the Job Clearly

Every job is a combination of several tasks that must be done each day or at least on a regular basis. In order to hire the right people, it is necessary that jobs be well defined. Often just by reading a job description the prospective employees will see they are not qualified and eliminate themselves. Even hearing verbal job descriptions during interviews is not as effective as seeing them in black and white.

We once interviewed a young man for a position as a telephone marketer with our organization. He was intelligent, well mannered, and articulate — all necessary qualifications for any position with our ministry. He also was enthusiastic about coming to work for us and mentioned the opportunities we offered many times during the interview.

When he was shown the written description of the job, which consisted of answering telephone responses from interested customers, disillusionment was evident on his face. The supervisor asked, "Do you think you could do that job all day long?"

"Well, I think so," he replied. "But how long would I have to do this before I would have the chance to do something more interesting?"

"Like what, in particular?" he was asked.

"I really want to teach and counsel people!" he replied with enthusiasm. "I would be willing to do this if I could be trained in those areas as well."

The supervisor thanked that young man and dismissed him. We needed a telephone marketer, but we didn't need to invest several thousands of dollars in training someone who was likely to leave (probably disgruntled) after a few weeks or months. He was a typically naive young college graduate who was looking for a foot in the door, rather than the job we had to offer.

2. Hire the Best Person for the Job

This may sound too simplistic, but most small businesses seldom hire the best person. Instead, they hire someone who is available. I have done this more than once in the past and usually regretted it.

I recall when I first started to develop the ministry of Christian Financial Concepts, I found myself in great need of help but with little available cash to pay anyone.

A Christian who was out of work came in for counsel and, discovering that I needed help, volunteered. Over the next several months the financial situation improved, and I was in a position to hire someone to do what he had been doing. The obvious conclusion (on both our parts) was that I would hire him.

Looking back at the situation, I realize now that I really wasn't happy with his performance, but because he was a volunteer I didn't complain. I also realize that I completely skirted the normal hiring practices that I had used in business because he was already in place. Otherwise I would have checked his references, inventoried his personality, and evaluated his skills.

To say the least, I lived to regret my lack of thoroughness. I soon found out that the man was misplaced and unhappy. That attitude reflected in nearly everything he did and ultimately led to a confrontation. My error was accepting someone who was less than the best for the position he held. He was unhappy, I was unhappy, and we both eventually were forced to face the truth.

I now try to follow a precept taught in Proverbs: *"Do you see a man skilled in his work? He will stand before kings; he will not stand before obscure men"* (Proverbs 22:29).

3. Match the Person to the Job

In earlier years I was not a great believer in personality tests and the like. However, after many attempts to put the right person in the right job (and many failures in doing so), I searched for anything that might help. Other businesspeople seemed to have a good grasp of personalities, and hiring the right people didn't seem to be a problem with them, but for me it was.

Then one day, while attending a conference on management I took a brief personality evaluation that divided the temperaments into four basic types.

I hurried through the test, discounting it as just another waste of time. But when the instructor evaluated the sheet I had completed and then used the results to describe my personality, I was totally shocked. That evaluation fit me to a T.

I spent the next few weeks studying the material. Then I proceeded to give the test to everyone I knew well enough to have a good grasp of their basic personalities and abilities. To my surprise, the test was accurate in every case.

After this trial, I knew I had a tool to help me hire employees properly. This evaluation tool, which takes only a few minutes, has virtually revolutionized our staff and several hundred other businesses with whom I have shared it.

It was that experience that led to our development of the Career Direct^{TM} assessment program mentioned earlier. More than 60,000 individuals have been served by this program since 1990. As an outgrowth of the individual assessment, we have developed products specifically to help companies identify the strengths of potential employees. We now have two personality assessments that are offered to businesses through our RightPath Resources division.

Longer, more complex evaluations are available, but I have found none that accomplish what our *ViewPoint Profile*^{TM} does with such a small investment of time and money. We use it with all potential employees in our organization. We also have found this type of profile to be absolutely essential in counseling. Understanding the personalities of those we are counseling helps both us and them to understand why they react the way they do.

The *ViewPoint* evaluation divides personalities into four dimensions, which are more precise than the normal Type A or Type B often used to describe people. For the sake of convenience, I will describe these four dimensions, using some simple analogies.

a. Directing versus *Adaptive.* This dimension is about control of the work agenda. The "D" or *Directing* personality type wants to set the agenda and is typical of the entrepreneur who makes decisions quickly, becomes easily bored with routine tasks, and hates to follow detailed instructions. The best description of this personality type is "often wrong, never in doubt." *Directing* personalities can be recognized easily. If they buy a swing set for their kids, they will spend three hours trying to figure out how to assemble it, rather than spending ten minutes to read the instructions.

Those on the other end of this dimension follow an *Adaptive* style. They are willing to cooperate with the agenda of others, so by nature they tend to be good team players. They are not motivated to control their work environment so they are able to adapt to the situation at hand.

b. Interacting versus Reserved. The *Interacting* personalities are outgoing, friendly, and talkative, and they love to associate with successful people. The "I" personalities are easily recognized because they smile easily and often. Also, on their bedroom, kitchen, or office wall they will have everything they ever achieved displayed. *Interacting* personalities are motivated by the desire to please others and to be accepted by them. They often become salespeople and do quite well in such positions because of the network of relationships they develop. An *Interacting* person is strongly attracted to social organizations and usually is characterized as warm and friendly.

The *Reserved* personality is just the opposite. They aren't motivated to meet new people and, in fact, frequent interaction will drain them of energy. *Reserved* personalities prefer to work in more solitary settings with few interruptions.

c. Supportive versus Objective. *Supportive* people like to help others and especially like harmony in the work environment. They tend to be the ones who keep the wheels of an organization greased, because their nature is to be loyal, hardworking, cooperative, and dependable. Their only real fault is that they usually lack imagination and the drive to attempt new things. They are easily recognized because they take fewer breaks than other people, rarely argue with anyone, are always present to do the jobs no one else wants, and rarely get recognized for their accomplishments.

As a side note, I've noticed that *Supportive* personalities are the only types that can marry someone like themselves and make the marriage work. They tend to be patient and good listeners. All other marriages of like personalities seem to end up in war. You can recognize the *Supportive* personalities because they hate to make decisions. If a husband asks the wife, "Where would you like to eat?" she says, "I don't care; you decide." If he is an "S" too, he will reply, "No, I don't care; you decide." This is likely to continue until they have a "High D" child, who will totally dominate their lives.

The counterpart of this dimension is the *Objective* profile. They tend to be very active, impatient, and even aggressive in their response to the challenges in the work environment. They prefer to make decisions based on logic, rather than feelings, and usually don't have difficulty making the hard decisions, especially when people are concerned.

d. Conscientious versus Unconventional. In most instances, a person with the *Conscientious* personality is known as a perfectionist. "C" personalities are easily recognized because they diligently adhere to all rules and become extremely frustrated when there are no rules to follow. If a "High C" buys a swing set that requires assembly, he or she will first lay out every part, largest to smallest, then thoroughly read the instruction manual, correcting all the spelling errors.

At the other extreme is the *Unconventional* personality, who is just the opposite. They don't like to spend a lot of time rehearsing or preparing; they like to "wing it" and can be pretty good at it. If you need someone who is not bound by procedures but can make a quick assessment and give you an opinion on the spot, look for someone with an *Unconventional* personality.

Obviously no one has a personality with one single characteristic; we are all combinations of all these traits. But usually there are one or two dominant traits that can help determine how that person will function in the job environment. Pinpointing these traits can greatly enhance your hiring practices. Knowing how various temperaments interact is essential to organizing a productive and efficient company.

Let me demonstrate how we use this information in employee recruiting. If we are looking for a particular position, say a receptionist, we first detail the job requirements. For example, a receptionist's duties would involve answering incoming calls, routing them to the appropriate departments, or taking messages. Additional duties might include updating supporter files, adding statistical information to computer files, and occasionally typing letters. A receptionist's typing skills, therefore, are as important as his or her verbal communication skills.

To find out what combination of personality traits will make the best receptionist/typist, we develop a benchmark for the position. This can be done by identifying a number of people who have been successful in the position and examining the commonalities in their personality profile. If it is a new position, we might solicit a profile from another company, consult a human resources expert, or develop our own predicted benchmark profile by prioritizing traits we think would be needed in the position. This benchmark is used then as a guide to hiring the receptionist we need. Through some research and experience, a profile can be compiled for virtually any position.

Obviously there are other factors that must be considered in the hiring process, such as previous work experience, job skills, dependability, vocabulary, and education. But I am convinced that the best employees are those whose jobs match their basic personalities.

I learned this lesson the hard way too. One business I owned had a need for a bookkeeper to assist our accountant. The young woman who was our receptionist at the time was bright and very quick to learn, so I thought I would have her cross trained in the accounting department. That situation was a disaster almost from the first day. Although she learned the accounting procedures quickly and was extremely accurate, she rarely worked for more than 10 minutes at a stretch. Then she would need to get a drink of water or go to the restroom—any excuse to leave the small, isolated cubicle where she worked. Along the way she would stop and chat with anyone available and then return to her "dungeon," as she called it.

It was clear that she would never be content as a bookkeeper, working in isolation from others, so I put her back at the front desk answering the phones and meeting visitors, where she was totally content. Only later did I realize that she was a "High I" (*Interacting*), with a fairly "High C" (*Conscientious*) element. In other words, she was an extrovert with a high degree of perfectionism. She turned out to be a great receptionist and typist—but a terrible bookkeeper.

4. Make Hiring Policy Decisions

The chore of finding qualified employees and hiring them will be made easier if you examine your attitudes on certain issues and make some basic policy decisions ahead of time. Some of these decisions will be influenced by federal guidelines and company policy (if you are a manager). But thinking through some of the more controversial issues can help you sort out the more complicated decisions. For Christians, two of the trickier hiring policy decisions are whether to hire non-Christians and whether to hire women.

Should I hire only Christians? Many Christian businesspeople assume that by hiring only Christians they can avoid many of the problems that plague normal businesses. After operating a ministry that employs only Christians for 21 years, I can now say with absolute conviction that such a notion is really naive. Not that we don't have some great people; we do! But the problems with Christian employees are really no different than with non-Christians.

Many Christian employers believe that they should employ only Christians. I personally believe that to do so stifles one of the greatest ministries available to Christian employers: evangelism of employees.

The biblical principle of not being unequally yoked (see 2 Corinthians 6:14) has sometimes been used to justify the exclusion of non-Christian employees. Clearly no yoke relationship is created between an employee and employer. A simple explanation may help to define the relationship in which one person is yoked to another.

The apostle Paul compares such a relationship to two oxen who are harnessed together; neither can do anything without affecting the other. If one moves left, the other has to follow. If one stumbles, the other falls too. The weight must be distributed equally and borne by both. Clearly this is not a picture of an employee/employer relationship, which is closer to the master/slave relationships described in Scripture than to the yoke. The only legitimate way to remove all unbelievers from a Christian's business is to get them all saved. In the hiring process the only criteria that should be used are whether the person can do the job and follow the rules established for all employees.

The same principle should apply in business that Paul applied to the church at Corinth. He had admonished the believers there about some of their behavior that was dishonoring to the Lord and instructed the leaders to remove the unruly ones from their midst. In their confusion they apparently removed all the non-Christians from their fellowship.

In 1 Corinthians 5:9–10 Paul wrote to correct this error: *"I wrote you in my letter not to associate with immoral people; I did not at all mean with the immoral people of this world, or with the covetous and swindlers, or with idolaters; for then you would have to go out of the world."* Without unbelievers in the business (or church), evangelism tends to be a little fruitless.

Should I hire married women? In Christian circles there has been a great deal of controversy about women working outside the home. That controversy has taken on a distinctly bitter flavor since the advent of "women's lib." Many assume that for a woman to work outside the home today implies that she is self-willed and independent. I would like to share a few observations from God's Word on the subject.

A description of the perfect wife. A description of the perfect wife is found in Proverbs 31. She is reported to plant her fields and sell the crops, weave clothing and belts and sell them, act as a helpmate to her husband, and manage her household in a manner that brings her honor. It seems to me that the woman described here is involved in activities other than normal household duties!

The Scripture doesn't imply that every wife has to do these things, but neither does it imply that for her to do so is a sin. I believe that God has assigned the right to make this decision to the husband and his wife. For one woman the decision to work outside the home may be wrong, but for another it will be right.

The apostle Paul's message is often quoted as an instruction for women to work only at home: *"That they may encourage the young women to love their husbands, to love their children, to be sensible, pure, workers at home, kind, being subject to their own husbands, that the word of God may not be dishonored"* (Titus 2:4–5).

I do not believe this was Paul's intent. Instead, he was admonishing women not to neglect their work at home, as was the custom of some who were busybodies and rebellious toward their husbands. Certainly Paul was not discussing the issue of women working outside the home, because very few did so in his day. In an era of few conveniences, their labor was vitally needed in the fields where the family's food was grown.

It is not this book's purpose to discuss whether or not women should work outside the home, with or without children (I covered that subject in my book, *Women Leaving the Workplace*, Moody Press). I will not elaborate any further on this subject here, except to say that I do understand the problems that can occur in families where both the husband and the wife are working and the children are virtually abandoned. Such neglect is causing a crisis in America, and it results primarily from the desire for an indulgent lifestyle. But having said that, I still believe it is not unscriptural for a woman to work outside her home if she and her husband agree.

This point is critically important to me as an employer. If I believed that God's Word instructed married women not to work outside the home, I would not hire a married woman in our office, because doing so would place me in the position of causing another to sin. However, I repeat, such decisions are left to the husband and wife to make — not me.

5. Establish a Trial Period

I encourage you to establish a 90-day trial period for new employees, during which the employees can be evaluated for job performance and compatibility. Obviously no one wants to leave one job and start another with the possibility that he or she might be terminated after a 90-day trial period, and good hiring practices can virtually eliminate this necessity. Yet the best hiring practices in the world will not totally eliminate hiring errors. It is better for the company and the employee that corrections be made early if necessary.

I recall such a situation with an individual I hired to manage our 200-hundred-acre training center in North Georgia. We had screened nearly 40 applicants and selected the five most qualified for the position for personal interviews. Among them was a man in his middle 30s, with an engineering background, who seemed perfectly suited for the position. He was a Christian, loved the outdoors, was highly praised by his present and former employers, and had the ideal personality profile for the position. After screening many other applicants, we made him an offer that matched his present salary, and he committed to the job.

For the first month this man did a great job and seemed enthusiastic about the work and the people who visited the center. Then I began to notice a change in his countenance. He was moody and withdrawn and often outright rebellious. When I would confront him about his attitude, he would seem to change for a week or so, then the moodiness would reappear. I repeatedly asked what the problem was, but he refused to admit that there was one.

Then one day a friend from our church who had spent some time with the manager and his wife came to my office to share what was going on. It seems that the manager's wife hated the isolation of the center and the lack of daily fellowship. In a word, she was homesick, and she continually nagged him to go back home. Caught between a discontented wife and his work commitment, the manager had subconsciously convinced himself that somehow we were at fault for his problems. I resolved the conflict by asking him to resign, which he did willingly.

There are factors other than personality and skill level that must be considered when hiring. In this case, for instance, we should have verified that the wife was also committed to the move.

From my experience, hiring is one of the biggest challenges you will face. A bad hire can be very discouraging for both the individual and the organization. That's why it is so important to take your time to be sure you know what type of person you really need for the position and then gain as much information as possible before offering someone a job.

Don't forget prayer as a key part of your human resources program. Spend time in prayer with your key staff and ask God to bring the right people and then give you the assurance that the people match the available jobs.

Ultimately, a well-thought-out hiring process will save you many headaches and heartaches and will enable you to have the teammates you need to achieve your vision.

11

Firing Decisions

I have found over the years that most Christians in the business world are confused about the responsibility of employers to their employees. I have met many Christian employers who believe they could never dismiss an employee for fear it would be a bad witness. I also have met many Christian employees who believe that because they work for a Christian they should be guaranteed permanent employment, regardless of their performance or demeanor.

A friend shared with me his experience of how one such employee failed in his responsibility to his employer.

"We hired a young graduate of a Christian college to work in our materials shipping department. Like many recent graduates, he had anticipated that his business degree would guarantee him at least a starting position in middle management. And, although he had been told that his position was that of shipper, he assumed he would be promoted in only a few weeks.

"In truth, we were considering creating a separate department of the materials area and eventually would need a manager. However, I had long since learned that a college education in business today signifies only that the recipient had the stamina to stick to one thing for at least four years. In no way does a college degree in business prepare a student to make good business decisions or to direct other people.

"Within a few weeks Greg [not his real name] had developed a belligerent manner and walked around with a perpetual scowl on his face. He did his job and did it quite well, but his attitude virtually eliminated him from any consideration for a more responsible position. His attitude continued to deteriorate, and finally he was dismissed.

"During the time this young man was employed, I occasionally found notes on my desk accusing me of failing to live by the biblical principles and many other accusatory statements about my 'horrendous crimes against God,' including using the New American Standard version of the Bible instead of the 'authorized' King James version. I could never be sure he was the author of these notes, but they ceased when he left.

"I personally felt that we had failed with this young man. He had good potential and might have become a valued member of our organization, except that he suffered from his own ego and biases."

On the other side of this issue, of course, are Christian employers who neglect their employees and treat them in a decidedly un-Christlike manner. They dismiss people they don't like; trade older, higher salaried people for younger people at reduced salaries; and fire people with the casualness of someone trading an automobile. In the process, they do untold damage to their witness and to the cause of Christ.

Malcolm was such a person. He owned and operated a construction company that employed more than 400 people, most of whom lived in daily fear for their jobs.

Malcolm professed to be a Christian and gave generously to a variety of Christian causes. He believed himself to be a fair man but, in reality, he had grown accustomed to being "the boss" and refused to accept any criticism from others.

Being extremely moody, Malcolm fluctuated from being the most amiable person anyone could meet to being a tyrant toward everyone around him, and his employees rarely knew when the change would take place. At one meeting he might ask for the opinions of his management team and appear to genuinely appreciate them. Yet those managers who were still around had learned that after such a meeting Malcolm might fire any manager whose input he perceived as critical.

The changes in Malcolm's attitude were usually related to how well the company was doing at that particular time, although few of his employees made the connection. The company might still be making money, but Malcolm's attitude would change if it wasn't making as much as it had previously. He suffered from an acute fear of the future, caused by an equally acute lack of trust in others. When business went well, Malcolm felt great; but, when business slowed even slightly, he would plunge into despair and usually take out his frustration on those around him.

In his "up" stages, Malcolm often attempted to bring Christ into his business. He tried having company devotion times, sending employees to seminars, giving away Bibles, even bringing in a company chaplain, but nothing worked. Many times his up cycles lasted several months, and just when it seemed to some of his most loyal people that he might really have changed he would fire a secretary or some other lower-paid employee for some slight mistake that cost the company money. Then his whole program went down the tubes again.

Malcolm's company had contracted with the Navy to make struts for a new fighter aircraft. The contract could easily double the previous year's business, but it also carried some stiff penalties for failure to deliver on time or for defective workmanship. As the company worked on the Navy project, Malcolm was both elated and frantic most of the time. He could see the potential, but he also could sense the inherent risks to his business. To ensure the project's success, he established a new manufacturing facility in a separate building and placed his most experienced managers in charge.

Things went along very well for several months, and the profits from the Navy contract doubled the company's previous best quarter. Then suddenly Malcolm's world came tumbling down. He received word from the Navy that one batch of strut parts were not up to Navy specifications and several parts were actually defective. The Navy told him that the parts would have to be re-fabricated at his cost. They also told him that any subsequent problems would result in stiff fines and a cancellation of his contract.

Malcolm was fit to be tied. He stormed out of his office and yelled so loudly at his startled secretary that the entire office staff looked up as he said, "I want that plant manager for the Navy contract in my office in ten minutes! You tell Stu [the plant manager] that if he's not up here in ten minutes with the production reports from last month, he can kiss his job good-bye!"

Everyone in the office knew Malcolm's statement was not an idle threat, even though a few months earlier he had praised Stu before the entire company and stated that he had complete trust in Stu's ability to head the Navy project. The fact that Stu had been with Malcolm almost from the beginning of the company made no difference. Malcolm had been known to fire long-term employees and later refuse to reinstate them even when he was shown to be in error.

Ten minutes later Stu showed up, carrying the production reports. As they went over the list of defective components, together they quickly discerned that all were from one shift.

"Who's the line supervisor on that shift?" Malcolm boomed, loud enough to be heard in a sawmill.

"That's Johnson," Stu replied, adding, "He's our best supervisor. He's been with the company four years and ran an entire project in Georgia."

"I don't care if he's been here since the beginning of time!" Malcolm shouted. "I want him off that job today, you hear? You take his shift if you have to, but I want him fired today."

"But, wouldn't it be better to find out what's happened?" Stu argued. "He's one of my best people. I know something has to be wrong."

"Yeah, and I know what it is. He thinks he can become buddies with the people on his shift and let them get away with this," Malcolm said as he slapped the Navy report down on the desk. "You fire him or I'll do it myself."

"No, I'll do it," Stu replied dejectedly as he got up to leave. He could just see Malcolm storming into the plant and firing Johnson in front of all the other employees.

Stu made his way back to the plant and called Johnson into his office. "I'm afraid I have some bad news. We just received word from the Navy that several of the struts from the last batch were defective and will have to be replaced. Our records show that they were all from your plant shift. What do you have to say?"

"Nothing really, Stu," Johnson replied dejectedly. "I've been having some personal problems, and I guess I just haven't been handling the quality control well enough."

"Johnson, you have to learn to leave your problems at home. The work we do is so critical that it takes total concentration."

"I know, Stu. I'll try to do better in the future. It's just been a difficult time for me the last month or so."

"I'm very sorry, but I've been instructed to let you go. This problem is going to cost the company a lot of money."

"But I've always done a good job in the past," Johnson said, trying to keep his voice steady. "I just can't afford to lose my job right now. Our money's really tight."

"I really am sorry," Stu confessed. "But I don't have any choice in the matter."

"I understand," Johnson mumbled as he got up. "I guess ole Mr. Self-righteous needs someone to crucify again."

"What do you mean?" Stu asked, shocked to hear the very statement he had been thinking himself earlier.

"Everybody knows that the boss relieves his tensions by firing people. I guess if it weren't this now, it would happen some other time. It's just rotten timing, that's all."

"That's the second time you mentioned that, Johnson. Tell me what the problem is."

The next ten minutes Johnson told his plant manager the details of what had been going on in his life. Stu waited until the man had left his office, and then he called Malcolm.

"Yeah, Stu, have you fired that supervisor yet?"

"Yes, Sir, I have, but I think you need to hear about what he's been going through the last few months."

"I don't care," Malcolm shouted over the phone so loudly that several people in the main office looked up. "You fire him, or it'll be you who gets fired."

"Is that your final word?" Stu asked politely.

"You're right. It is!" Malcolm gruffed, resorting to the profanity he used occasionally, whenever anyone challenged his decisions.

"Okay," Stu replied briskly. "It's done." And with that he hung up the phone. He was busy writing out his letter of resignation when the two production line supervisors who worked for Johnson came into his cubicle.

"Is it true that Johnson has been fired, Stu?"

"Yeah, and I've just written my letter of resignation too," he responded. "I know what Johnson is going through, but I can't do anything about it."

"But he's taking the blame for what someone on the line screwed up," one of the assembly supervisors said angrily. "It should be one of us that gets it, not Johnson."

"But he's the supervisor in charge, and he's the one who has to take the heat. I wish I could help, but I can't," Stu replied as he sealed his resignation envelope.

"That's kinda what we all figured," the supervisors said as they handed Stu a sheet of paper.

Stu let out an inadvertent gasp as he read the letter. On it were the names of every day-shift worker under Johnson's authority. At the bottom of the page was a scratchy statement that read, "We all quit. We won't work for a hypocrite like Malcolm Bloom no more."

"Are you sure about this?" Stu asked.

"We sure are. Money ain't everything in life. We would rather collect welfare and keep our integrity than work for a hypocrite who talks about Christ and then fires a decent man who's going through what Johnson's going through! You know, that poor guy hasn't missed a day because he feels so responsible for the work here!"

When Stu asked the secretary to see Malcolm, the owner was still fuming in his office. "What is it now?" he asked with obvious irritation.

Stu closed the door and sat down. "Here, Malcolm, you read this first."

As he read the note from the employees, Malcolm turned red in the face. "Why those ungrateful . . . I'll . . ."

"You'll what, Malcolm? Fire them? You can't do that; they all quit."

"They can't all quit," Malcolm sputtered. "We need them to get this job out. It will ruin me, Stu. You need to talk to them."

"Not me, Malcolm," Stu replied. "You need to open the other envelope. I quit too."

"What! You can't quit, Stu. You're my best manager. Why are you quitting? I didn't blame you for the foul-up."

"Malcolm, you fire people indiscriminately whenever things don't go totally your way. You're the boss, but you're not God. You wonder why more of the employees don't come to your devotionals and the other Christian activities you provide. It's because they see your faith through your actions and they don't want anything to do with it. I know you're basically a decent man, and I think you even care about people—but only when it's convenient.

"Your Christianity is based on giving, not serving. And the Lord dealt with that issue when He confronted the Pharisees. I think I can even quote the verse: *'Woe to you Pharisees! For you pay tithe of mint and rue and every kind of garden herb, and yet disregard justice and the love of God; but these are the things you should have done without neglecting the others'* (Luke 11:42)."

"Okay, you made your point, Stu, and I have to agree that I do fly off the handle sometimes. I'll try to control my temper in the future. But let's get this shift thing straightened out. Would it help if we just gave the supervisor a few days off?"

"You still don't understand, do you, Malcolm? The company comes first in your life. The way you handle people just reflects outside what you believe inside. The supervisor has a name: Johnson. And he has a family: a wife, Thelma, and a daughter, Missy, both of whom have terminal cancer; and he has twin boys, Matt and Luke.

"Malcolm, this guy has been driving a hundred miles each evening to visit his wife and daughter at the cancer center and shuffling the twins from family to family so he can still work. The medical bills are nearly $200,000, and his deductible is nearly $40,000 so far. He has not used his sick leave because he knows he'll need it when his wife becomes totally incapacitated. He has worked weekends without pay to keep his shift's paperwork up to date so the contract wouldn't be jeopardized. And in the middle of all this, I had to fire him!"

"You mean all this was going on and none of the people in the plant told you or me?" Malcolm said as he collapsed into his chair. "I would have helped."

"I believe you would have, but the people who work for you were afraid you might fire him because of his problems."

"What? Do they think I'm some kind of ogre or something?" Malcolm muttered, more to himself than to Stu.

"All they know is that Johnson got fired, just like they expected," Stu replied as he started to leave.

"Just a minute, Stu. I'm going to need your help if I'm ever to get this problem solved. And I mean my attitude problem, not the contract."

That afternoon, Malcolm went over to the plant and personally apologized to the entire shift. He then went to Johnson's home, apologized to him, and asked that he return to his job after the medical crisis was over. Malcolm granted him an unlimited medical leave at full pay and later personally paid all of the medical bills not covered by the company's insurance. He had learned a lesson that many businesspeople fail to learn in an entire career: *People are more important than profits.*

BIBLICAL PRINCIPLES FOR FIRING

Acting fairly and humanely toward employees is one of the most important responsibilities of a Christian businessperson. But an employee's responsibility to an employer is an equally important principle. When an employee refuses to conform to company rules, dismissal may be necessary.

What does the Bible say about firing? Obviously there were no corporations, as we know them, when the authors of the Bible were transmitting God's words to us. But application of the principles found in God's Word will answer the vast majority of the questions related to the dismissal of an employee.

Let me start by redefining the prerequisites any Christian owner or manager must meet before the dismissal of an employee should ever be considered.

1. Have a clearly defined job description.
2. Have a clearly defined set of job standards: time, dress, expected output.
3. Communicate your expectations clearly.
4. Communicate your dissatisfactions clearly and quickly—in writing.
5. Have a trial correction period.

Before getting into the details of how to handle a dismissal, I would like to discuss two of these points that I find most Christian businesspeople violate: communicating expectations and communicating dissatisfactions.

THE NEED TO COMMUNICATE

Too often, an owner or manager who wrestles with the balance between leadership and Christianity will allow grievances to build up until they become intolerable; then that person will unload on some unsuspecting employee who should have been corrected long before. It is vitally important, therefore, that you get a firm understanding of just what the Scriptures say about how to handle people and avoid the procrastination that comes with doubt.

A friend I'll call Peter needed a field supervisor for his commercial plumbing business. He had tried several of his better plumbers, but none of them did a particularly good job of managing the projects. Then at a breakfast Bible study a mutual friend of ours mentioned that his son was leaving the staff of a prominent Christian ministry and was actively looking for a job. The young man had worked for my friend during the summers while in college and impressed Peter with his ability to learn quickly and his diligence in getting a job done. So Peter asked our friend to have his son contact him as soon as possible.

Later Peter told me that he had hired the young man, Brad, to be his field supervisor. Peter was particularly excited because Brad had suggested that he could organize a morning Bible study at the job sites and that perhaps they would see some men come to the Lord.

I asked Peter if he had clearly described to Brad his job expectations. "Oh, yes," he said. "Brad will work out great. We have a complete meeting of the minds."

Unfortunately, that is rarely true, even part of the time. Usually whatever can be misunderstood will be, and this time was to be no exception.

At first, however, things seemed to be going well. Each week Peter kept me informed on Brad's progress, and for the first month he was enthusiastic. Brad had made an overall good impression on the work crews and had spent most of his time in the field getting to know the men.

But then Peter confided to me at one of our breakfast meetings that he was having a little problem with Brad. "What's the problem?" I asked, after all the other men had cleared out.

"He seems to be spending too much time with a few men who are having some family problems, and some of his Bible studies at the work sites are lasting too long."

"Then tell him exactly how you feel," I suggested. "You can't lose with total honesty. You might hurt a few feelings up front, but if you allow the situation to go on, you'll end up hurting a lot more."

Instead of confronting the issue, however, Peter tried using psychology on Brad. He "suggested" that perhaps some of the studies should be limited to 15 minutes. Brad apparently interpreted this to mean that he should take the matter under consideration. But great things were happening at the studies and lives were being changed, so he decided against cutting the meetings short.

Peter skipped two weeks of breakfast meetings; then he came to see me. "I can't keep Brad on the payroll," he said bleakly.

"Why not? Isn't he working out like you expected?" I asked.

"It's a disaster. He spends most of his time talking with men having marriage and family problems. In fact, he has become the resident counselor on the job sites, and men from other companies ask him questions. He hardly has time to fill out the reports I need from the job sites."

"Have you confronted him with this?" I asked.

"I tried, but it's really hard because he shares how many lives are being changed, and I know that's true. I can't fault what he's doing. It's just that he's not doing what I hired him to do."

"You need to sit down with Brad and confront this directly and honestly," I said. "You're not being honest with Brad. Either confront the problem or learn to live with it, but don't just keep talking about it."

Peter couldn't bring himself to face the issue of the young man's evangelizing on the job, so he finally decided to take the coward's way out. He planned to call Brad in and fire him on the pretext that he couldn't afford his salary.

When Brad came in the next morning, Peter asked him to come into his office. He began the conversation by saying, "Brad, I need to talk to you about your job." Then, stalling for time, Peter asked, "How do you think it's going so far?"

Since Peter was so discouraged with Brad, he just naturally assumed that Brad was feeling the same way. So he was floored when he heard Brad answer, "I think it's going great, Sir. I believe we're right on target."

Peter almost drenched himself in the coffee he was holding. He stammered, "What?" Then he asked a very penetrating question. "Tell me what your job is, Brad. Exactly what are you doing?"

Brad looked a little confused, but he replied, "Well, I've always assumed that you want me to share Christ with the men at the construction sites. I've shared with our friends at church what a great idea it is to bring Christ to these men, who will probably never hear the message otherwise."

Peter was genuinely amazed. Brad was serious! "But . . . Brad, don't you realize that I hired you to oversee the jobs themselves and that your evangelism and Bible studies are interfering with the work?"

Now it was Brad's turn to be shocked. "No, Sir, I really didn't know that's what you were expecting. Why, you must think I've been wasting company money and time. Do you?"

"I guess I'd have to be honest and say the thought had occurred to me. But I would still like to try you as the site foreman."

"I appreciate the offer, Sir, but I believe God wants me to stay in the field of evangelism. I took the job because I thought you wanted to start evangelizing at the job sites. Perhaps God used this opportunity to show me what can be done there. If you'll let me, I'd like to stay on as long as my money holds out and try to train one of the other men to take over when I leave."

Brad resigned and left Peter's office. Later that week, Peter called me to talk about their discussion. "I just can't get what he said out of my mind. I know he is having a great impact on some of those men. But I really do need a site supervisor."

"Have you ever thought about getting some of the other Christian businesspeople together and cosponsoring Brad as a kind of roving Bible teacher-evangelist?" I asked.

"No, I haven't, but that sounds like a great idea," Peter replied.

Within a week, Peter had arranged for three other businesspeople to help underwrite Brad's salary, and the young man was engaged as a full-time site evangelist. Brad has now become a well-known and highly sought-after business evangelist.

Peter's mistake was one made by many, if not most, business owners: He assumed that he and the other person were thinking on the same wavelength. That is almost never true. You must learn to communicate your expectations, approvals, and disapprovals clearly. Most important is never to let the sun go down on a problem without making a promise to handle it.

Sometimes it is better to let a little time pass if the issue is very emotional. Over the years I've learned that if I react to something when I'm angry, I'll almost always say something I'll later regret, so I give it some time. But if I wait too long, I won't deal with the problem and it will eventually get worse.

Two proverbs have helped me to reach the correct balance: *"Like a city that is broken into and without walls, is a man who has no control over his spirit"* (Proverbs 25:28); and *"A man's pride will bring him low, but a humble spirit will obtain honor"* (Proverbs 29:23).

12

Justification for Dismissal

Problems with employees need to be dealt with, not allowed to drag on. People problems almost never get better when left alone. In time, the problems usually compound. The Lord told us, *"A little leaven leavens the whole lump."* When you allow a dissenter, a thief, or a slacker to continue uncorrected, it will encourage others to follow his or her example.

REASONS FOR DISMISSAL

The following is a list of biblically justifiable reasons for dismissing an employee. It is not meant to be all-inclusive, but it should be useful in pointing out the most common justifiable reasons for dismissal.

1. Dishonesty

The Lord tells us in Matthew 9:13 that we should always lean more toward forgiveness than toward seeking retribution for sins against us. In a business, I believe this means that we should forgive someone who is repentant for his or her misconduct and who truly wishes to change. But when dishonesty is tolerated or overlooked, the wicked prosper and the honest suffer. *"He who walks in his uprightness fears the Lord, but he who is crooked in his ways despises Him"* (Proverbs 14:2).

During my first year of college I worked at a large sporting goods store. The manager was a nice guy who was great with the buying and selling end of the business, but he was not good at disciplining his people. The company did a lot of wholesale business with schools and other sporting goods stores in the area; thus, it employed several outside salespeople.

It was not uncommon for these salespeople to come into the warehouse and load up their cars with samples of all kinds of athletic equipment. The owner required that they sign for what they took, but the manager was very lax about this rule. As a result, most of the equipment taken was never checked out.

This lax attitude about sales samples influenced some of the younger employees to develop a similar attitude toward their use of company merchandise. The problem grew to alarming proportions when the annual audit showed the loss of nearly $50,000 worth of inventory.

The company owner secretly hired a detective to investigate the losses, and the detective's report pointed to employee pilfering as the culprit. One of the employees was caught selling company goods along the roadside of his route. His excuse was, "I thought it was okay, since nobody cared how much stock we took out."

After that, all inventory was carefully checked in and out, and the employees who had taken merchandise were given a chance to pay for the goods or resign. A lot of missing stock mysteriously reappeared on the shelves.

It is management's responsibility to establish and maintain rules that reduce such temptations and that includes firing employees who break these rules. The correct procedure for dismissing a dishonest employee is, first, be sure the standard for acceptable and unacceptable conduct is very clear to everyone. Then, if a theft is discovered, confront the issue in the open with anyone who is involved.

In many situations, employee dishonesty will involve such non-cash issues as misuse of the company telephone; equipment, such as copiers; or available supplies, such as paper and pencils. In such cases, confronting the dishonesty may be all that the situation requires. If the confrontation is done with an attitude of caring and the goal is to restore and salvage the individual, this action can be a positive witness for the Lord.

However, if the offense involves blatant theft of money or materials, it is important that the punishment fit the crime. Our society often condones crime, and the negative effect it has had on society should make any Christian ready to follow God's principle. God's Word says,

"Where there is no vision, the people are unrestrained, but happy is he who keeps the law" (Proverbs 29:18).

2. Disobedience

There are many degrees of disobedience when it comes to employees. Open rebellion is simple to spot and relatively simple to deal with: the employee either stops rebelling or is asked to leave the company. However, subtle disobedience is more difficult to ferret out and infinitely more difficult to control.

Some years ago I experienced this problem and faced the challenge of handling it without undermining the morale of the other employees. The situation involved a secretary who, although very good at her job, had a habit of undercutting the authority of her supervisor. Hers was never open rebellion but, rather, it was a series of subtle comments made to other employees, such as "Have you noticed that Mr. Smith and Rhonda are spending a lot of time together?" or "I heard that Julie can't be fired. It makes you wonder why, doesn't it?"

Usually this secretary would ensnare one of the younger women by making a comment that the other person would agree with. Later, if the comment was traced back, it would always be attributed to the younger employee.

I began to notice after a while that, although this secretary was never named as the agitator, she was always involved somewhere. When any disciplinary action was taken against any hourly employee for tardiness or absence, this secretary would immediately go to console the person and fill him or her in on what she perceived to be management's blatant violation of the Fair Labor Standards Act governing hourly employees. I found myself defending my decisions at staff meetings for nonexistent abuses.

I was at a loss as to how to deal with the problem, since the secretary would always deny having any part in the dissension. Finally I felt the best way to handle the situation was to be totally honest with the others who were involved. I made a habit of reminding them where the comments originated, who ended up with the blame, and who ended up with the denials. Once the others began to see what this person was up to, they began to confront her about everything she said about anyone else.

They made a practice of calling the other parties into the discussion and asking the secretary to repeat what she had just told them, which she always refused to do. Within a few weeks of my initiating this action she resigned. The old maxim proved to be true: In the face of truth, a lie (or liar) will always flee.

3. Laziness

Proverbs describes this problem as *slothfulness*; but, however you describe it, laziness is undoubtedly on the rise in American industry. The average American worker produces approximately 30 percent less than his or her Asian counterpart. Fortunately, we have been able to make up some of the inefficiencies by improved technology (computers and word processors in the office environment).

It has been said, in fact, that if modern American workers had the same tools to work with that their fathers did in the fifties, they would have to work a 90-hour week (for the same wages) in order for their employers to make a profit and continue paying them.

Apparently, through advanced technology, we have eased the burden of working and have failed to instill a healthy work ethic in the younger generations. Or perhaps the problem lies in the fact that so many people have taken on jobs they dislike and are constantly seeking to escape.

It is unfortunate that many employers are now inheriting the progeny of parents who failed to instill in their children a Christian work ethic, which evolves from the three basic principles: honoring authority (Romans 13:1); doing the best job possible (Proverbs 22:29); and putting energy into one's work (1 Peter 4:11). As a result, today's businesspeople often struggle to run businesses with employees who show little respect or loyalty to their employers.

Whatever its origin, the trend toward laziness in our society adds impetus to the need to evaluate and place employees and to establish rules that promote efficiency. Then you need to discipline those who don't perform up to their potential.

General George Patton had a problem with lazy parachute packers during the European campaign in World War II. Several pilots were killed when their chutes didn't open because of sloppy packing. An inspection of in-use parachutes showed that as many as 30 percent were improperly packed.

In his inimitable style, General Patton quickly solved the problem. He charged into the central parachute packing depot and commanded all the packers to take the last chutes they had packed and come with him. He then herded them into a waiting C-46 aircraft and had them jump over the practice range, wearing the chutes they had just packed.

He continued this practice for the remainder of the war and never again had a problem with slothful parachute packers.

Every effort should be made to motivate and redirect slothful employees. If, after a reasonable effort has been made, there is no change, the only solution may be to remove the problem employee.

Roland ran a chain of hamburger restaurants, where he employed several dozen teenagers. He also had young shift managers who were permanent employees (more or less). It seemed to him that slothfulness was the rule with the kids who worked for him. It wasn't that they couldn't do a good job. When he was around, they worked hard and did quality work, but when he left, the quality went down and complaints went up. He also had to cope with constant employee turnover. The kids knew that if he fired them, they could go to work for his competitor down the street because there was a perpetual need for personnel.

On the advice of a friend who had attended one of our business seminars, Roland called our office one day. Deeply frustrated, he was seriously thinking about selling the restaurants and getting into another business. He said he was convinced that his problem was one of a degenerate generation of young people, both Christian and non-Christian. He said, "I can see little difference in the basic work ethic of believers and nonbelievers."

"Do you think it's a problem with all teenagers?"

"No, obviously not," he replied. "But the kids with the good work habits can find better, higher-paying jobs, so we rarely see them apply for work."

"Why do you think they take the other jobs?" I asked.

"I guess because they pay more and are perceived to be prestigious."

"Then you'll just have to raise the perception of your business," I commented.

"I don't know how to do that," Roland responded with irritation in his voice. "We sell hamburgers. We don't build rockets."

"Well, I guess you probably won't be able to attract any rocket scientists then," I quipped, "but if you never need rocket scientists, that probably won't be a great loss. Why don't you start by offering wages that are competitive with the so-called prestigious jobs?"

"But that would mean I would be paying more than any other fast-food place in town. I don't know if I can afford that."

"Is your business losing money right now?"

"No, in fact, we do quite well, in spite of the high turnover in personnel."

"Then why don't you give it a try? Perhaps you'll find that the extra cost in wages will be more than offset by the lower turnover rate."

Roland took the advice and raised his starting wage by nearly 40 percent. Then he raised the experienced people another 20 percent. He also instituted a scholarship program that awarded students a $1,000 scholarship for each additional year they worked after the first year.

As a result of the changes Roland made, the college-bound students flocked to his businesses, and his personnel problems virtually disappeared. He also instituted a profit-sharing program based on each restaurant's growth and lack of complaints. These incentives attracted better employees, who worked hard and treated customers better.

In the short run, Roland's profits declined, but within a year they were higher than ever and now they exceed the national average for all similar businesses. The firing process gets a whole lot easier when you take steps to attract the right people initially!

4. Incompetence

One of the most difficult situations to deal with from a Christian perspective is that of an incompetent but cooperative employee. Anyone who has been in business for any number of years has been faced with this situation at one time or the other. When I worked for General Electric at the space center in Florida, we had a standing joke that the civil service administration was created to provide jobs to those who were incompetent and uncooperative. That's probably unfair, but the government civil service system does seem to thwart any effort by competent managers to remove the incompetent.

To allow a person who clearly cannot do the tasks assigned him or her to remain on that job is a disservice to both the employee and the company. But before dismissing the incompetent person, you should first attempt to determine if he or she may just be misplaced. Sometimes a change in job responsibilities can solve the problem.

A doctor I'll call Jerry hired Nancy, a registered nurse, to work in his office. Her job was to interview the patients and prepare them for the appointment with the doctor. Additionally she was required to routinely give shots and take blood or urine samples. Any of these tasks could be easily handled by a trained nonprofessional, but she quickly proved herself completely inept at handling them.

During her first week on the job, Nancy gave the wrong patient a vitamin shot (fortunately with no harmful consequences), mismarked two blood samples (one of which tested positive with hepatitis), and mismarked two patients' charts. The situation deteriorated from there. Nancy was so disorganized that Jerry soon learned he could never entrust any important or critical tasks to her. Over the next several weeks he found himself working around her and giving her normal duties to others on his staff.

Each time he talked to her about her shortcomings, Nancy was pleasant and apologetic. Virtually every patient praised her for her helpful attitude and willing spirit. None of the other office workers trusted any paperwork she had touched, but they all agreed she was about the nicest person they had ever met.

Jerry was faced with a dilemma: what to do with this sweet but highly inefficient nurse. I suggested shifting her to the reception area where she could meet and schedule patients. He did that for two days and was faced with several double bookings and numerous wrong appointments.

Finally Jerry called her into his office to confront the issues with her. "Nancy, why did you become a nurse?" he asked over her tears.

"Because I really want to help people," she replied. "I just love working with people."

"How did you get through nurse's training?" Jerry asked, knowing that each prospective nurse must intern in a hospital before being certified.

"Well, I had to study about three times harder than anyone else in my classes," she replied between sobs. "And I repeated some of the labs several times until I passed them. But I really want to be a nurse. If you fire me, I may never get another chance."

"But, I can't allow you to risk injury to a patient," Jerry said. He was really feeling bad now, but he still had every intention of firing her.

Then he had a brainstorm and asked, "Nancy, if you could do anything your heart desired, what would it be?"

"Oh, I'd love to work with older people in a nursing home," she replied as her face lit up. "I helped my grandmother while she was alive, and I really enjoyed it."

"Okay," Jerry replied. "You go back to work and we'll talk again." She left as puzzled as Jerry was. Both of them had expected her to get fired at that meeting. But as Jerry sat there, he remembered a doctor he had met at a conference of Christian physicians. This doctor ran a sizable nursing home and had spoken on the problems of getting nurses to work in elderly care because of the long hours and short pay.

Jerry immediately placed a call to the other doctor and told him about Nancy. Then Jerry presented his idea. If the other doctor would be willing to give Nancy a trial period at the home, Jerry's clinic would absorb a part of her salary for the first month. The other physician agreed, and Nancy was ecstatic.

Two weeks later the doctor called Jerry to say that they would not need his salary supplement. He had hired Nancy permanently and was totally thrilled with her.

"But how in the world did you get her organized?" Jerry asked.

"We have permanently assigned a nurse's aide to do her paperwork and scheduling," he replied. "Did you know she is dyslexic?" he asked.

"No I sure didn't, but that explains a lot of things."

"Yes," the doctor replied. "But it doesn't matter to us. The cost of a student helper is insignificant compared to the positive effect Nancy has on our patients. If you come across any more like her, send them our way."

Cases like Nancy's are not unusual in many businesses. The difference in her case was the necessity to deal with the problem quickly and her employer's willingness to search for a creative solution.

Maintaining people in jobs for which they are neither qualified nor motivated is a disservice to both the company and the employees, yet many Christians do so out of a misguided sense of ethics.

I want to conclude this discussion of firing with a reminder: When in doubt about what to do, lean heavily on God's wisdom and show mercy. In situations in which an employee must be dismissed, the dismissal should be carried out in an attitude of love and concern.

In addition, mercy means being concerned about the financial needs of anyone under your watch care, even ex-employees. Be sensitive to God's leading about helping those you dismiss, even for valid cause. Several times I have felt God's leading to assist ex-employees financially, even though I never would have considered them for rehire. So have other Christians, like Thomas West (not his real name), who have faced the issue of needing to help an employee they dismissed.

Thomas had employed an elderly man, Oscar Roper, to deliver packages to various customers around his city. At first the delivery volume wasn't very large, and the old fellow did pretty well. He was slow, but since he worked on a per diem basis, it didn't really matter. But as

Thomas's business picked up and the volume increased, customers began to complain about their orders being delayed.

Then customers began to call with stories about the delivery man sleeping in the hallways outside their offices and about mysterious damage done to vehicles parked close to the delivery zone. An inspection of the delivery van revealed a whole variety of scratches and dents on the front and back bumpers.

Finally Thomas called Oscar into his office and told him that he would have to let him go: "I'm afraid you just can't do this job, Oscar," he said to the older gentleman.

"Yes, Sir, I know you must be right. I get lost a lot lately, and sometimes I have to rest before the next stop."

By common consent, Oscar's services were terminated. After the employment contract with Oscar was ended, Thomas contracted his parcels with a delivery service. The business prospered and deliveries were processed on time.

Then, a few months later, Thomas woke up in the middle of the night with this old gentleman on his heart. He was certain that the Lord wanted him to check on Oscar. The next day he went to the address he had listed in the employees' records and knocked on the door of the run-down apartment.

"Why, Mr. West, come on in," Oscar's wife said as she opened the door. "What brings you out here?"

As Thomas entered the apartment he shuddered. It was colder inside than the 38-degree temperature outside. He also noticed half-burned candles placed around the threadbare room. "Don't you have any heat, Mrs. Roper?" Thomas asked.

"No, Sir. The electric company turned the power off. We can't pay the bill."

"Is Oscar home?"

"No, Sir, he's out looking for work. We can't live on his pension. But it sure is hard for an old man to find regular work these days."

"Would you please have him call me when he comes in?"

"Yes, Sir, but we don't have a phone. He'll have to walk down to the grocery store. They took his drivin' license away last week 'cause he couldn't pass the test. But I'll have him call."

As Thomas hurried away from Oscar's apartment, he knew God had sent him to that house to learn that people were more important than profits. Thomas later told Oscar that he had qualified for a pension from his company (although he had worked less than two months).

From that month on, he provided the Ropers with an additional $350-a-month income.

Three years later, when Oscar died, Thomas told Mrs. Roper that the pension would be hers for life, and he continues to pay as of this writing. He has taken to heart what the Lord said, *"And the King will answer and say to them, 'Truly I say to you, to the extent that you did it to one of these brothers of Mine, even the least of them, you did it to Me'"* (Matthew 25:40).

STEPS FOR DISMISSAL

Now that we have considered the reasons for dismissal, I'd like to suggest the essential steps that should be taken prior to dismissing any employee.

1. Institute a Trial Correction Period

When you realize that disciplinary action must be taken and dismissal may be necessary, you should first give the employee an opportunity to change. A trial correction period should be established and the employee told the exact purpose for the trial: It is a precursor to more punitive action. The minimum requirements should be detailed (in writing) and the meeting documented in the employee's personnel file.

If the trial period is to be for a period of more than 30 days, there should be at least two additional face-to-face reviews during that period.

2. Conduct an Exit Interview

If the trial period does not work out, the immediate manager should confront the employee with the necessity of dismissal. I always recommend that once the decision to dismiss has been confirmed, it should be executed quickly and the employee removed from the business environment. Adequate compensation should be provided in the form of severance pay or extended pay for a predetermined period.

3. Provide Job Referrals

Assuming the dismissal did not result from a problem that would prohibit a future job referral, the exit interview should include providing a letter of recommendation and perhaps even the offer of assistance in locating another job. Remember, the fact that someone did not work out for your company in the particular position he or she held does not automatically mean that person will not work out somewhere else.

REASONS TO ABORT A DISMISSAL ACTION

You may sometimes find it necessary to reverse your decision to dismiss an employee. A part of being a Christian employer involves compassion as well as discipline.

There are several reasons why a dismissal action might be aborted. Remember, any action taken by a Christian employer should always be done in a spirit of love and concern for the others involved. Of course, if you think about your actions carefully and try never to indulge in resentment or anger toward an employee, you won't have to repent and apologize very often. The damage that an angry, vengeful employer can do is sometimes irreparable. *"There is one who speaks rashly like the thrusts of a sword, but the tongue of the wise brings healing"* (Proverbs 12:18).

1. The Conditions of the Trial Period Are Met

This may sound ridiculous to mention, but if you establish trial periods for employees to conform to and they do, don't dismiss them. Unfortunately I have known employers who did just that. Why? Because they had their feelings bruised by some action of a subordinate, and the trial period was simply a formality to satisfy the federal Fair Labor Standards Act.

It is a wise person who can admit he or she is wrong—especially the boss. I have seen many employers who were so stiff-necked they would never admit an error in judgment. It was as if they believed others thought they were infallible. No one is, and employees don't think less of an authority who admits when he or she is wrong. They admire that person instead.

2. The Employee Shows a Repentant Attitude

In a dialogue with Jesus, Simon Peter asked, *"'Lord, how often shall my brother sin against me and I forgive him? Up to seven times?' Jesus said to him, 'I do not say to you, up to seven times, but up to seventy times seven'"* (Matthew 18:21–22). The principle behind the Lord's reply was to show that a Christian should go far beyond the requirements of society.

The same principle applies in business. If someone violates a company policy that merits dismissal but truly displays a repentant spirit, the dismissal should be set aside.

I recall a Christian I was counseling who suspected he was being robbed by his company accountant. He initiated an audit through an outside firm, and their findings confirmed his suspicions. At first the accountant denied everything, but eventually she confessed to pilfering small amounts from the petty cash fund over several months. The total amounted to approximately $1,200.

Her dismissal was immediate; the question was whether or not to prosecute. After discussing the situation with her pastor, he decided not to prosecute, since this was her first offense. *"Does any of you, when he has a case against his neighbor, dare to go to law before the unrighteous, and not before the saints?"* (1 Corinthians 6:1).

A few days later the accountant came to his office to ask his forgiveness and offered to start paying the money back each month as she could. She also offered him a note written on her car as collateral for the debt.

In the course of the discussion, he asked why she had stolen the money. She replied that her husband had left her and moved in with another woman, forcing her to fend for herself and their five children. It seemed that when anything broke, she never had the funds to fix it, so she had taken small amounts from petty cash.

At first she had only borrowed the money with the intention of repaying it from her next paycheck, but the next paycheck had come and gone without her being able to replace the money. Eventually she got in so far she couldn't pay what she had taken. She had stopped the pilfering several weeks earlier and attempted to confess several times, but the fear of losing her job and career stopped her.

The accountant had always been a scrupulously honest person and couldn't live with this sin on her conscience. She knew she had been wrong and asked his forgiveness. He offered her the job back again with the agreement that the money would be repaid from her salary at the rate of $100 a month. In the meantime he went to her pastor and worked out a method to help meet her expenses through the church without her knowing it. She continued to work as a valued employee and never repeated the offense. Forgiveness was the correct procedure in her case.

3. The Employee Is "Heavenly Sandpaper"

Another reason for aborting a dismissal is that God is using that person as "heavenly sandpaper" on you. Perhaps the classic biblical example of this is found in 2 Samuel, where Shimei is throwing stones at David and his men as they flee from Jerusalem. When Abishai wanted to attack him, David said, *"Let him alone and let him curse, for the Lord has told him"* (2 Samuel 16:11). David accepted Shimei as God's heavenly sandpaper to humble him.

I don't know if God has ever used someone as "heavenly sandpaper" in your life, but He most certainly has in mine. If you recognize this, don't dismiss that person. If you do, God will simply bring another just like him or her into your life to polish off those rough edges.

4. Outside Factors

As in the case in Chapter 11 of the shift supervisor in Malcolm's factory, there can be outside factors pressuring someone to react the way he or she does. Obviously, these can be used as cop-outs. Everyone is exposed to outside pressures, and they can't all be allowed to affect the job performance. But under extreme duress people will react differently from normal. Allow them the benefit of the doubt if the behavior is decidedly unusual for them.

One source of problems that is least understood by many business owners is a phase known as midlife crisis today. This is a real event in the lives of the majority of men between the ages of 40 and 50 years old.

Perhaps one of the best descriptions of this condition is found in Pastor Jim Conway's book, *Men in Mid-Life Crisis*. He describes his own feelings of inadequacy and failure as he realized that more of his life was behind him than was left before him, and he hadn't accomplished what he had thought he would. He found himself despondent and depressed over nothing in particular and sometimes unable to perform even the simplest tasks. In general, this is the transition period for men (and women to some degree) when they begin to realize that they are no longer young.

Too often those with the financial means to do so during this phase end up leaving their families and looking for a younger partner in an attempt to recapture one element of their youth. When you see a previously conservative 45-year-old businessman riding to work on his new motorcycle, wearing a black leather jacket, he's in a midlife crisis for sure.

Nobody fires the boss, but what about the employee whose performance drops off for no logical reason? Or the middle-aged manager who suddenly takes all his sick leave and vacation and still can't perform, when he had never missed two days in a row before? The common reaction is to dismiss that person, and in some cases that may be necessary. First, however, you need to make an effort to understand the outside circumstances that person is suffering.

I believe that too few Christian businesspeople understand or accept the principle: *"A friend loves at all times, and a brother is born for adversity"* (Proverbs 17:17).

Clearly, if our Christianity doesn't work like that, we need to question whether we really have it.

13

Management Selection
Decisions

Victor owned and operated a large printing facility. The business was growing, and he was beginning to breathe a little easier about the large debt he had assumed when he purchased the business from the previous owner. Victor was committed to operating his business according to biblical principles and consistently told his managers that if they did quality work, charged a fair price, and treated both the customers and the employees with courtesy and respect, the business would prosper.

Unfortunately the previous owner had established the policy that virtually all decisions were to be based on profits. His attitude was, any job that doesn't generate a profit is the manager's fault, and his or her salary will reflect it.

Pat, one of the managers, had been assigned a rush job to print posters for a political campaign. This job carried with it a penalty clause: if the materials were not delivered on time, the company would lose money. As luck would have it, one of the large presses in Pat's area broke down just as the rush job was being processed. So Pat, trying to stay with his timetable, requested the use of an identical press. Unfortunately, this press was being used by Max, another manager. The conversation went something like the following.

"Max, I need the use of your press for at least a day or so. If I have to wait for the factory to ship the parts we need to get the number-three press working, I'll miss my deadline," Pat said.

"Can't do it, Pat," Max answered. "I have a big job on the press, and it would cost me at least 40 man hours to clean the press and restart the job once you're through."

"But it'll cost the company $10,000 if this job isn't out by the meeting on Friday!" Pat protested. "That will be ten times the loss you'd have on cleanup."

"Yeah, probably so. But that's really your problem, isn't it?" Max replied callously. "This job comes off my bonus. What's the matter with your press, anyway?"

"Apparently the safety bar is broken. Even when the operator holds the bar down, the press won't run."

"No sweat; that's an easy fix," Max said. "You just go into the control circuit and bypass the safety bar. The press will run just as well without it."

"But we were told by the OSHA [Occupational Safety and Health Administration] people that any alteration to the safety system would jeopardize our certificate," Pat protested.

"Well, suit yourself, Buddy. But I've been around long enough to know that OSHA doesn't pay our salaries. Besides, the older presses didn't have all that junk on them. You just have to be careful around it. Look, it's just one job, anyway. Who's to know?"

If a Christian is to succeed in applying biblical principles to his or her business, there is no more important decision than the selection of managers. In any business the owner or chief executive officer establishes the basic policies, but the managers are the ones who will execute these policies. Good managers will support and enhance the leader's policies; bad managers will undermine and subvert them.

The ideal is to have managers who are spiritually and philosophically compatible with the head of any organization. That truly is just an ideal, because situations almost never work out that way, even if the owner sets out to hire only compatible management personnel. In the first place, it is very difficult to determine a person's true values up front.

Second, to discriminate by such subjective measures in most businesses is illegal. But there are some basic standards that will at least help make the hiring of new managers and the promotion of employees to management positions easier.

SHOULD ALL MANAGERS BE CHRISTIANS?

If you are operating a Christian ministry, as I am, most assuredly the managers must be Christians and very mature ones. Our whole function is to minister to people in the name of the Lord, and our right to hire only Christians is protected by law. This makes the process a lot simpler for me. But even so, I have had managers who were not spiritually compatible, even though they were Christians. They did as much to undermine the purpose of our organization as any non-Christian would have. So a policy of just hiring Christians cannot be expected to eliminate all management conflicts.

For most businesses it is illegal to discriminate on the basis of religion in either hiring or promotion, as well it should be. But that alone does not automatically prohibit the screening of incompatible managers. There are allowable criteria that will ensure that at least your managers will be of the moral fiber that is necessary to build a biblically based company. The guiding rule is to have clear, written criteria for managers and apply them equally to everyone.

Always bear this principle in mind: The law does not prohibit you from doing more for your people than the law requires. Once you establish an environment that fosters biblical principles within a company, those who are inalterably opposed to high ethical standards will leave.

LIFESTYLE CRITERIA FOR MANAGERS

What are some of the legally allowable criteria for managers? Most of them involve visible aspects of a person's lifestyle.

Look for managers who meet the minimum standards established for leaders spelled out by the apostle Paul: *"If any man aspires to the office of overseer, it is a fine work he desires to do. An overseer, then, must be above reproach, the husband of one wife, temperate, prudent, respectable, hospitable, able to teach, not addicted to wine or pugnacious, but gentle, uncontentious, free from the love of money"* (1 Timothy 3:1–3).

These are the standards given for an overseer. But, in reality, isn't an overseer a manager? With the exception of the requirement about marriage, the standards given by Paul could just as easily apply to any decision-level manager.

You certainly want your managers to be above reproach. This includes their morals, honesty, ethics, and reputation. Anyone who has ever hired a manager with a roving eye for women will certainly attest to this standard!

The following are some important lifestyle traits to look for in a manager.

1. Temperate

A temperate person is not given to wide emotional swings. Nothing is more disruptive to the everyday activity of a company than a manager who is up one day and down the next. Your best, most productive employees are generally those with the *Supportive* personality. An unpredictable manager will make these people nervous wrecks and will lower their capacity to produce.

2. Prudent

A prudent person, according to *Webster's Dictionary*, is one who exercises good judgment. No law prohibits you from using this standard for selecting managers. (I wish the law required this standard for all politicians.) The difficulty comes in devising a method to test a prospective manager's prudence. Unfortunately Victor, the owner of the printing business, never had that opportunity because he inherited his management team from the previous owner.

Pat walked back to his cubicle thinking about his options. He knew the new owner had been leery about taking on the political poster job anyway and had agreed only after Pat assured him that there would be no problem in meeting the deadline. Pat decided that he was not about to take a loss on the very first job he had bid on his own.

He spent the next half-hour studying the control circuits and satisfied himself that he could indeed bypass the safety bar with a couple of jumpers. He waited until lunch time and made the necessary changes then.

"Listen," Pat told the pressman when the press was ready to roll, "you just worry about doing your job. If you use your head, you won't have any problems. The machine runs fine without the bar. Just don't go beyond the red line while the press is in operation. Okay?"

"You're the boss, Pat, but I don't like working around that machine with the safety bar disabled. Man, if that thing ever got you, it would grind you into dog meat before anyone could shut it down!"

"Just use the switch box on the side of the press to shut it down when you reload paper," Pat instructed the operator. "There's no reason anyone has to go near the hopper otherwise. Now, if you want to keep working here, get on it."

About three hours later Victor heard the warning siren signaling an emergency in the press area. He rushed out of his office just as someone shouted, "Somebody's been caught in one of the presses. It looks like his arm is smashed!"

Victor rushed over to the number-three-press area. What he saw there nearly made him sick. The press was stopped, but the pressman's arm was caught in the paper feeder up to his elbow. Victor heard one of the other operators say, "Some idiot bypassed the safety bar on this press. Benny tried to load paper with the machine still operating and got his shirt caught. By the time they got the machine shut down, Benny's arm was caught in the feeder. It's really a mess."

The pressman ultimately recovered the use of his arm, but the lawsuits, combined with $100,000 OSHA fine, forced the plant to shut down. Victor's ethic was right, but without like-minded managers, his policies could not be uniformly implemented. Neither the courts nor the health and safety agency had any sympathy for the fact that Pat had acted on his own. As far as they were concerned, Victor, as owner and manager, was still responsible.

3. Respectable

Being respectable means displaying appropriate conduct or mannerisms. Managers who are known as drunkards, carousers, or liars elicit no respect from those around them. Subordinates do not seek out their advice and counsel because they don't respect them. This doesn't mean employees won't listen to a manager they don't respect. They will, because they have no choice, but they won't seek the manager's advice or offer helpful input. Quite often employees will talk behind such a manager's back and undercut his or her authority by ridicule.

Janet had just been hired by a major computer company as a unit manager over a sales group of 50 people. A friend from her church, where she served in the adult singles group, recommended her for the job, her first real management position, and she was excited to be part of a well-respected company.

Janet reported to Mr. Barnett, the district manager, who supervised 20 other unit managers. When she came to work the first day she was met by one of the other managers in her division.

"So you're the new unit head, are you?" he stated, more than asked.

"Yes I am. I'm Janet Koble."

"How long have you been involved with Barnett?" he asked sarcastically.

"I don't know what you mean," Janet replied somewhat defensively.

"Well, everybody knows he doesn't make any woman a manager unless there are some favors involved," the manager said in a condescending tone.

Janet was furious as she made her way to Barnett's office. Thinking back over the interview, she now realized that what she had interpreted as a friendly manner was actually a sexual advance. She also realized she would be the brunt of many office jokes because of her manager's reputation.

"Mr. Barnett, I just want to tell you that in spite of what you or anyone else thinks, I am qualified for the position I was hired to do. And if you think I'm going to perform any other duties just for you, you're sadly mistaken."

"I don't know what's eating you, Janet," Barnett said. "I thought we had an agreement when I hired you for this job."

"I don't know what agreement you had in mind, but I can assure you I have no interest in any relationship other than business. I thought you were a Christian and were just being nice to me. I didn't realize this business was your personal recruiting ground for women."

"Janet, if you ever want to go any further in this company, you'd better learn to cooperate with your bosses a little better," Barnett said with a smirk.

"Mr. Barnett, if that's what it takes, I'll pass," Janet said emphatically. "My integrity and self-esteem and Christian witness are worth a lot more to me than any job, even yours. I suspect you're a joke in your own department, and I believe you know it. Respect is hard to earn and easy to lose. You sold yours pretty cheaply."

Janet walked out of the office with the department manager blustering about how he would see to it that she never got another raise. Three years later, the company put a new regional vice president over Mr. Barnett's department, who saw the lack of productivity in the department. The new boss ended up replacing Barnett with one of his most productive unit managers, Janet, who clearly had earned the respect and confidence of her staff.

We could continue listing the attributes of good managers, but it is sufficient to say that you can apply biblical criteria without quoting Scripture or interviewing people with a Bible in your hands. Just establish your basic policies for managers in written format, identifying the minimum expected.

In this era of mega-million-dollar lawsuits for sexual harassment, knowing the character of a manager is very important. One bad manager can reflect on all the management. The sex scandals in the military in the late nineties certainly attest to that.

Of the tens of thousands of noncommissioned and commissioned officers, only a few abused their positions. But, because the leadership chose to overlook the reports of these offenses and, in fact, covered them up, the entire military hierarchy received a bad name.

The object lesson: *Have good rules and enforce them.*

WHAT TO DO WHEN A MANAGER REBELS

It has often been said, "A rebellious employee becomes a rebellious manager." In other words, a promotion almost never turns a problem employee into a good one.

What can you do when one of your managers ignores the rules? Disobedience on the part of a manager is really no different from disobedience on the part of any other employee, and you should deal with it similarly. You first need to communicate your policies in writing so they can be understood clearly.

Next, you need to evaluate each manager's performance against this written standard. To those who don't meet this standard, you need to communicate your dissatisfaction clearly and establish a review period during which you evaluate compliance. Last, you need to deal with any manager who still won't comply by issuing written reprimands and, if necessary, dismissal or demotion.

Andy was a graduate engineer who had started a plastics company that specialized in injection molding. As with most small companies, the company's policies were relaxed and informal in the beginning. Then, as the company grew and the rules became too complex to leave to verbal communications only, a policy manual was developed.

Reggie, one of the shift managers, was an engineer who had started with Andy. A product of the sixties, he had always shown a very casual attitude about his dress and authority. Because of his skill and abilities Andy overlooked his peculiarities for a long time. But as the company grew and more clients sent their buyers to the home plant to inspect the facilities, Reggie's attitude became more of a problem. Even when major potential clients were visiting, Reggie would show up wearing well-worn blue jeans and screened T-shirts. At client meetings he would prop up his sock-less feet on the conference table.

Finally, at his wit's end, Andy called Reggie into his office. "Have you read the new policy manual?" Andy asked, as the engineer propped his feet on the trash can by Andy's desk.

"Yeah, I read some of it. Aren't you gettin' a little picky in your old age, Andy? I mean, I dressed good enough to help get this company started; how come I need to wear a tie now?"

"Because we have clients who expect to see our managers look like professionals. That's why," Andy snapped.

Sensing Andy's irritation, Reggie pressed him harder. "Listen, Boss, I do my job, and you know I do it well. I know more about injection molding than you do. I think you could ease up on this dress code thing, don't you?"

"No, I don't, Reggie. I run this company, and I want to do it in a manner that will honor the Lord . . ."

Reggie interrupted, "Oh, now we're gettin' off on that religion thing again, are we? I knew when you said you got saved, you'd try to cram it down my throat."

"That's not true, Reg. That has nothing to do with it. Most businesses require a dress code of their managers. I'm going to put a note in your personnel file about this reprimand. Consider it a warning."

"Man, that's got me shakin', Andy. A letter in my personnel file! The next thing will be a note that I'll need to take home and have my wife sign," Reggie said sarcastically.

"No, the next thing will be a dismissal," Andy replied evenly. "If you don't wear acceptable attire on Monday, I'll have to dismiss you."

"Listen, Andy, if you think you can fire me just because I don't dress to suit you, let me tell you something. I'll take my case to the government and tell them you fired me because of religious discrimination."

"I hope you don't do that, Reggie, because it wouldn't be true. But I'll let you go now and take my chances if you don't dress appropriately the next time you come to work."

Reggie stormed out of Andy's office and spent the rest of that day yelling at any employee who happened to cross his path.

The next Monday when Andy came in, he was met by a line of plant workers. Reggie was at the end of the line wearing baggy dress pants and suspenders and a T-shirt with the impression of a tie neatly silk-screened down the front. The smirk on his face told the story: He was intent on defying Andy's authority, or at least testing its limits.

Andy walked past the line and into his office. After praying for several minutes he asked his secretary to have Reggie come to his office.

When the call came from Andy's secretary, Reggie was strutting around the plant, confident that he had backed down the boss. As he walked toward the office, several of the employees heard him say, "Well, here goes lecture number 20 on dress codes." Instead, when he sat down in Andy's office, he was handed his termination notice and the severance pay specified by the company's policy manual.

"I'm really sorry to have to do this, Reggie," Andy said honestly. "But considering your attitude, I believe it's best for you and for the company."

"I'll see you in court over this. You can count on that!" Reggie shouted. "I'll see that you lose everything you have, you hypocritical psalm singer."

"That's your right, obviously," Andy replied calmly. "But your dismissal has absolutely nothing to do with Christianity. I would dismiss a Christian who was as rebellious as you are just as quickly. No, maybe even quicker, because a Christian should know better."

Reggie did file a job discrimination suit against Andy. The case dragged out for nearly three years, while teams of government investigators circulated around the office and plant asking questions. In the end the judge decided in favor of the company and even assigned all court costs and attorney fees to Reggie. Andy could have taken every material asset Reggie owned; instead, he elected to close the issue and forget it. It was a high price to pay for integrity, but Andy said it was well worth it.

HIRING WOMEN AS MANAGERS

Two common questions I'm asked at business conferences concern using women in management positions. "Can a woman hold a position of authority over men according to Scripture?" And, "Should a Christian hire a woman who will exercise authority over men as a manager?" These controversial issues are further complicated by federal laws against sex discrimination.

In reality there probably is a great deal of *de facto* discrimination in business. This occurs when a particular group or class of people is simply eliminated from the hiring or promotion process because someone else is selected. Often they never know they were passed over. I often have felt this was true of women in management positions.

Let me start out by saying that I believe there are some times when discrimination on the basis of sex is legitimate. For example, the owner of a nationwide sales company asked what he should do about promoting one of his best saleswomen to the position of regional sales manager. In the course of the conversation I learned that the job required the manager to travel with new male sales personnel to help them establish their territories. This often meant driving together, flying together, and staying at the same motels. These trips often required several weeks on the road. The saleswoman under consideration was in her early 30s, was married, and had two young children.

I told this businessman something I had learned from the Bible: *"A prudent man sees evil and hides himself, the naive proceed and pay the penalty"* (Proverbs 27:12).

"I would suggest that you consider that wisdom well," I said. "In my opinion, to even consider putting a young mother on the road to travel with men for extended periods of time is asking for trouble. In fact, if it were me, I would divide my sales force by gender and never have anyone of the opposite sex traveling together. It may be the chic thing to do today, but I still say it's inadvisable."

In the end he didn't give the young woman the job as sales manager. Instead, he formed a team approach to training in which at least four people always traveled together. The young woman became his national sales training coordinator with the responsibility to ensure that potential problems such as that of members of opposite sex traveling together were avoided in the future.

As far as the basic issue of women managers goes, I personally believe that the apostle Paul's instruction on women in the church in 1 Corinthians 14:34–35 deals with precisely that: women and their roles in the church. I do not believe this is directly applicable to the marketplace.

I know there are many instances in which the transition from church to home to work is totally compatible between the biblical setting and the current application. (A good example is Paul's instruction on partnerships.) But in my opinion, such a transfer in regard to women in a business is to read more into God's Word than actually exists.

I must assume that if God saw fit to assign Deborah as a judge over Israel, there is no biblical conflict with a woman's exercising authority over men. It has been said that God put Deborah in power because there was no man in Israel with courage enough to stand as judge during that time. That may or may not be true. We can only speculate on such a conclusion. What we do know is that Deborah was married (her husband's name was Lappidoth) and that she exercised considerable authority over the nation.

In Proverbs 31 an excellent wife is described as one who does her husband good and not evil. She is also described three times as a merchant and businesswoman. Unless there are specific job considerations that would not make placing a woman in a management position logical, I can find no biblical principle that would prohibit doing so.

I have found that, individually, women can be just as good as managers as men. There are some women who wouldn't make good managers, but there also are some men who wouldn't.

14

Employee Pay Decisions

Ron owned a medium-sized manufacturing plant that employed 200 hourly employees, most of them assembly line workers. These positions were normally filled by women for two basic reasons. First, the women were usually more detail-oriented than men, and the assembly work required great detail. Second, women would work for less than men would because their income was often supplemental.

The difficulty was that some of the women on the assembly line didn't fit the "supplemental income" profile. Some were single parents who, as a result of a divorce, desertion, or the death of a spouse, were the sole supporters of their families.

Jennifer was just such a person: a 34-year-old mother of three, whose ex-husband had spent time in the state penitentiary for handling drugs and refusing to support his family. Jennifer worked hard and was a valued employee, but her minimum wage job just wouldn't stretch to meet all the bills. She never complained, but twice during the year she had worked for Ron the claims court had issued a garnishment on her wages, once for a past-due credit-card bill and a second time to pay damages for a minor automobile accident.

Ron called Jennifer into his office to ask her about the latest garnishment.

"Jennifer, I received a note from the small claims court that we must garnish your wages for a car accident. Don't you carry liability insurance?"

"I used to, but I just couldn't afford to renew the policy, and it lapsed. I'm really sorry about the notice, Sir. Will this cost me my job?"

"No, Jennifer," Ron replied as he saw the panic in her eyes. "I wouldn't fire you over this kind of thing. You're a good worker and I just want to help if I can. Would you be willing to see a financial counselor who may be able to help you manage your money a little better? If you keep driving without insurance, you'll lose your license."

"I'll be happy to talk with anyone, Sir. If I lose my license, I don't know how I'll be able to get to work."

Ron knew that Jennifer's value to the company was worth paying for her car insurance, but the union that represented the hourly workers would never have agreed to his giving her a bonus or a raise without doing the same for everyone else. He was stumped. He wanted to raise her pay because she needed the money, but he couldn't.

The next week Jennifer's counselor called Ron as they had agreed. Without revealing any of the details, he told Ron that Jennifer appeared to be a good money manager who simply didn't make enough to cover all of her expenses. "In fact," he said, "it will take another $125 a month just to buy the necessities for her family."

Since Jennifer didn't attend a church regularly, Ron knew he couldn't count on her church helping much. So he made up his mind that he would help if he could come up with a way that wouldn't violate union rules. After discussing the problem with his pastor and the financial counselor, Ron came up with an idea: He would give the money to his church and the church would pay Jennifer's bills under the counselor's supervision.

Even when the counselor told Ron that he couldn't write off the gifts as tax-deductible contributions, he never hesitated. "I didn't intend to claim them," he responded. "I believe God will bless the gift, not the government."

For nearly three years Ron continued to supplement Jennifer's monthly income without her ever knowing the source. She joined the church that was helping her. And eventually she moved into a supervisory position, with a salary adequate to meet all of her family's needs. Later Ron negotiated an employee-run benevolence plan with the union that allowed both the company and the employees to contribute to the needs of other employees.

BIBLICAL PRINCIPLES FOR PAYING EMPLOYEES

"Behold, the pay of the laborers who mowed your fields, and which has been withheld by you, cries out against you; and the outcry of those

who did the harvesting has reached the ears of the Lord of Sabaoth" (James 5:4).

Many Christian businesspeople are familiar with this verse, but I sometimes wonder if they understand what it means and practice its principle in their businesses. Some do; most don't.

If you were to do a search of all the Scripture passages dealing with paying employees, you would find an abundance. When I made a detailed study of all these references, I came to the following conclusions.

1. God does not require that everybody be paid the same amount.
2. Those who do better work should be paid more.
3. God simply demands fairness in paying employees, as He does in everything else a Christian does.
4. A Christian employer has a responsibility to meet the minimum needs of the employees.

Each of these conclusions gives rise to a whole new set of questions. What really constitutes someone's minimum needs? How can you reward extra effort in a union environment? What is "fair" when it comes to paying people? Should you reward loyalty?

I don't pretend to have all the answers to these questions, but I do think I can help you settle some basic issues. Remember, though, our relationship to the Lord is not just following a set of predetermined rules.

The Jews attempted to do that and came up with "the handbook of the Pharisees." They had rule heaped upon rule, and the Lord told them, "[You] *strain out a gnat and swallow a camel"* (Matthew 23:24). You must always go to the Lord and ask for the wisdom to apply God's plan fairly and consistently.

WHAT ARE MINIMUM NEEDS?

Defining the need level of another person is no simple task. One person may consider a microwave oven a need, but someone else may struggle to have one good meal a day. What someone in India considers a luxury may be determined the barest necessity in America. I will leave the discussion about meeting the needs of the truly poor in other countries to another author.

Suffice it to say, as Christians living in America, we have a standard of living that is the envy of many nations around the world. Generally speaking, we have lost the distinction between needs, wants, and desires.

One of the most helpful ways I have found to determine other people's minimum needs is simply to put myself in their position and see if I could live on what they are earning. If employers would do this with their employees (and be honest about it), most would have to admit they aren't paying a fair wage.

Nothing in the Bible says that we should all make the same wage or that an owner can't make more than his or her workers. But the Bible does speak against cheating the workers of what is due them. *"Woe to him who builds his house without righteousness, and his upper rooms without justice, who uses his neighbor's services without pay and does not give him his wages"* (Jeremiah 22:13).

This principle became real to me while sitting in my study working on the material I was to teach at a business seminar. I was reviewing a list of questions submitted by the attendees of a previous seminar. One question dealt with this issue of paying a fair wage to employees. The businessman was obviously wrestling with the concept of fairness: Should he, as an owner, make so much more than the people he employed? I have often wrestled with this issue and still haven't come to a definite conclusion, except to quote Luke: *"Everyone who exalts himself shall be humbled, and he who humbles himself shall be exalted"* (Luke 14:11).

On this particular day what stuck in my mind was Big Joe, a printer we once hired. We paid him more than he had been making; in fact, it was the highest wage he had ever earned. I thought about his sizable family. On his monthly income, he would never be able to send the children to college or even buy an adequate home. He was poorly educated and probably would never earn more than we were paying him. He was a willing and cooperative worker but not a particularly good printer. In addition, at the time I was seriously considering shutting down our printing operation.

As I thought about Big Joe, I felt the Lord was asking me to do something totally illogical and economically unsound: give him a raise. I wrestled with what seemed to be a senseless idea and argued with myself that this was just in my mind and that God wouldn't require such an absurdity. But several years before when I had prayed to receive Jesus Christ as my Savior, I had made that promise I mentioned earlier: "If You'll make Your will for my life clear, I'll do it, no matter what!"

So I ended up giving Big Joe a raise of nearly $500 a month, a good portion of which was totally by faith, since the funds weren't there. I believe that God was testing my willingness to obey His instructions and care about the needs of others under my watch care. It was a rewarding experience for me to see God provide what was needed each month. Later Big Joe accepted another job at a lesser salary because he didn't want to be a printer any longer. Since I had made the decision that if he ever left I would shut down the printing operation, his decision worked out well for all.

I have since done a great deal of counseling with people who were poorly paid, often by Christian employers. As a counselor, I believe that if money can be stretched to cover expenses, I can find a way to do it. Certainly many people create their own problems by overspending; the resultant debt is a symptom, not a problem. But if I place myself in the other person's position and cannot find a way to make the available money stretch to meet the minimum needs of that person's family, then he or she is being paid too little.

Try this line of thinking with some of your employees. I expect it will be enlightening.

SITUATIONAL ECONOMICS

Is it fair to replace long-term employees with younger, lower-paid workers? Few situations better reflect the ethics and motives of those in authority than what I call *situational economics.*

A company may have many loyal and dependable employees who have been with the business a long time. The fact that they have been employed with one company for a long while usually results in two things: (1) They are making higher wages than a new employee would command; (2) They are older and perhaps a little less aggressive in the jobs. Pure economics would dictate replacing them with younger, more aggressive (and lower-paid) employees. This is the same financial logic that dictates replacing outdated equipment. That's one reason there are often mass replacements when a company is bought out or merged with another.

But there are some serious problems with this kind of thinking. In the first place, it is thoroughly nonbiblical and unethical. The Bible makes this clear: *"Let your heart keep my commandments; for length of days and years of life, and peace they will add to you. Do not let kindness and truth leave you; bind them around your neck, write them on the tablet of your heart. So you will find favor and good repute in the sight of God and man"* (Proverbs 3:1–4).

In the ethics of a Christian, kindness and justice play predominant roles, and the practice of dumping long-term employees is neither kind nor just.

But there are other, more practical, problems as well. Developing long-term company loyalty is difficult or impossible in a "wear 'em out, then replace 'em" atmosphere. Much has been said over the last two decades about the decline of the unions, but I believe we will see a resurgence of union activities if this mentality doesn't change in America's businesses. (Not much has been, or will be, reported in the media about this activity because the communications companies that run the media are some of the biggest culprits.)

A classic example of the problems such thinking brings a company can be seen in the airline industry during the late eighties. With many airlines in financial trouble, it was both necessary and logical that some of the weaker companies be absorbed by the stronger. But few were prepared for the furor that broke out when Frank Lorenzo took over Eastern Airlines. Word quickly spread that his policy was to replace the older higher-paid employees with younger ones.

In great part, many of the changes Lorenzo instituted, including some salary cuts, were necessary; the airline hadn't made a profit in over 15 years and was notorious for its inefficiencies. But when the attitude of the owner was transmitted through the ranks of management, it came out: "We just don't care about our employees."

Later, when management needed the support and cooperation of the employees, it wasn't there. The employees decided they would prefer to see the company fail and lose their jobs rather than help their enemy. These employees weren't stupid, as some have reported; they simply saw management (the spokesmen of the owner) as an adversary. When such a situation exists, all logic goes out the window.

I saw the principle of sowing and reaping (in terms of employees) demonstrated graphically in two construction businesses during the seventies. Whenever there is a downturn in the national economy, the home construction industry usually follows; a major portion of the construction business shrinks immediately because of the interest rates and the scare of the potential buyer.

The owner of the first construction company was a woman I'll call Mary. She was raised in her father's construction business but had always wanted to be in the business herself. However, since the construction business is a male-dominated industry, she had few opportunities to start her own company. After her father died, she attended a vocational/technical school, where she studied home construction. She began working for a contractor, first in the office doing estimating and purchasing and gradually working her way up to being project supervisor.

She was very successful at working with the subcontractors and owners, but after five years of working for someone else she decided to start her own company. She determined that she would try to operate her company on biblical principles. She had been a Christian since she was 11 years old and had been taught to live her life according to God's Word. She was determined to make her business a testimony for the Lord.

She took a personal interest in her employees and made them a part of the team. She hired Christians and non-Christians alike, based on their qualifications. Her business theme: to put others first—a definite rarity in the construction business. Her goal was to build a quality structure at a reasonable price and make a fair profit.

Mary did extremely well for several years, growing to 30 full-time employees and several part-time employees. She had more work than she could accept and things were going great.

Then the 1990 recession hit. The Fed tightened lending and raised interest rates. When interest rates rise, home buying goes down; consequently, home construction goes down. As the jobs were completed, it was clear there would be fewer new contracts, and Mary knew she was going to have to let some workers go.

In an effort to salvage some jobs, she initiated a split week: some of the employees would work 25 hours one week and the others would work 20 hours; then she would reverse it. Salaried employees were asked to take a 20 percent pay cut and Mary took a 50 percent pay cut.

When possible, she built a few spec houses, selling them at cost to keep her employees busy. She bid small commercial jobs, at cost, just to cover her overhead. Often she personally extended loans to her employees so they could make their monthly payments.

When the economy picked up and interest rates declined, home construction perked up. Mary was off and running again. Most of her people had stayed with her and the company began making money again.

A couple of years later Mary bought a piece of property to develop her own subdivision. She did it right, paying cash for the land and obtaining the proper building permits and subdivision permits. Then one day she received notice that her property had been declared a wetland by the corps of engineers and they had secured a development injunction against her. The subsequent lawsuit cost Mary her company, her home, and everything she had. Ultimately, the corps of engineers made her remove all the top soil, at a cost of more than $400,000, and restore the land to its original condition. Mary was out of business.

Mary was determined to go back in business. She started out of a rented apartment, back to building one house at a time. Most of her original employees returned and requested to work for her part-time. In addition, several offered to work one day a week free. They committed to do whatever it would take to get her business profitable. Some of them even offered to lend her money, because they believed in her. Within three years, her business was larger and more profitable than ever, and the demand for her houses was overwhelming.

Today, Mary is one of the largest home builders in her city, with an incredible reputation for quality, integrity, and honesty. Without fail, Mary gives the glory to the Lord.

Mary's story is in direct contrast to an ex-textile mill owner I'll call Robert.

Robert operated according to the situational economics principle; in other words, he took every advantage the economy provided. At the time, the economy was in the doldrums; jobs were scarce, and employees were plentiful. During that period he replaced many of his higher-paid people with cheaper labor. To avoid violating union rules, he did this through selective shift assignments and shutdowns. The unions objected, but in reality they could do very little about it. If they had organized any walk off, it was quite possible the employees would have voted to abandon the union altogether. After all, a bad job is better than no job at all.

Robert, a Christian, rationalized his actions as being logical for the times. His attitude was not unlike that of many Christians who interpret God's will for their benefit: "This must be God's will. He must have arranged the economic slowdown so that the higher-paid employees could be replaced" (a convenient philosophy when the events are going your way).

Two years later the economy picked up and the textile business came under intense foreign pressure. Within a few months the carpet industry plunged into the deepest recession since the Great Depression. Not only was business down, raw materials prices skyrocketed. At one point the domestic textile industry teetered on the verge of collapse. Robert appealed to the union for wage concessions and even a short-term loan to save his company. Both were voted down by his employees. They said they would rather lose their jobs than help him.

Robert found himself in deep financial trouble with nowhere to turn for help. Ultimately he borrowed at interest rates of 24 percent, gambling that the rates would drop before he had to pay. He lost. The company was dissolved and sold for partial settlement of the outstanding debt. Robert filed for personal bankruptcy and lost virtually everything he owned.

THE POWER OF REWARD

Most people in authority are "High D" personalities (*Directing*— see Chapter 10) and, as such, are quick to criticize but slow to reward the work of their subordinates, either with praise or with money. I find that this is usually due to a personality flaw, rather than any fault with the employee's work. "High D" personalities need to be reminded to praise others, especially a "High D" who is also a perfectionist.

"The guy I work for never sees anything extra I do," Susan declared as she ate with the other secretaries in the company cafeteria. "I can do 99 percent of the work perfectly, and he'll always comment about the 1 percent that's not perfect. I just wish he were as critical of his own work as he is of mine. He keeps contracts on his desk for months at a time."

"That's really too bad," Sheri replied, thinking of her own boss. He could be tough and always demanded her very best, but he always made a point of complimenting her work before correcting any errors she might have made. And unlike Susan's boss, Mr. Rhone never criticized her in public.

She still remembered her first day on the job, when the new boss said, "I know you'll do great, Sheri. This is your first real job out of high school, and I'd like to help you get started on the right track. I'll correct your work from time to time if I see something that needs improvement, but I'll always try to do it constructively." Three months later he gave Sheri a sizable raise and praised her efforts.

That had been three years ago, and Mr. Rhone had corrected her work often. The first few times she had gone home crying and worried about her job. But over the years he had proven his concern about her as a person. He corrected her, but he never humiliated or demeaned her. As a result, she developed into an efficient, confident secretary.

Sheri hadn't always felt secure, even at home. Her father was a successful businessman too and a Christian. But he had always used his position to rule rather than lead people. She remembered his saying one time, "I fired the whole office today. We had someone stealing, and I offered them a choice: confess or everybody will lose their jobs. No one confessed, so I fired them all."

Sheri remembered thinking how unfair that was and saying so to her father. "Listen, Sheri," her father replied angrily. "When you're in charge of a business, you have to be tough. If you give employees an inch, they'll take a mile. It may be a little tough on some of them right now, but they'll remember next time and will be on the lookout for thieves."

From that point on, Sheri had secretly harbored a fear that maybe God was like that too. She had decided that when she was out on her own she would stop going to church, and she had. But in Mr. Rhone she had been given a different view of a Christian employer: firm but fair. Mr. Rhone obviously cared more about protecting the innocent than punishing the guilty.

"Sheri, I want you to remember Proverbs 22:29: *'Do you see a man skilled in his work? He will stand before kings; he will not stand before obscure men.'* That will carry you a long way in this world. You may run into bosses now and then who won't recognize your hard work and loyalty, but they're the exception. Always be ready to give a good testimony for the Lord, but remember that the best testimony a Christian can have is a love for others and good work habits."

REWARDING DIFFERENT ABILITIES

Each of us is equipped to do at least one thing well. Sometimes that ability will yield monetary rewards, and sometimes it won't. It is interesting what things we consider important and valuable in our society. We reward a good athlete with millions of dollars to carry a football or dribble a basketball, but then we pay a good teacher or social worker a few thousand a year.

As I mentioned in an earlier chapter, we value the abilities of an average pastor higher than those of an excellent janitor. There is nothing particularly unscriptural about paying different rates of pay, but I question whether the Lord values job classifications the same way we do.

Some years ago a well-known book called *The Peter Principle* (Laurence J. Peters and Raymond Hull, Wm. Morrow & Co., 1969) presented the theory that most people will eventually be promoted beyond their "level of competence" (ability to perform). To some degree this is true. Someone who is particularly good at one thing will eventually attract the attention of management and then will be offered a job that may be beyond his or her skill level.

Harvey was a classic example. An excellent salesman, Harvey eventually was offered a job as regional sales manager for the company he represented. It was common knowledge that if anyone turned down a management position he or she would not be offered any further raises or subsequent positions. Turning down the boss was considered tantamount to disloyalty.

So Harvey accepted the managerial position and became an instant disaster. He was a "High I" personality (*Interacting*), which served him well as a salesman but became his biggest liability as a manager. He was not able to direct a sales team, many with much stronger personalities than his.

The sales for Harvey's area fell to less than half of what they had been the previous year. This was partly because they lost their best salesman (Harvey) and partly because other salespeople were floundering for lack of good direction. Ultimately Harvey was dismissed from the company.

Harvey was discouraged by this experience and felt more than a little defeated by his obvious failure. Determined to prove himself, he hired on with a competitor as their regional sales manager. Within three months it was obvious that Harvey wasn't going to make it with that company either, and he began to look for another position—again as a sales manager!

He was interviewing for a position in yet another company when the owner, Adam Yates, happened to come by the personnel office. He had met Harvey on several occasions at trade shows and had been impressed by the way he conducted himself. Harvey had a nearly perfect memory, especially for names. He usually could recall the names of people he had met only one time, years earlier. This had particularly impressed Adam, who had a difficult time remembering all of his employees' names.

"Harvey, what are you doing here?" Yates asked as he stuck his head into the personnel manager's office.

"I'm applying for a job, Mr. Yates," Harvey responded in a voice that reflected his total lack of confidence.

Sensing something was wrong, Adam told the manager, "I'll talk to Harvey. I've known him for several years."

"Yes, Sir," the manager responded quickly. "Here's his file."

"Come with me," Yates said as he walked down the hall, reading the file he had been handed.

"Harvey, it says here that you're applying for the regional sales manager position. Is that right?"

"Yes, Sir," Harvey replied, looking at the floor.

"Why?"

"Sir?"

"Why are you applying for a manager's job? It looks like you've tried twice and failed. Do you really like management?"

Harvey had to stop for a minute to think. He really hadn't ever thought about it since a management job was the next step up the ladder. Then he knew the answer: "No, Sir, I guess I really don't like management." He knew he had just blown his chances of getting the job, but he also knew that his answer was correct. He really didn't like management. He was a salesman, not an office type.

"Well, I'm glad to hear it," Yates said with a grin, "because I can hire a hundred managers, but a good salesman is hard to find. Would you consider coming to work here as a territory salesman?"

"Yes, Sir, I sure would." Harvey knew that he had made the right decision. For the first time in nearly two years, he didn't feel as if his insides were knotted up.

"Harvey, one thing you'll find different here," Yates said. "You'll be paid according to your ability as a salesman, and a good salesman can easily make as much or more than a good manager."

"Thank you, Sir. That would be a refreshing change, if I may say so."

"You're a Christian, aren't you?" Yates had often noticed that Harvey never walked around at the sales conferences holding a glass of liquor.

"Yes, I am. How did you know?"

"I guess I always thought you might be. I'm a Christian too."

"You're a Christian?" Harvey exclaimed.

"Yes, the Lord can save guys that run companies, too, you know."

"I didn't mean it that way, Sir."

"Well, the sales manager you'll report to is not a believer yet, but he's a good man who does a very good job. I'm sure you will get along with him just fine. He's a good family man and totally honest and ethical."

Adam Yates thought back to some of the discussions he had had with his management team about his Christian principles. He knew that most of them thought he had gone off the deep end right after he was saved. But he had received some good advice from another Christian he met in a Monday night Bible study: "I would encourage you to take at least two years to learn a little about the Christian life before you try to implement any principles into your business, Adam. A lot of new Christians make the mistake of trying to share something they don't really understand themselves. As the boss you can bruise a lot of feelings in a hurry."

Adam had taken that advice to heart. Instead of telling his employees what they should do, he concentrated on practicing as many of the principles in his own life as he could.

One of those principles was to pay well for excellence, regardless of company hierarchy. He told his management team, "No job has a salary limit except to the extent of each person's abilities. In other words, if salespeople generate income, they can earn more than their managers."

At first, Adam's managers had a problem with that concept but soon they realized that what he was doing was encouraging each person to utilize his or her best talents fully. Each manager was likewise compensated as the overall sales in his area increased. A few people became angry with the policy and quit but, in general, the system worked well. Thus a person like Harvey was allowed to do what he did best without the pressure to move into a management position.

The final salary-related question we'll look at is, "How should I reward loyalty?"

REWARD LOYALTY

Loyalty can be defined as "a commitment to a person or company, even in the face of adversity." By that definition, loyalty is a rare commodity today. If you find a loyal employee, you should do everything in your power to promote that quality. Remember that loyalty begets loyalty, so it must flow both ways.

God's Word supports honoring those who are loyal to authority, and that includes paying them extra. Clearly God did this for David, purely on the basis of David's loyalty to Him. Throughout the Bible there are literally dozens of examples of God's rewarding loyalty and punishing unfaithfulness.

What is it worth to have employees who are loyal and think the best, rather than the worst, of your decisions? Anyone who has ever worked around disloyal employees can answer that. It's worth whatever you have to pay.

I know a Christian leader who found himself in the middle of a large scandal created by a member of his family. He himself had nothing to do with the wrongdoing; his only error had been refusing to listen to the rumors about his relative until it was too late to correct the situation privately.

When the scandal broke, the majority of this man's staff, both leaders and employees, revolted against him and demanded his resignation. He was devastated and withdrew in shock, shaken to the core by this onslaught from people he believed to be loyal.

Fortunately a pastor who knew him well remained totally loyal to him, believing he had done nothing wrong. This pastor took over temporary control of the organization. He allowed each staff member to air his or her concerns but would not hear any accusations against the leader that were unsupported by witnesses or verifiable facts.

After two days of frustrating interaction with the rebellious staff who, as the Pharisees did with Jesus, shouted first one thing and then another without any convicting evidence, the pastor finally had enough. He gathered all the staff together in one room and said to them, "Thus far I have examined all the accusations against this man and found nothing of any substance." Then he drew an imaginary line on the floor and said, "Everyone who is loyal to him step over this line. Everyone who isn't willing to support him without reservation stay where you are."

The group was fairly evenly split between those who stepped over and those who did not. To the latter he said, "Please see the accountant on your way out for your severance pay."

The evidence that God was in that decision is still being confirmed by the changed lives of those who are touched by the Christian leader's teaching. God simply cannot work with disloyal people. He was willing to wait 40 years to see if the next crop of Jews would be more loyal to Him than the ones who came out of Egypt were.

God's total staff among the rebellious Jews consisted of Joshua and Caleb, who were willing to remain faithful to their authority. If you have it in your power to pay loyal people more, do so. If you don't, then find a way to show them how much you value their loyalty.

Loyalty is a characteristic that can neither be taught nor bought.

15

Borrowing Decisions

In recent years I have actually heard many intelligent people, who profess to understand such things, state that the national debt doesn't really matter and that we can go on expanding it indefinitely. They also point out that, as a percentage of our gross national product (GNP), the debt is actually less than it was 10 years ago.

That's a little like watching someone who has been shot, noticing that the flow of blood is slowing, and concluding that the wound is getting smaller. If you watch long enough and the flow stops totally, you could even surmise that the patient is healed. But if that patient doesn't get up in a few hours and resume normal activities, you probably could draw a different conclusion!

The primary reason the actual debt is a smaller percentage of the GNP is that the government has found a way to borrow massive amounts of money without all of it being reflected in the category of national debt. How has this been accomplished under the watchful eye of the Congress?

The most obvious way has been to borrow the funds from the Social Security Trust Fund, the Railroad Trust Fund, and the Federal Employees Retirement account. *This has accounted for the better part of $200 billion since 1986.* Another method has been to delay a portion of the debt until the first day of the next fiscal year, then the next year delay a little more until the following year, and so on. It's called "creative accounting."

At present our government owes these various trust funds nearly $1.5 trillion (that's with a "t") and by 2007 this amount will be nearly $3 trillion. When this debt begins to come due in 2008, as the baby boomers begin to retire, the financial strain on our economy will be horrendous.

In our generation we have come to practice Proverbs 22:7 as no generation has since the early thirties: *"The rich rules over the poor, and the borrower becomes the lender's slave."* As I said earlier, the pendulum has swung its full arc, and we're back in the position of jeopardy that characterized the generation of the Great Depression.

The nation as a whole is beginning to be aroused from its apathy about compounding debt upon debt and has begun to realize that a debt-run economy has its limits. We haven't discovered exactly what those limits are as yet, but we will. Volumes will be written by many hard-core debt advocates about how the leaders of America should have been able to foresee the coming calamity and warn the people. Presently they themselves are the biggest fans of debt expansion—but only until it becomes uncontrollable.

One thing is critical to understand about debt: The increase in borrowed money is the single most direct component of inflation and, contrary to popular opinion, inflation has not been eliminated in our economy. Eventually, inflation will return with a vengeance and will once again dominate headlines. When this will happen is anyone's guess, but the rules of economics have not been changed.

Inflation is the borrower's friend (in the short run), because as inflation increases the overall GNP goes up, even with no more production. In fact, production actually may have gone down, but the overall figure in dollars is higher because overall prices went up.

So the trick is to borrow more money without its being reflected in the national debt figures, then wait for that money to drive up inflation. The result is a lower debt-to-GNP ratio. It's a little like watching a magician with the colored scarves: Now you see it, now you don't.

IS BORROWING UNSCRIPTURAL?

In recent years several well-meaning Christian teachers have stated that borrowing money is not in line with the Bible. That is wrong. I sincerely wish that there were such an instruction in God's Word; it would make teaching on this particular topic much simpler. But borrowing is not scripturally prohibited.

I would like to cover the primary arguments presented by what I call the absolutists—those who believe that all borrowing is a sin.

First, they correctly point out the inherent dangers in borrowing. The following are some of the results of debt.

- The demise of countless marriages
- The ruin of millions of lives
- The destruction of countless businesses
- The undermining of the American economy
- The waste of billions of dollars that could otherwise have gone to the Lord's work

Second, since most of them have borrowed and suffered tremendous financial losses in a bad economy, they correctly point out that most borrowing is based on the unwarranted presumption that the future is predictable. James warned us against that: *"Come now, you who say, 'Today or tomorrow, we shall go to such and such a city, and spend a year there and engage in business and make a profit.' Yet you do not know what your life will be like tomorrow. You are just a vapor that appears for a little while and then vanishes away"* (James 4:13–14).

The Scripture that is most quoted by the absolutists: *"Owe nothing to anyone except to love one another; for he who loves his neighbor has fulfilled the law"* (Romans 13:8). It is unfortunate that this verse doesn't mean what is implied at first glance. The apostle Paul was a most cautious writer when it came to biblical principles.

When writing on any fundamental doctrine, he leaned heavily on Old Testament teachings, and any time he felt the necessity to add to or detract from some previous doctrine he made it abundantly clear. Sometimes he even went so far as to clarify that what he was saying was his opinion, as one who was strong in the Lord (see 1 Corinthians 7:25).

If Paul had been teaching in Romans 13:8 that all borrowing is wrong for a believer, first he would have presented the contrary evidence from the Old Testament: the necessity of a year of remission and a year of Jubilee, when all debts were forgiven, both of which would have been totally unnecessary if borrowing were an Old Testament prohibition!

Therefore, Paul's teaching would have been a new doctrine and he would have said so, just as he did in Romans 7, where he described how the Old Testament law related to Christians. Another example of the establishment of new doctrine is found in Matthew 19:8, where the

Lord overturned the Old Testament law of divorce. *"He said to them, 'Because of your hardness of heart, Moses permitted you to divorce your wives; but from the beginning it has not been this way.'"*

In Romans 13:1 Paul was dealing specifically with the raging debate over whether Christians should pay taxes to the heathen government of Rome. (Sound familiar?) In Romans 13:6–8 Paul was saying to the Christians, "Don't be left owing anyone anything, even taxes to Rome."

SCRIPTURAL PRINCIPLES FOR BORROWING

Borrowing is not prohibited scripturally, but neither is it encouraged. It is always presented in a negative context and with many warnings about its misuse.

I believe there are three fundamental scriptural principles related to borrowing.

1. Avoid Borrowing Unless Absolutely Necessary

In our generation most Americans accept borrowing as a necessity. Because of this attitude they borrow perpetually. Both home and automobile loans reflect this attitude. The average American family will spend nearly $300,000 on car loans in their lifetimes, more than half of which will be spent on interest alone. This is a new phenomenon that staggers the imagination. Most Americans could retire on what they waste on car loans.

What would the price of new cars be if it wasn't for borrowing? That's hard to estimate, but it wouldn't be anywhere near the current prices. The car manufacturers understand the debt mentality very well. That's why they offer low-interest loans and leases as incentives to buy overpriced automobiles.

The typical Christian businessperson is as deeply in debt as the typical non-Christian. Neither one has any real goal for being debt-free, and consequently both are totally vulnerable to any downturn in the economy.

A good example of this was Jake, a successful businessman who operated a chain of shoe stores in Houston, Texas. As his business grew and became more profitable, he elected to borrow to expand the operation.

Jake had always been a conservative businessman. At one point he had even considered the idea of using the company's growing profits to pay off all his outstanding debt. A quick discussion of this idea with his accountant convinced Jake that tax-wise it was a bad idea.

"You want to do what?" Jake's accountant asked in disbelief.

"I was thinking about using some of the surplus to pay off all the debt in the company."

"The government will kill you on taxes if you do that, Jake," the accountant replied.

"You'll be a lot better off using your money to expand the business. I thought you were going to open some more stores this year."

"Well, I probably am," Jake replied. "It's just that Margie would like to see us get out of debt totally. She really wants me to pay the house off too."

"That's crazy, Jake. About the only tax break left is deductible interest. You would get stuck for a lot more taxes without any tax breaks."

"Yeah, I guess you're right. It's just that Margie keeps hearing some guy on the radio talking about getting out of debt, and she's all keyed up about it."

"You tell her to call me, and I'll explain the benefits of using the interest to offset taxes. You just use your cash to expand your business."

Jake decided that his accountant's counsel was better than the counsel of his wife, at least where business was concerned, so he continued the expansion of his wholesale shoe outlets. After all, business had never been better, and the prospects for the future looked great. The oil embargo of the late seventies had really launched his business, which had begun in 1978 as a small local shoe outlet. During the embargo his business had exploded, because rising oil prices had boosted Houston's economy.

By the early eighties Jake had two flourishing stores in Houston. He decided to branch out to several other Texas cities, and those stores flourished too. By the mid-eighties he had 20 outlets throughout the Southwest, and his business was booming. The debt load bothered him and panicked Margie, but the business had no difficulty meeting the payments. Jake's accountant assured him that with a few more years of growth the business would be the largest brand-name outlet chain in the country.

Then, with almost no warning the price of oil began to fall and, with it, the Southwest's economy. The biggest boom since the

California gold rush came to a screeching halt. Jake saw his sales plummet from nearly $13 million at their peak to less than $6 million. He closed store after store in a desperate attempt to keep the business solvent. But long-term leases backed by company assets continued the cash drain. A business that could have been debt-free two years earlier ended up going under.

Jake saw the assets auctioned off for a fraction of their original cost, and the residual debt wiped out every asset he and Margie owned. (An interesting side note is that Jake's ex-accountant sued for his payment too.)

Jake learned the expensive way what God's Word tells us free of charge: *"For while you are going with your opponent to appear before the magistrate, on your way there make an effort to settle with him, in order that he may not drag you before the judge, and the judge turn you over to the constable, and the constable throw you into prison. I say to you, you shall not get out of there until you have paid the very last cent"* (Luke 12:58–59).

2. Avoid Signing Surety on a Loan

Webster's Dictionary defines *surety* as "a formal engagement (as a pledge) given for the fulfillment of an undertaking; one who has become legally liable for the debt, default, or failure in duty of another."

In biblical times it was not unusual for borrowers to pledge their only asset of any value—themselves—as guarantee to repay a loan. If the borrowers failed to pay according to the agreed-upon terms, they forfeited their freedom. A survey of the Proverbs will reveal many references to surety and many observations of the judge about what happens to those who are foolish enough to assume such a risk.

The judge's advice to one in surety is found in Proverbs 6:1–3: *"My son, if you have become surety for your neighbor, have given a pledge for a stranger, if you have been snared with the words of your mouth, have been caught with the words of your mouth, do this then, my son, and deliver yourself; since you have come into the hand of your neighbor, go, humble yourself, and importune your neighbor."*

Today we no longer put debtors in prison or indenture their families for failure to repay a debt, but the creditors still have a right to collect their money or to recover whatever property has been pledged as surety (collateral). And when you endorse a note personally, you pledge all of your assets as collateral. This is *personal surety*.

Most people sign as surety on the debts they incur and don't consciously realize it. For instance, most home buyers believe the loans on their homes are collateralized by the dwellings themselves, but that is rarely true. Although the homes are pledged as collateral, virtually all the mortgages created since the eighties also require the personal guarantees of the buyers. Therefore, if the home buyers can't make the payments and the mortgage companies foreclose and sell them at a loss (less than the outstanding debt), the companies can sue the buyers for the deficiency.

Most people would say they don't worry about that since the value of homes has traditionally increased over the years. However, the experience of thousands of ex-homeowners in the "oil patch" a few years ago shows that this assumption doesn't always hold. For instance, foreclosed homes in the Houston and Dallas area sold for less than one-half the outstanding mortgages. In Oklahoma and Louisiana some went for a third of the existing mortgage.

Signing personally on a debt indicates two things: (1) the seller doesn't think what you're buying is worth what you're paying for it, and (2) the seller is a lot smarter than you are. As long as any portion of that debt exists, everything you own is at risk. That is the worst possible case of presuming on the future.

Roger was a businessman who owned and operated a steel building fabrication company in Tennessee. He had a line of credit with a large commercial bank, which he used to buy materials for the jobs he had in progress until the customer paid him.

At any given time Roger might have $300,000 to $400,000 borrowed against this credit line. The business had prospered well, and he usually had a balance in his money market account of $600,000 to $700,000, which he used as collateral for the line of credit. What he didn't realize, or perhaps just didn't care about, was that each of the notes he signed was endorsed personally. Thus, he was a guarantor on every debt.

Almost any financial adviser today would say, "So what?" After all, he had the cash in the bank to cover any money he borrowed. But why did he borrow when he had the cash? I have asked that question of many people who were doing the same thing. The normal answer is, "Just in case." I'm not sure what the "in case" is and usually neither are they.

Roger's business was doing well, and the economy was strong for his type of business. Then one Friday Roger's bank closed its doors and never opened them again.

"Not to worry," the Federal Depositors Insurance Corporation (FDIC) told the depositors. "The bank failed because of massive fraud on the part of some bank officials, but the FDIC is guaranteeing all deposits, up to $100,000." Unfortunately for Roger, that left him about $500,000 shy of what he had on deposit.

Roger felt terrible. After all, a half-million dollars is a lot of money to lose. Many times over the next few weeks he wished he had given more to the Lord's work—at least that money would have been out there doing some good. "But," he decided, "no sense in crying over spilt milk."

Then about two months after the bank closed, Roger got the shock of his life. An agent from the FDIC came to his office, demanding total payment of the $400,000 note he had with the bank.

"But I don't have the money," Roger argued. "When the bank closed, I lost all of my ready cash. Besides," he said, "since the bank really owes me more than I owe it, I don't see how you can ask me to pay."

"Sir," the agent said in a very matter-of-fact tone, "the assets of the bank [Roger's note being one] now belong to the FDIC. The debts of the bank [Roger's $100,000 insured account] will be paid through the liquidation courts. You must either pay the note or we will foreclose on your business and your personal assets."

The liquidation was averted because Roger was able to work out another loan to satisfy the FDIC. Unfortunately the loan became such a financial strain on the business that he was forced to sell out at a substantial loss within a year.

Roger learned some bitter lessons about debt: First, there is no principle of offset in banking. In other words, no matter how much you have on deposit, that balance will not offset your debt unless it is pledged as the total collateral for the loans. Second, the friendly, cooperative banker you deal with during good times probably will be gone during bad times.

I cannot leave this section on surety without telling you the story of a Christian businessman who attended a "Business by the Book" seminar in Sacramento, California. When Henry heard me teach about surety and, specifically, what God's Word says in Proverbs 6:1–3 (just don't do it), he was flabbergasted.

He was in the automobile business and, regularly, he personally guaranteed notes for his automobile dealership. He asked to have dinner with me after the conference and reviewed each of the verses on surety very carefully. It was clear that Henry was convicted by what he had heard. He asked me what he should do.

"Just do what God convicts you to do," I replied. "You're not responsible to me; you're responsible to God." I certainly wasn't going to tell him God's will for his life. So Henry left, determined that he was going to do whatever God's Word said.

He first went to his bank and told them that he was not going to sign surety on any more notes. They responded, "That's fine, then we won't finance any more loans for you."

So Henry went to another bank and said, "If you'll not require me to sign surety on the business loans, I'll give you all of my business." They quickly agreed.

Several months later the first bank came back and said, "We've reconsidered and if you'll give us half your business we won't require a personal endorsement either and, in addition, we'll release you from the personal endorsements you already have with us." Henry quickly accepted their offer.

Thirteen months later I received a letter from Henry with a big "Praise the Lord" written across the front of it. In slightly more than a year Henry was completely free from all surety. As God's Word says, *"You do not have because you do not ask"* (James 4:2). Henry eventually sold his business, leased the property, and went into full-time ministry. God demonstrated that obedience to the Word will deliver you from jeopardy.

3. Avoid Long-Term Debt

"At the end of every seven years you shall grant a remission of debts" (Deuteronomy 15:1).

In an era of 30- and 40-year, and even longer, mortgages, avoiding long-term debt sounds almost impossible. But remember, such long-term debt is a relatively new idea. Our grandfathers, even many of our fathers, would have balked at loans that extended for three or four decades. They knew what this generation will eventually find out for themselves: If you stay in debt long enough, you will eventually get wiped out. There are a few exceptions to any rule, so there always will be some businesses that take on long-term debt and survive.

Unfortunately those are the ones that get the publicity, not the multitude of others that fail miserably.

Edgar, a committed Christian who was known for his giving to the Lord's work, was a successful stockbroker who felt the Lord wanted him to go into real estate development. So he left a lucrative job with a major brokerage firm to go into the land development business. Unfortunately, this happened just prior to the real estate crash of the mid-seventies.

Almost immediately after starting his business, Edgar was plunged into personal financial disaster and was unable to make even his house payments. But, with the tenacity that often characterizes the movers in any society, he stuck it out and began to look for the opportunities that a negative market provides.

During this time Edgar and his wife came under assault from some of their so-called friends, who confronted them with every sin that might be the cause of their financial problems. I recall that Job's friends did something similar for him. It is amazing how perceptive some people are about finding the dust speck in someone else's eye.

Edgar and his wife came in for counseling at the request of a mutual friend. Their only violation of biblical principles that I could find was the misuse of credit cards. Like so many young couples, they had used their credit cards to fill in the income gaps during the previous year. Unfortunately Edgar's untimely career change had severely affected his income, so they owed several thousand dollars. When I pointed out the inconsistency of walking by faith but using a creditor's money to do so, they made a commitment to cease all further credit card use and to live on what God provided, in plenty or in lack, as the apostle Paul once said.

Once they made this decision, times really got lean. Edgar shared that he and his wife and their two children once sat down to a meal of just popcorn. In the midst of this situation, however, they continued to share God's vision of developing a real estate business. Several of Edgar's friends gave up on him because of what they interpreted as his blatant disregard of the obvious: get a job. One frustrated friend even went so far as to say, "Well, you enjoy your popcorn. I'm going home to have some steak. When you are willing to face reality, give me a call."

Then, in the mid-seventies, Edgar saw an opportunity he had been looking for: a run-down apartment building in one of the older sections of his city. The project had been repossessed by the lender, who was desperate to get the project off his hands. With no assets and no experience, Edgar tried to convince the lender to sell him the project. The terms were simple: no money down, no personal liability, no payments until the project was renovated and rented, and enough up-front money to renovate the property. In other words, Edgar asked the lender to sell him the property and finance the remodeling with no personal liability. And, unbelievably, the seller agreed.

Edgar's new business was off and running. Over the next five years he acquired several more properties through the use of limited partnerships with other investors. As the economy improved, the properties soared in value. Edgar was giving hundreds of thousands of dollars a year to the Lord's work, and the business continued to grow rapidly. Unfortunately, as often happens when things go well, Edgar forgot one of the principal rules of economics: Whatever benefits you short term can become your worst nightmare long term.

As the values of the properties soared during the economic recovery of the early eighties, Edgar could have sold a few properties and held the others debt-free. Instead, the temptation to borrow against the appreciated values was too much, and he borrowed most of the equity out of the properties. He was able to return virtually all the investors' capital, plus a sizable profit from most of the investments. Since the return was in the form of loans against the properties, it was not taxable. In an era of tax shelters, that temptation was irresistible.

Then, as suddenly as the boom market in apartments started, it ended, with the 1986 Tax Reform Act. This act removed most of the tax advantages from rental properties, and values dropped suddenly. Even worse, the occupancy rate of apartments also plummeted. Many other projects already under construction became available, and panicked landlords slashed rents and offered incentives to attract renters.

Edgar's properties were in trouble. In an attempt to keep them going and protect the investors' money, Edgar borrowed more money against the properties. But in the final analysis, the lenders always win with long-term debt: the properties began to default.

This created a dual problem. Edgar's income was severely reduced as his management fees fell. At the same time, the defaulting properties created massive tax liabilities. The tax codes treat the forgiveness of debt as income. So when one of Edgar's investments failed, the entire outstanding debt became taxable income to Edgar and his clients.

The last chapter of Edgar's situation has not been written; he is still struggling to overcome his problems. But the reality of Proverbs 22:7

has been confirmed once again in his experience: *"The rich rules over the poor, and the borrower becomes the lender's slave."*

God created the year of remission discussed in Deuteronomy 15 for a logical reason. If you stay in debt long enough, you will get wiped out. If the Lord deemed it prudent for the Jews to limit borrowing to seven years or less, we should adopt the same guidelines.

THE BOTTOM LINE COMMANDMENT: REPAY WHAT YOU OWE

I trust that by now you realize that although God never prohibited borrowing for His people He did establish some principles to guide us. I call these the "don't principles."

- Don't borrow needlessly.
- Don't sign surety.
- Don't take on long-term debt.

Note that I called these statements *principles*. God's Word normally breaks down into two broad categories: principles and commandments. In general, principles are instructions for making intelligent decisions; they are not absolutes. The book of Proverbs, for example, contains more than a dozen warnings about cosigning for the debts of others. These are not commands; they are principles.

In other words, to cosign is not a sin; it's just dumb. As Proverbs 20:16 says, *"Take his garment when he becomes surety for a stranger; and for foreigners, hold him in pledge."* Anyone who has cosigned for the debts of someone who then defaulted understands the wisdom of this principle. But if you still want to cosign for someone else's debts, feel free. Just don't expect sympathy from the Lord.

God's Word does contain clear absolutes as well as principles. The most important scriptural absolute about borrowing: *You must repay what you owe*.

There is no option for the Christian when it comes to repaying a debt. Since the law no longer imprisons those who default on their debts, we tend to downgrade this as a sin. But the Scripture is very clear when it equates the breaking of a promise (vow) with sinning. The Bible describes the person who does not repay debts as being an evil person: *"The wicked borrows and does not pay back, but the righteous is gracious and gives"* (Psalm 37:21).

The lender has an implied authority that includes the right to punish the faithless borrower. In Matthew 5:25–26 the Lord instructed debtors to beg the forgiveness of their creditors. Obviously there is a deeper spiritual meaning in this instruction, but He was drawing the analogy from real life. When it comes to borrowing, the bottom line in Christianity is that you must repay what you owe.

George ran a restaurant with his wife, Martha. George was not a Christian and had no respect for most of the people who were. Martha was a Christian, and George had seen her friends from church "stiff" her for a lot of meals. At least that was the way George put it. Because of the numerous bad checks they had written, he had long since stopped taking checks from the after-church crowd. His basic evaluation of most Christians: "They're a bunch of freeloading hypocrites."

As George and Martha's restaurant prospered and they were able to hire more help, Martha began a catering business to assist local businesses with their staff parties. She also began catering for various church groups around Christmastime.

George predicted, "It's only a matter of time until some church group stiffs you for your fees."

"I guess if they do, I'll just remember that I'm doing this for the Lord and not for people," Martha replied.

To George's surprise it wasn't a church group that failed to pay its bills; it was a large company that had been doing a lot of business with their restaurant. The company owed them nearly $6,000 for catering and prepayment of food they had ordered for the upcoming holiday season.

Then one Monday morning, as George was reading the paper, he saw an article stating that the company president had filed for bankruptcy protection. When he contacted the company office, George heard the bad news: "Sir, I'm afraid that your bill will not be paid in the near future. The secured creditors have forced a total liquidation of the company, and the debts exceed the assets by a wide margin."

"Stiffed again," George muttered to Martha as he put the receiver down. "But at least this time it's not by one of your religious friends. I know the company president, and he may be a crook, but at least he doesn't pretend to be religious."

Nearly a year later George suffered the first of several heart attacks, which left him unable to work regularly. Martha was unable to run the restaurant by herself, so they tried to sell it. But there were few prospects in their town that had both the ability and the cash.

One day George was at the restaurant going over the books, in anticipation of closing the business and selling off the equipment and property. Hearing a knock at the front door, he wheeled his chair around, unlocked the door, and saw the president of the bankrupt company standing there.

"What are you doing here?" George asked contemptuously. "I thought you left town after your business folded."

"Yes, I did," he replied. "We moved back to Vermont, where my wife's family lives."

"Well, what are you doing back here?"

"I came back to apologize to you and the other people I owe money to. I know I did wrong by not warning you about my financial troubles."

"I don't guess you did any worse than anyone else has," George said bitterly. "Everybody kicks the little guys when they're down."

"I really didn't mean to leave the people I did business with holding the bag. I guess I always considered myself an honest man, and now I've come to realize I was only honest when it was convenient."

"Well, what do you want from me?" George snarled.

"Nothing," he replied. "I heard about your health problems and wanted to help. I have become a Christian . . ." He hesitated when he saw the look of disdain on George's face.

"Well I guess you round out the group," George muttered as he started to close the door. "You weren't religious when you stiffed us, so you went out and got religion."

"Wait, George," he said as he pushed the door back open. "What I wanted to tell you is that I want to pay you back everything you lost when my company folded."

"How's that?" George asked as he released the door. "You want to pay the money back? But I thought you went bankrupt."

"I did, but that doesn't relieve my requirement to repay my debts. Christians always repay what they owe. The Bible teaches that it's the right thing to do."

"Boy, that's the first time I ever heard that one," George quipped. "I always thought it was the church people that invented the word *deadbeat*."

"I guess it must seem that way sometimes. A lot of people watch Christians to see if they do what they say."

"I don't know what you're trying to pull, but I'll tell you this: I'm not lending you any more money to try to get back what I already lost," George said sarcastically.

"I don't want to borrow more money. Actually I'd like to pay you some of what I owe."

"Some of that money sure would help right now," George said a little more politely.

"Well, I don't have all that I owe you, but here's $5,000. When the sale of our home is complete, I should be able to pay the rest."

"You sold your home?" George asked.

"Yes. The home was in my wife's name, so I was able to keep it out of the bankruptcy. But the Lord has convicted me that I should lay everything at His feet. So we put the house up for sale, and we're using the profits to repay everyone who lost money in the bankruptcy."

"Well, I'll be!" George said. "That beats anything I've heard of."

"I also heard that you're trying to sell your business here," he said to George. "I'd like to talk to you about buying it. We won't have a lot of money left after paying everybody off, but we should have a few thousand. I know the restaurant business because my family has run one back home for 30 years. And you two could stay on and watch the operation until you're sure we're capable of running it."

The conclusion to this story came a year later when George became a Christian just two weeks before his fatal heart attack. The new owner continues to make an impact on his community through the application of biblical principles in his life and business.

THE PERILS OF CREDIT

As the examples in this chapter have shown, the misuse of credit can be hazardous to your personal and corporate finances. But, in reality, there are potential dangers associated with any use of credit, not just its misuse. Before closing this chapter I would like to cover three of these potential perils.

1. Borrowing Can Cause You To Miss God's Direction

The use of credit can easily cloud your view of God's direction for your life. There's no indication in Scripture that God ever directed anyone through the use of a loan.

A few years ago, God allowed me to observe firsthand how a credit mind-set can cause us to miss out on God's best. A Christian businessman came to my office for counsel. He had made a considerable profit on a real estate transaction and wanted to give a large part of it to the Lord's work. His church had a building fund drive to develop a youth center, and he wanted to give the money to that fund. But he had a very strong conviction about not borrowing in general and particularly his church not borrowing.

He told me, "I'll give the church the money for the building if you can convince the pastor to build it debt-free without his knowing about the gift."

What a dilemma! I knew that all the money the church needed was already committed and available, but I had to convince the pastor not to borrow without revealing what I knew. The pastor and I were friends, so I asked him to have lunch the next day and to bring along the chairman of his board of deacons.

At that meal I did everything I could do, within the restrictions given me, to convince the pastor to make an absolute commitment to build the youth center debt-free. I thought I was making some head-way with arguments like, "Don't stifle God's ability to bless your people" and "If you can't trust God for the money you need, do you really trust God?"

I knew the pastor basically wanted to build debt-free and was willing to do so with the youth center, provided he had the support of the church leadership. Financially speaking, the building was beyond the ability of the membership to fund outright, at least while they continued in their established lifestyles. (Heaven forbid that anyone should forego a vacation or a new car to build a church building!)

Near the end of the luncheon the pastor asked the deacon, a local businessman, what he thought about our discussion. He replied, "If I tried to run my business by the principles he just outlined I would be broke today. If we try to build this youth center debt-free, our kids will be grown and gone before the walls are up. Pastor, it's a great theory, but it just won't work in this generation."

The pastor caved in under the logic of this argument and walked out with a commitment to present the plan to borrow the money to the congregation that evening.

I wanted to shout, "But if you'll believe God for it, the money is already provided!" But I couldn't.

The next day the potential donor presented another ministry a check for more than $200,000. His church went on to borrow the money for the youth center and paid on the debt for the next 15 years or so.

One day you and I will stand before the Lord, and He will reveal all the blessings He had available to us but was unable to give because of our unbelief. I wonder how many of us will see that our dependence on credit was what blocked us from receiving His best gifts.

2. Borrowing Can Delay Necessary Decisions

Often a business that is in financial trouble because of poor management or other problems will sustain itself by borrowing until it is too late, instead of resolving the real problems.

God's Word says, *"The prudent sees the evil and hides himself, but the naive go on, and are punished for it"* (Proverbs 22:3). The use of borrowed money can provide a false sense of security that allows a correctable situation to grow into an out-of-control problem. Credit has allowed many businesses to continue losing money until assets that could have been salvaged have been lost.

To verify this principle you don't have to look much further than the example of what happened to Eastern Airlines in the late seventies. Eastern had been losing money even before the deregulation of the industry, but because of appreciating equipment and other assets the management was able to borrow more and more money to sustain operations. In the absence of available credit, the company would have been forced to face reality: to reduce overhead or close its doors.

Instead, the borrowing continued well into the next decade, at which time the company was sold to a speculator who cut the company into pieces and sold them off. The net result was the loss of thousands of employees' jobs and the disruption of many lives.

Borrowing merely delays necessary decisions; it does not avoid them. When a family borrows to buy a new car because they can't afford to keep their old one going, they don't really avoid making some fundamental changes to their budget; they merely delay these changes and often make them more stringent.

Cory was operating a retail hardware store that also sold at wholesale to local building contractors. The business began to drift into financial trouble because Cory was not a particularly astute manager and didn't control his inventory closely. He often would overbuy on building materials and then end up selling them at a loss to generate income. To make up the difference, he borrowed against his inventory at the local bank.

As small town bankers are sometimes prone to do, the banker did not require an outside audit of Cory's actual inventory but took Cory's word for how much inventory he had. Over a period of three years Cory accumulated a debt of nearly $200,000 at the bank. He was able to pay the interest only by borrowing more money on the nonexistent inventory.

Then the local bank was sold to a larger outside chain, and new management was installed. A review of the outstanding loans revealed an ever-increasing debt, being accumulated by the local hardware store owner. "Don't worry about that loan, Mr. Simpson," the loan officer said with confidence. "Cory Wallace is as good as gold. He never misses a payment, and he has a growing business."

"But it looks as if he continues to borrow every quarter," said the accountant-turned-bank president. "In fact, it would appear that he's borrowing to pay the interest on his loan. If so, that's illegal."

"No, he's borrowing to increase his inventory. His wholesale business is doing great, and he needs the materials to expand."

"Do you have a copy of his most recent financial statement?"

"No, Sir, we've never needed one so far. But I asked him for a copy of the inventory, and it shows nearly $400,000 in stock now."

"Let's go over to that store. I want to see that inventory myself," the president said.

The loan officer called Cory and set up a meeting. Once inside the store the banker said, "Mr. Wallace, I'm a little concerned about your outstanding loan balance. Would you mind showing me the material warehouse and the inventory that is pledged as collateral?"

Cory felt the panic inside as the banker asked his questions. For two years he had been issuing phony inventory statements to the bank to get new loans—always hoping that things would turn around and he would be able to repay some of the debt. But instead of turning around, things had gotten worse. He had always been able to "good ole boy" his way around the previous president's questions, but he realized that this new banker was all business and no nonsense.

"This is the only building I own," Cory replied meekly. "The inventory is in the rear of the store."

As they walked toward the rear of the building the banker asked, "Do you have a current financial statement?"

"No, I don't do but one a year, and the last one I have is from last December," Cory said as the panic began to show in his voice.

"I'd like a copy of that statement, then," the banker said very curtly. "Is this the total extent of your wholesale inventory?" he asked, looking at the sparse materials on the crude wooden shelves.

"Yes, it is," Cory replied. "But I have some outstanding accounts for materials the builders have picked up."

"Unless you have about $300,000 in receivables, I think we have a problem here," the banker replied.

That afternoon the new bank president ordered an official audit of the store's inventory and Cory's books. Within a week the facts were clear: The total value of all the assets owned by Cory Wallace, including the building itself, would barely total $150,000. Under court order the property was seized and the assets liquidated at public auction.

The banking firm charged Cory with fraud. Tried and convicted, he received three years in prison for fraud and lost every asset he had. His decision to borrow had not solved his problems; it had made them infinitely worse.

In most cases borrowing is a symptom rather than a problem. And in many instances credit becomes a substitute for trusting God in facing hard decisions.

3. Borrowing Can Create Unnecessary Pressures

I don't know of anyone who would disagree that living with debt is a lot more stressful than living without it. Not being able to do all the things you would like to do may be somewhat irritating, but the threat of having your home and business sold out from under you is really stressful.

The Bible says, *"There is a way which seems right to a man, but its end is the way of death"* (Proverbs 14:12). I believe this applies to the credit habit. Debt may not lead to physical death, but it surely can lead to financial death, and living under a death threat can wear any person down.

The only people who don't believe debt is stressful are those who never have been debt-free. People who live under pressure long enough no longer remember what true freedom is. In recent years many studies have been done on the correlation between stress and health problems, particularly heart disease and cancer. I believe that much of this can be attributed to debt stress in our generation.

There never has been another generation of people so addicted to borrowing money as ours. At some point God's people must break out of this debt trap and become lenders again, rather than borrowers.

Remember, debt is not a problem; it is a symptom. The problem is the consistent and systematic disregard for biblical principles. Debt is the result.

16

Lending Decisions

If you are in business, you are in the lending business, whether you realize it or not (unless you ship everything prepaid only). Many good businesses have failed because of poor credit policies. But since the extension of credit has become a virtual necessity in our generation, the questions any Christian has to ask are: to whom and how much?

TO WHOM DO YOU EXTEND CREDIT?

One question any Christian must ask is, "Should I extend credit if I don't believe in borrowing?" The answer to this question is really found in the previous section on borrowing. Since borrowing is not prohibited scripturally, then it is not wrong to lend. That is, unless you have a strong personal conviction about it and you would violate your own conscience by lending.

The use of credit cards is the most common means of extending credit to customers, at least in most retail businesses. Although this takes the burden of collecting off the merchant, it does not remove the merchant's responsibility to qualify those who can handle credit.

How do you do that if someone wants to purchase your merchandise with a credit card? Actually, the only control you have is to ensure that you don't use advertising that promotes the use of credit by those who can't afford it.

I saw an example of such advertising recently in a store that advertised a credit card for people whose credit was up to the limit with other companies. This is a clear example of preying upon the weaknesses of others. The result of this can be seen in the escalating personal bankruptcy rate.

Contrary to popular opinion, I am not personally opposed to the use of credit cards; in fact, I carry one or more myself for personal and business use. Because I've often pointed out the problems associated with the misuse of plastic money, I'm often misquoted as saying that credit cards are evil.

A few years ago a national radio ministry, on whose program I had appeared several times, decided to allow the use of credit cards for the purchase of their materials. The outcry from their listeners was immediate and negative. The listeners thought they had heard me say that the use of credit cards is unscriptural. I've never said that, because it is not true. It isn't the use of credit that is unscriptural; it's the misuse.

WHAT HAPPENS WHEN PEOPLE DON'T PAY?

When extending credit there is one important rule to follow: Never lend more than you can afford to lose. You will discover that if you live by God's principles your ability to collect a delinquent debt will be greatly curtailed, because many common means of collection are unscriptural. It is important, therefore, that you determine how much you can afford to lose before extending credit to others.

I was counseling with Blake, a Christian physician, who was having a typical Christian physician's problem: collecting his fees from some of his Christian patients. He also had some non-Christian patients who didn't pay, but because he was more prone to be lenient with those who said they were Christians, those patients tended to accumulate the bigger deficits.

"I don't know what to do about these bills," Blake said in my office one day. "I don't want to sue to collect the money, but I can't afford to write all this off either."

"Are you sure your fees are in line?" I asked him, as I have asked of virtually every doctor I know. It's an honest question that a Christian in any business needs to address. If the prices or fees for a needed service are too high, they need to be adjusted. Doctors, lawyers, dentists, and businesspeople are not exempt from God's principles any more than are pastors or bricklayers.

"I think so," Blake replied. "I could actually lower my fees if I didn't have so many delinquent accounts. Unfortunately, most of the accounts are Christians from my own church."

"Do you think it's a case of can't pay—or won't pay?" I asked.

"I believe it's mostly a case of not paying the Christian doctor," Blake said. "I have to be honest. I have a problem treating some of them when I know they won't pay their bills and, yet, they drive cars that cost $40,000 or more."

"Have you tried to collect the money?"

"Yes, I have my receptionist bill each patient at least once a month. Some will pay a portion of their bill, but my outstanding accounts are nearly $150,000 now."

"I would suggest two things to help this situation. First, I would have your collections person call each delinquent patient personally and request payment of the bill or work out some payment plan. Second, I would suggest that you institute a cash-only policy, except by prearrangement for selected patients."

"But won't that cost me a lot of patients?"

"Probably so. I suspect that all of those who don't presently pay their bills will go to another doctor."

In fact, that's exactly what happened. Some of the patients paid their bills quickly. A few asked to negotiate a time payment plan. And the rest found other doctors.

If you're faced with a situation in which one or more debtors simply won't pay their bills, then what? How far should you go in collecting the money owed you? Should you use a collection agency? What are the guidelines for suing or not suing to collect?

As a lender you do have a right to collect money that is legitimately owed you. The decision about what tactics are to be used in the process is what separates a Christian creditor from other creditors.

The principle I stress here is, *"But if you had known what this means, 'I desire compassion, not a sacrifice,' you would not have condemned the innocent"* (Matthew 12:7). When seeking the correct balance, remember always that God is more concerned with the salvation of people than with the collection of debts.

Whatever you do, always try to put the other person first and, when in doubt, give that person the benefit. It would be better to suffer the loss of all debts than to needlessly offend someone who cannot (as opposed to will not) pay. With that said, let me outline some considerations that have worked for many businesspeople I know.

COLLECTION CONSIDERATIONS

1. Consider Individual Circumstances

Obviously there can be extenuating circumstances that would limit someone's ability to pay his or her debts. It's important to offer such people the chance to discuss their difficulties.

I've often heard a businessperson or credit manager say, "Well if the person had a legitimate problem he (or she) should have said so." But, if you ever have been on the other side of that fence and have been rebuffed by a discourteous credit manager, you can appreciate why some people will simply ignore the issue until it's pressed by the creditor. It's not that people are dishonest or don't want to pay. Often, they fear the confrontation and rejection. Remember the personality traits discussed in Chapter 10. Someone with the "High S" (*Supportive*) personality hates conflict and will avoid it at all costs.

I know of several cases in which a "High S" wife was married to a "High D" (*Directing*) personality. He would ignore the problem until it developed into a major crisis and then assign the dirty work to his timid wife. Under the pressure of debts that could not be paid, she would develop a myriad of physical symptoms that only added to the anxieties. Often this is true of men as well, except that rarely will the creditors attempt to intimidate a man the way they will a woman.

I suggest establishing a relationship with a good financial counselor in your area who will meet with delinquent debtors at your request and determine if they're able to pay and, if not, work out an alternative plan. If a debtor refuses to follow the plan you suggest, including seeing the counselor, you'll need to proceed to the next step: a collection agency.

I was attending a morning Bible study with some other businessmen, discussing these very same topics, when the issue of collecting debts came up. One of the men in the group, Glenn, said that he had a great many outstanding accounts from his car service center and had a policy of turning all accounts over 30 days old to a collection agency.

I knew of the agency from some of the families I had counseled and asked, "Do you think that agency represents your ethics well?"

"What do you mean?" Glenn asked.

"I have dealt with that agency many times, and their position is, 'Pay up now or we'll take you to court.' Several times I tried to discuss a client's problems, but they didn't want to discuss anything except a cash settlement. At least three families they sued were having severe financial problems and couldn't pay."

"Well, if my clients were having problems, they should have come to me," Glenn said defensively. "I would have worked out something."

"But you don't understand what a poor sense of self-worth people in that situation often have, particularly if they knew when they used your services that they wouldn't be able to pay the bill. Many times they feel totally defeated and dishonest and just want to run from the problems. Most people are honest and want to pay their bills."

"What would you suggest?" Glenn asked.

"Why don't you have your bookkeeper contact the delinquent accounts and at least offer them the alternative of meeting with one of our counselors to determine their ability to pay?"

"That sounds fair enough. I'll contact the collection agency and tell them what I'm going to do."

"They probably will object," I said. "They make their money by collecting, and your method won't fit their pattern."

True to form, the collection agency did everything it could to dissuade Glenn from sending the accounts to a counselor. I received at least a half-dozen nasty calls from everyone up to and including the president of the company. In truth, most of the clients refused the offer to see a counselor, and the company proceeded with their normal collection procedures. But at least 10 of the families asked to see a counselor and were willing to work out any kind of reasonable plan to repay the debt. Ultimately these people repaid their debts, and they continue as Glenn's valued customers.

One of the families who agreed to see a counselor had been hit by a series of financial disasters that would have wrecked anyone's budget. They had three little girls, ages two, four, and six, all of whom had been diagnosed with leukemia. All were undergoing chemotherapy at a children's hospital in another state, and the cost of travel and lodging alone was over $600 a month. In addition they had no medical insurance, and the cumulative medical bills were nearly $250,000, even with the hospital donating its services.

When Glenn received the counselor's report on this family, he was visibly shaken. At our next meeting he shared this family's plight with our group and announced that not only was he canceling their bill but he would continue to repair their old car as long as necessary at no cost.

Over the next several weeks the group continued to ask about the family and their needs. Then one day Glenn asked if some of the other men would like to contribute to a fund his attorney had set up to help with the medical expenses. Everyone agreed enthusiastically and not only contributed but helped Glenn in raising additional funds. Within six weeks, all the medical bills were paid and enough money was set aside for several months' expenses.

Glenn had learned a lesson about debt collecting that went far beyond the money involved: People are more important than money. He also decided to change collection agencies, concluding that his good name was far more important than his collections. *"A good name is to be more desired than great riches, favor is better than silver and gold"* (Proverbs 22:1).

2. Analyze Your Motives

If you sincerely believe that everything you have belongs to God and that you are just a manager for Him, then you must make every decision with that in mind. If the motive behind your system of collections is greed, anger, and resentment, then it is your money you're collecting, not God's.

You have a right to the money that is owed you, but if in recovering that money you are willing to violate the very principles God has established, your loss is much more than a financial one.

Phil and Cindy ran a small lettering company whose primary business was painting personalized door signs for office buildings. Phil had a contract with a commercial developer of some large office complexes to do all of his buildings. One building he had worked on for over six months should have netted him over $60,000. But just as he was finishing the building the developer sold the complex to a large insurance company from Canada without paying him.

Phil contacted the developer about getting his money and was basically told, "Get it from the new owners." So he contacted the new owners, who also refused payment, saying the bill was not shown as an outstanding account at the time of sale and they were not responsible for it.

Phil again called the developer, who stated flatly that he did not feel responsible for the bill. He was retiring from business and would not need Phil's services again. To a relatively small company like Phil's this was a severe financial blow, and he immediately filed suit in court against the developer. Within two days of the time the papers were served, Phil received a call.

"I thought you were a Christian, Phil," the developer said curtly.

"I am, but what does that have to do with anything?" Phil replied.

"You're not supposed to sue another Christian, are you?" the developer asked in a sharp tone.

"Why do you ask? Are you saying you're a Christian?"

"I sure am," he replied. "I go to the Hidden Hills church here in town."

"But if you're a Christian, how can you refuse to pay the bill you owe me?" Phil asked in an angry tone of voice.

"I really don't owe you the money, Phil. If you didn't have a lien against the building when it was sold, you're out of luck."

"But you didn't notify me that the building was being sold," Phil complained.

"I posted the legal notices in the paper that are required," the developer replied. "If you didn't see them, that's your problem." And with that he hung up.

Phil sat at his desk for a long time, thinking about the conversation he had just had. His attorney had already told him he had a good chance of collecting the money, plus attorney's fees, since what had happened was a clear case of deception. At the very least, the court would place a mechanic's lien against the building and pressure the insurance company to make the developer pay up. Their final payment to the developer was not due until midyear, and the insurance company wouldn't want any hassle over their property.

Phil called his pastor, who referred him to our office for help. After hearing Phil's story, I placed a call to the developer.

"Hi, I'm a Christian counselor and I have Phil Lindsey in my office . . ." Click. The line went dead as the phone on the other end was slammed down.

"I get the distinct feeling that he doesn't want to discuss this issue, Phil."

"I got the same feeling when we tried to call him from my attorney's office yesterday," Phil responded. "What do you think I should do?"

"I think you should sue him," I replied.

"Oh," Phil said in surprise, "I thought you would say not to sue."

Then I asked, "But you only asked what I thought. Would you like to know what God thinks?"

"Certainly," he said. "That's why I'm here."

"God thinks you shouldn't sue, Phil, even though it's not fair. If the man says he is a Christian, then leave the decision in the Lord's hands."

"I thought that's what you would say," Phil responded with a sigh. "But what if he isn't really a Christian?"

"That really is an impossible question to answer. You just have to go with the direction the Lord gave us through the apostle Paul: *'Does any one of you, when he has a case against his neighbor, dare to go to law before the unrighteous, and not before the saints?'* (1 Corinthians 6:1)."

Phil wrote the developer a note saying that he had decided not to sue and explaining why. He also attempted to confront the issue through the local church but was rebuffed by the developer's pastor, who refused to discuss the issue.

I'd like to be able to report that this sacrifice on the part of an honest Christian businessman resulted in some supernatural event that returned the money. (I do know of some that did!) But Phil never collected the money he was owed, because the developer died a few months after all this happened.

We still don't know for sure that the man was a Christian; only the Lord knows for sure. But we do know with certainty: he won't show up before the Lord claiming that a Christian businessman named Phil was a stumbling block to him in this lifetime. And after all, that's the bottom line on our balance sheet.

3. Be Willing to Forgive

When you're confronted with a refusal to pay a debt, it's always best to try to contact the debtors directly rather than making contact with them through the mail or through a collection agency. That way most of the confusion will be avoided. Once you or one of your staff have done this and have offered an alternative plan and the debtor still refuses to pay, then turn the situation over to a third party if necessary. In all of this process, however, remember the principle taught by the Lord in the parable of the debts: If you expect forgiveness, you must be willing to forgive others (see Matthew 18:21–35).

SUING TO COLLECT

Most Christians believe the question of suing can be divided into a black or white decision. If the debtor is a Christian, you probably should not sue; if he or she is not a Christian, it is okay to sue. Unfortunately arriving at a biblical answer is not that simple.

Many well-meaning teachers say that 1 Corinthians 6 does not apply to the collection of debts at all. If not, then what is the application? Paul didn't use any qualifiers in his instructions when he said, *"Actually, then, it is already a defeat for you, that you have lawsuits with one another. Why not rather be wronged? Why not rather be defrauded?"* (1 Corinthians 6:7). I conclude from his arguments that Christians are simply not to sue one another.

But what about suing non-Christians? I don't believe that the Bible teaches (directly) that you cannot sue a non-Christian. However, the fact that there are no direct instructions not to sue someone does not automatically impute the right to do so. Every decision has to be made in light of the fact that our primary function is to share the ministry of Jesus Christ with others. If that ministry is impeded by your suing another person, then do not sue.

Before you make a decision to sue anyone over a personal loss, I encourage you to read the following verse: *"Give to everyone who asks of you, and whoever takes away what is yours, do not demand it back"* (Luke 6:30).

With rare exception, I have never seen a lawsuit involving a relatively small amount of money that benefited anyone other than the attorneys. If an individual will not pay a legitimate debt without being sued, that person usually will default through bankruptcy or some other "sleight of hand," even if you get a judgment against him or her. There are obvious exceptions, such as recovering real properties or evicting someone who will not pay rent. But most lawsuits are pursued out of an attitude of anger, revenge, or greed. Lawsuits with that motivation—even against unbelievers—are unlikely to further God's purposes.

The most common question asked of me by Christians in business regarding lawsuits is, "Can I sue a corporation?" Since there were no corporations in existence when the Bible was written, the best we can do is relate the principle to the closest parallel of that time: a government agency.

It seems clear from the book of Acts that Paul recognized both the authority and the responsibility of the government of Rome. Twice when he was falsely arrested he relied on application of Roman law to regain his freedom.

He also used the law to deter his antagonists (see Acts 16:37). When he was falsely accused by the Jewish leaders in Jerusalem and jailed by the Roman authorities, to defend himself he appealed to Caesar on the basis of his citizenship. The Roman government was an entity, not a person, so Paul felt he was clearly within his rights to use Roman law against that entity.

A corporation is also an entity, not a person. And although the entity is controlled and sometimes solely owned by a person, in my opinion the corporation has no rights under biblical guidelines except the rights of prevailing law. Therefore I would say that to sue a corporation in order to require that it meet its legal responsibilities is not unscriptural.

A good example of this would be an insurance company. Any company exists only as a legal entity and can be totally dissolved by law. It executes contracts in its own name and operates by applicable contract laws. A case could be made that if such a corporation is owned and operated by a Christian (alone), then suing the corporation is tantamount to suing the owner. I believe this argument is invalid. The use of the corporate shield supersedes the individual's ownership.

Throughout God's Word believers are admonished to keep their vows: *"You shall be careful to perform what goes out from your lips, just as you have voluntarily vowed to the Lord your God, what you have promised"* (Deuteronomy 23:23; also see Psalm 22:25 and Ecclesiastes 5:5). When an individual voluntarily elects to be treated as a corporation, he or she has made a new vow. God warned Israel about doing this when they asked for a king but acknowledged their right to do so as free-willed people. Once they made that election they were bound by the rules of the king (except where that authority conflicted with the fundamental laws of God, such as the ban against the worship of idols).

Again, the fact that God's Word allows a Christian to sue a corporation does not automatically impute such a right in every instance. God may ask us to forego that right for a bigger cause.

SETTLE OUT OF COURT, IF POSSIBLE

Too often what keeps us from settling a dispute out of court is pride. If the other party is at fault, it is common to assume an adversarial position. In some cases this may be justified because the other party is either uncooperative or belligerent. But often the issues are not clear and both parties genuinely believe they are in the right. In these cases arbitration can serve both sides better than the courts.

The Peacemaker Ministry, Billings, Montana, exists for the purpose of arbitrating issues between Christians who take seriously Paul's instruction not to sue one another. This group and several other similar organizations have branches throughout most areas of the country. I urge every Christian who has a dispute with another believer to contact Peacemaker Ministry and avoid the court system.

WHAT ABOUT WHEN YOU ARE SUED?

Fortunately, most of us will not be faced with having to sue a corporation or anyone else. However, in this litigious age we might find ourselves facing a lawsuit.

I have known Christians in business who would sue anyone at the drop of a hat and who used countersuits as a weapon if anyone sued them. Their image to the outside world was like that of the wolverine: fiercely protective of its territory and very combative.

But I have also known those who were so confused by the admonition to put others first that they were totally vulnerable to any charlatan in business. They often allowed others to steal from or cheat them with impunity. As a result their businesses suffered and they actually encouraged more cheating. Mercy should always be our strong point as Christians. But mercy without justice is weakness, not meekness.

Mike was a Christian CEO in charge of an electronics firm. Several of the products his firm sold were proprietary in nature and protected by patents. Mike had started the company when he was not a Christian, and in those days he was known for his combative spirit and ruthlessness in business. After his conversion Mike devoted most of his prayer and study time to conquering his arrogance and self-first attitude. In his zeal to resolve this personality flaw, Mike concluded that to sue another person or company would be wrong, and he made a point of stating his conviction publicly several times.

One afternoon Mike received a call from one of the sales companies representing his product line. It seemed that another company had produced a competitive product using his company's patented design.

Mike called the owner of the other company: "Keith, this is Mike at Electron. One of my sales reps called to say that you have a new product on the market that uses some of our designs."

"I've got a new product out, but it doesn't use your design. It's one I worked out myself," Keith asserted belligerently.

"Would you mind telling me how you accomplished that? I happen to know that we have the only design that has ever worked," Mike replied combatively.

"Listen, Pal," Keith retorted, "if you think I stole your design, sue me."

"I sure will," Mike shouted. "You don't have the brains to build a crystal radio set, much less do your own designing. You've been robbing other people's designs since you began!" With that Mike slammed down the phone.

He had no sooner done that than he began to realize that his old nature had assumed control again. Thoroughly confused about what he should do, he decided to just wait and see what action the other company would take.

Over the next few months Mike's company began to lose sales as the other company's products saturated the market. It was clear that Keith expected to be sued and was trying to sell as much as possible in the interim. Meanwhile, Mike stalled in making the necessary decisions about suing or not suing over the patent infringement. The delay cost his company millions of dollars in lost sales. Several of his managers encouraged him to file suit, as well as two of his board of directors who heard about the patent infringement.

Mike was sitting in his office one Friday when a process server appeared at his door. "Are you Mike Billings?" he asked. When Mike nodded he said, "Mr. Billings, I have a summons for you to appear in court."

Mike was almost in shock as he read the document. It was a lawsuit filed against him by several of his stockholders, including the two directors. The stockholders clearly took a dim view of Mike's inactivity. They construed it to be a threat to their ownership in the company, as indeed it was.

Ultimately Mike was required to compensate the stockholders several hundred thousand dollars for what the court interpreted to be his failure to protect their interests. The stockholders also filed a lawsuit against the offending company and had all the profits from the sale of the pirated equipment assigned to their company. The owner of the other company then filed for personal and corporate bankruptcy and never paid one dollar to the rightful owners of the patent.

Mike learned a costly lesson about being the responsible authority and not allowing his personal convictions to be confused with biblical principle.

I recall a class discussion from one of my business management courses in college. The professor posed this hypothetical question: "If you were the captain of a ship that had just sunk and were in the only lifeboat with 39 other people, but the boat was designed to only hold 30 people and would sink with 40 people aboard, would you use your authority to force 10 people over the side?"

I answered the question as honestly as I could: "I don't think I could make that choice." To those of us who responded negatively the professor said, "Then don't ever become the captain of a ship, because you might be faced with such a decision one day." The same principle holds true with being a fiduciary.

HANDLING LAWSUITS AGAINST YOU

What should you do when someone decides to sue you? Are you required as a Christian to never defend yourself in a court of law? And what if the person suing is a Christian also? Is defending yourself in court the same as taking another person to court?

The first question you need to ask yourself if you are being sued is: Am I guilty? If so, then you need to confess your guilt and offer to make restitution to the injured parties. As the Lord said, *"Make friends quickly with your opponent at law while you are with him on the way, in order that your opponent may not deliver you to the judge, and the judge to the officer, and you be thrown into prison"* (Matthew 5:25).

I once counseled a Christian in the real estate business who was being sued by another Christian over what the latter said was a blatant default on a contract to purchase some land from him. In the course of our conversation he asked, "Do you think it's wrong for one Christian to sue another?"

"Absolutely," I replied. "All it does is expose Christians to the ridicule of the world."

"That's how I feel too," he said. "Would you be willing to call this individual and tell him that?"

"Let me ask you something first," I said. "Did you default on a contract you had with him?"

"Yes, I did," he replied. "The economy had changed and I felt the property was no longer worth what I had offered."

"But did you have a contingency clause in your agreement that would allow you to back out of the purchase?"

"No, but it wouldn't make any sense to buy property at twice what it's worth in this economy. I just want you to tell him that he should not be suing me as a Christian."

"I'm afraid I can't do that. Obviously, he's wrong in suing you, but you're equally wrong in breaking your vow to him. I'm not going to referee who is the most or least wrong. You need to complete your contract as written, and then he won't have a reason to sue."

"That's not right!" he protested. "He's trying to force me to buy land that's not worth what I'd have to pay for it."

When he finally decided I was not going to try to talk the other party out of suing him, he left. The subsequent lawsuit forced him to complete the contract. In this case both parties lost because they were wrong. As the adage goes, "Two wrongs do not make a right."

DEFENSE IN COURT

Late one evening I received a call from a businessman I'll call Sidney. It seems he and another Christian were in a metal trading business together. They bought and sold lead, zinc, and copper all over the world and had developed a very good business, as well as spotless reputations. As the business grew, Sidney, the financial backer, put in more money to allow them the option of buying product and storing it for future use. He knew this was risky, because if they guessed wrong and the prices went down they could sustain considerable losses. But, since they purchased for cash only, the most they stood to lose was what they had invested.

Without Sidney's knowledge, however, his partner began to trade in options on the commodity exchange. Since he was then leveraging the investments by depositing a small amount of money against a large purchase (option) the potential profits were enormous, but the potential losses were just as great.

By using the company's inventory as collateral, Sidney's partner was able to acquire a large portfolio of options. These had the potential to bring in several million dollars' profit if an anticipated upswing in price occurred.

Instead, the price plummeted as a rumored strike at the major supplier's mines failed to materialize. Suddenly Sidney's partner found himself facing losses of several hundred thousand dollars, much of which he couldn't cover.

When the truth finally came out, Sidney was confronted with irate traders who wanted their money. It cost him nearly $400,000 to pay off all the losses and sell out the remaining contracts. By selling off the last of their metal inventories he was able to recover about half of his money. He then dissolved the partnership and went back to his regular vocation (a commodities broker) as a wiser, if poorer, man.

Then Sidney was served with a summons to appear in court. His ex-partner was suing him for unlawful conversion of assets. He claimed that Sidney had directed him to buy the options and then had stolen the inventory to benefit himself. He was asking for the value of the inventory (about $200,000), plus $1 million in damages.

Since Sidney and I had known each other for a long time, he called me. "Larry, I want to know what I should do about this situation. I probably have a case against my ex-partner. I never authorized him to trade in options and can easily prove that his doing so violated our agreement. My attorney recommends that we countersue. What do you advise?"

"Is your ex-partner a Christian?" I asked.

"I would have said so before this situation came up," he answered. "Yes, I'm sure he is, but he's caught up in greed and fear right now. He lost everything he owns in this deal."

"Have you studied what Paul said about suing another Christian in 1 Corinthians 6?"

"You know I have. But my attorney says that if we don't do something, he just might find the ear of a sympathetic judge who would give him damages. I don't want to countersue, but don't I have the right to defend myself in court?"

"Have you approached him about taking this issue to arbitration?"

"Yes, but his attorney won't even discuss it. He has obtained the services of a pretty high-powered attorney who is quite obviously not a Christian."

"Do you have a Bible with you?" I asked.

"Yes. Why?"

"Turn to Acts 25." Then I began to discuss Paul's situation. "The Pharisees had accused Paul of violating their law, including bringing a Gentile into the temple to worship. They had appealed to the local Roman government to allow them to try Paul according to their customs. Paul realized he would get more justice from the hands of the Gentile government than from a bigoted group of hypocrites.

"Being a Roman citizen, he had the right to appeal to Caesar for any final judgment, particularly in the case of a death sentence, which this certainly would be. In verse 11 he wrote, *'If then I am a wrongdoer, and have committed anything worthy of death, I do not refuse to die;*

but if none of those things is true of which these men accuse me, no one can hand me over to them. I appeal to Caesar.'

"Clearly, Paul had the right to use the prevailing law to defend himself. God must have concurred, since this was all a part of His greater plan to plant the apostle in Caesar's household. One point that must be kept in perspective is that Paul never counterattacked the Jews who were accusing him. A defense in court does not give a Christian the right to countersue."

"I agree," he replied, obviously relieved. "I don't want anything from my ex-partner, but I also don't want to lose any more money for something he did without my knowledge."

Sidney rebuffed all attempts by his ex-partner's attorney to settle out of court for various amounts down to $100,000. "No," he said the last time, just before the trial, "I won't settle for even one dollar."

By then the costs had become so great that the attorney had no choice but to pursue the matter in court. When the case came to trial, the judge asked to hear the opening statements from each attorney. The plaintiff's attorney presented Sidney as a greedy, selfish man who had robbed his client of his due portion of the partnership. Anyone listening to the pitiful condition of the poor, deceived partner probably would have granted him anything he asked for. That's the principle of "The first to speak always sounds right, until another is heard."

The judge asked Sidney if he had anything to say for himself after his attorney had presented his side.

"Yes, Sir, I do," he replied. "I don't want anything from these proceedings except to clear my name and reputation. I believe I can show evidence that I never authorized the trades that took place and that I willingly absorbed all the losses from them."

His attorney then offered two full boxes of information from the brokers who had handled the trades as well as the authorizing documents with his forged signature on them. His partner had neglected to clear out a filing cabinet that had been stored in the record closet.

When he saw the evidence, the ex-partner paled. He had assumed that all the evidence had been destroyed. He immediately motioned to his attorney. In two minutes the attorney asked the judge to allow them to withdraw the suit.

The judge, leafing through the files, looked up and said, "I should think so." Then, looking at Sidney, he asked, "Are you planning to file a countersuit against this thief?"

"No, Sir," Sidney replied. "I just want to be done with this business."

The judge, looking at the partner, said, "I believe you are a thief. If he would file charges against you, I would see to it that you were prosecuted to the full extent of the law. Since he will not, the most I can do is assign to you all of the court costs, including all attorneys' fees. Now I would suggest that you get out of my court before I decide to find something I can try you for."

Any Christian who is faced with a lawsuit has a legal and biblical right to bring the truth to light. Often we won't get biblical justice in the world's court, but sometimes God works even through the unsaved.

17

Discounting Decisions

"I'm sorry, Ma'am, but I can't cut the price on that car any more," Kris Burgess whined. "As you can see from the dealer invoice I showed you, we're at rock bottom. Check with any other dealer in town and you'll see we're always the lowest. I'll only make a hundred dollars on the sale, and that's hardly enough to keep the doors open."

"I wouldn't want you to lose any money," Elizabeth Evans responded. "I know you have to make a living too. I guess I'll take it. If you're only making a hundred dollars, surely no one else could beat your price."

"That's for sure, Ma'am," Kris replied.

Standing outside the sales manager's doorway, Chuck Crouse, the general manager, chuckled beneath his breath, "Boy, Kris is the sharpest salesperson I've ever had. He could talk a dog out of his fleas, I'll bet."

Chuck knew that the invoice price Elizabeth Evans had been shown was only partially accurate. It was true that the amount the invoice showed was what the agency was billed. But with the special dealer incentives and service charges, the sale would net several hundred dollars for the company. Chuck Crouse walked away pleased that he had what it took to make his dealership successful.

Soon after Elizabeth signed her contract, including the essential service extension, the local county commissioner, Marvin Terrell, came into the dealership.

"Say, Chuck, I need to buy a new car, but I want your best deal, you hear me?"

"No problem, Marv," Crouse said with a wink. "I've really got a deal for you. I'll have Kris draw up a contract at our absolute cost."

"I don't want any of that dealer cost junk, Chuck. I don't mind your making a hundred or so, but I don't want to pay for your kid's college education."

"No sweat, Marv, I'll guarantee you a thousand less than Mrs. Evans just paid for the same car."

"Well, I hope you made enough off her that you don't need to stick it to me too," Marvin chuckled.

"Sure did," Chuck said as he nudged his friend. "Hey, the only thing little old ladies need to be sheep is a wool coat."

They both laughed.

That was a fairly accurate description of what a Christian salesman overheard at the agency he had just gone to work for as he sat in his office studying the sales literature on the cars he was to sell. He had taken the job because the owner was a member of his father's church and they served on the deacon board together. He was reported to be an honest businessman and a faithful Christian.

In all probability if someone had challenged that owner on the ethics of what he was doing, he would have justified it by saying, "It didn't really hurt anyone. Mrs. Evans did get a good car, and she was satisfied with the deal she got. And besides, Marvin's a better nego- tiator."

We are told, *"A false balance is an abomination to the Lord, but a just weight is His delight"* (Proverbs 11:1). I submit that Chuck Crouse has a different weight in his bag for different customers.

ARE PRICE DIFFERENCES HONEST?

The principle behind differing weights is a simple one. In biblical times it was common for street merchants, such as those selling grain door-to-door, to have two sets of weights in the bag that hung around their waists. When they sold grain in the poor community, they would use the lighter weight to measure out the portions, because they knew the poor wouldn't have their own weights to verify the measure.

However, when they sold in the more affluent areas, they would use the proper weights, because often buyers would take out their own weights, to check the salesperson's honesty. Being caught with a short weight would often result in a short trip to the rock quarry!

In many societies bartering or haggling is a common practice. I can recall visiting in Mexico and shopping at an outdoor bazaar. Very quickly I learned that the initial asking price was highly inflated and often the merchant would settle for a fraction of his original offer.

I doubt that most of the Mexican merchants who sold to the tourists ever thought about whether what they were doing was ethical or biblical. To them it was a tradition they had grown up with and everyone followed.

But is that the philosophy a Christian should adopt? When we begin to allow our standards to be adjusted to the world's norm, we run the risk of becoming just like the world. When someone makes a habit of price bargaining, it becomes difficult to tell whether he or she is being truthful.

In the case of the Mexican merchants, I quickly realized that I could never really depend on what they said. They would say, "This is my very bottom price. I won't go one penny lower." Then when I began walking away, they would drop their prices even lower. They probably didn't consciously think that what they were doing was dishonest, but it was.

Essentially there is no difference in the majority of merchants in America and the Mexican street merchants. The price charged often depends on the negotiating ability of the buyers. If buyers are particularly shrewd and know the real cost (and value) of the items, they can get the very best price. But if, like Elizabeth Evans, they really don't know the bottom line, or if they tend to trust the person they're dealing with, they'll pay a higher price.

The acid test of differing weights for a believer is really twofold. The first is whether you would want someone to deal with you on the same basis that you're dealing with others. The biblical guidelines for this can be found in the New Testament: *"You shall love your neighbor as yourself"* (Matthew 22:39). From this principle is drawn one of the most common adages in Christianity: "Do unto others as you would have them do unto you."

The second test is whether you're willing to tell the less knowledgeable buyer that someone else has been given a better deal. Suppose, for instance, that an unsaved woman bought a washing machine from you and was allowed to believe she got the best deal possible, then later learned from another friend that she had paid a premium for her appliance.

Now, also assume that you were the last person on Earth with the opportunity to share the message of Christ with that woman before she died. Would she receive the words from your mouth as the literal truth? This puts a slightly different perspective on being careful about what proceeds out of our mouths, doesn't it?

I have a friend who travels to Afghanistan regularly. He would like to help some of the people there start their own businesses and export goods to the West, but he's handicapped by the pervasive lying in their society. It's considered an honor in some religions to lie to a "foreign devil" and, therefore, they diligently practice lying to Westerners. As a result they will remain poor because virtually no Western businessperson can trust them.

I can envision this same mentality taking control of our society, unless we guard the words of our mouths carefully: *"The integrity of the upright will guide them, but the falseness of the treacherous will destroy them"* (Proverbs 11:3).

WHAT PRICE DIFFERENCES ARE LEGITIMATE?

There are many ethical reasons why a merchant might charge one person more (or less) than another.

1. Volume Discounts

Many businesses offer discounts based on the quantity purchased. This is an honest and acceptable practice, provided everyone is allowed the same opportunity to receive the discount. If I purchased an item at one price and then later heard that someone else had bought 10 of the same item and paid a lower average cost, I wouldn't feel cheated at all, particularly if the salesperson explained that I could get the same discount by buying 10 or more. There would be no intent to deceive me and, therefore, no differing weight.

2. Cash Discounts

Many merchants offer discounts to customers who pay in cash. Often in business the same offer is extended to payments made within a certain time period, such as 10 days from the date of billing. As long as this offer is extended to all customers and they know of the policy, whether to pay the higher price becomes their decision, so it is not what Scripture would call "differing weights."

3. Class Discounts

Discounts are offered to senior citizens, college students, the unemployed, and so on. Although this policy may not always be in the best interest of the merchant, it is not the equivalent of a differing weight, as long as this policy is clearly posted and available to anyone within the selected class. I said it may not always be in the merchant's best interest, however, because customers may abuse such privileges. Unfortunately, this is often true when a Christian businessperson offers discounts to vocational Christians, such as pastors and evangelists.

I'm sure you see the common thread in the examples given. If the discounts are based on established policies and available to anyone who qualifies, there is no intent to deceive and thus no "differing weight." The Lord usually is more concerned with the intent of our hearts than He is with our actions, although more often than not our actions reflect our intentions.

A FAIR PRICE STANDARD

Wouldn't it be great to be able to buy something, knowing that you received as fair a price as possible? If the salesperson said, "That's as low as we can go and make a profit," you'd know you could believe him or her. That should be the norm for a Christian's business and the model for all secular businesses in our country. There appears to be a growing trend in America to resurrect this philosophy. Many companies now advertise that if their customers can find a lower price for the exact item they will refund the difference.

For men like J. C. Penney, such a policy was the standard. He sold an item at a fair but firm price and stood behind his word. That's why you still can't go into a Penney's store and negotiate a better price. If a sale is offered, it is advertised and available to every customer. That was the standard conduct in American business for decades—until the media generation took over. Now it's "let the suckers beware."

Just remember, stick to God's standards, not the media's. God's Word says, *"A good name is to be more desired than great riches, favor is better than silver and gold"* (Proverbs 22:1).

Harry and Mark were in the electronics business; they manufactured equipment used by large companies to test their own electronics products. They built very good equipment that, unfortunately, didn't sell very well. It was so specialized that highly trained technical salespeople were required to demonstrate its use effectively.

After trying several sales representative firms, they finally decided to limit sales to their own individual efforts. Still, their sales hovered just above the disaster level for their company, because they lacked the skilled salespeople to cover enough of the market.

One afternoon Mark received a call from a man representing himself as a potential buyer of several million dollars' worth of their equipment. He asked if Mark and Harry could meet with him later that day for an early dinner.

At six they were waiting at the restaurant when Nathan Shadburn, the caller, arrived. Over dinner he outlined his idea to build a special type of test equipment for the government, using Mark and Harry's design as the key component.

"But there's one thing," he said as he finished his presentation, "we'll have to raise the price of the equipment from $8,000 to $40,000 a unit."

"But why is that?" Harry asked. "Our costs won't be any more for the government model."

"Well, first you need to understand that the government always pays more for what it buys. I mean, it's practically un-American not to charge the government at least four times what industry pays. Your equipment won't be considered any good if it doesn't cost at least $30,000."

"I just don't think it's right to charge the government more than we would any other customer, unless there are higher costs involved," Harry said.

"There will be some additional costs associated with selling to the government, but basically it's whatever the traffic will bear," Shadburn said with a wink.

"Well, I won't do it," Harry said with finality. "I've always believed that you charge a fair price for a good product and people will appreciate it."

"I can see you've never done business with our government," Shadburn said. "They don't appreciate cost savings. In fact, they'll usually turn down the lowest bid just because they think there's something wrong with the product."

"Come on, Harry. Grow up," his partner said in an irritated voice. "Listen to what the man is saying. It's not like we're trying to rob little ole ladies. The government buyers are big guys. If they want to pay more, what's that to us?"

"I guess it's just a matter of ethics," Harry replied. "As long as I own half of this company, we'll stick with the policies the Bible teaches. You know too, Mark, it doesn't matter whether other people know we cheated them; the Lord will know."

"Listen, if you guys aren't willing to let me mark the equipment up, I don't want to handle it," Nathan Shadburn said as a challenge.

With that Harry got up to leave. "I guess we really don't have anything else to talk about, then."

Shadburn was flabbergasted. "Wait a minute. You don't mean you're actually going to walk out on this deal, do you? I know you guys need the business. I can use maybe $20 million of your equipment over the next few years."

Mark's face paled as he heard the figures. "Twenty million! Harry, that would make the company. Be reasonable."

"I'm sorry," Harry said as he started to walk away, "I guess my beliefs are worth a lot more than $20 million. We'll be glad to do business, Mr. Shadburn, but not at trumped-up prices."

Over the next few weeks, Shadburn called to talk with Harry several more times. He was convinced that Harry had some scheme to make more money off the equipment. But, in spite of every offer he made, Harry turned him down. When Harry realized what Nathan Shadburn was thinking, he said, "Mr. Shadburn, you need to realize that I am not negotiating for a better deal with you. As a Christian I must follow the principles of God's Word, one of which is charging each customer fairly. I can't arbitrarily mark up a product just because the government is the buyer, any more than I could if it were someone else."

"I guess I don't understand that kind of logic," Shadburn said. "If you don't get it, someone else will. It's a policy in the government to always spend all the money allocated in the budget."

"Then I guess they'll be accountable for their decisions," Harry replied. "But I won't violate what I believe to be right."

Another month passed before Harry heard anything further from Nathan Shadburn. In the meantime Mark had been seething and in a perpetually mad mood. He avoided Harry whenever possible and gave him dirty looks when they passed in the hall. One afternoon Mr. Shadburn called and asked Harry if he and Mark could have lunch with him. Harry agreed and left a message at Mark's desk.

Harry looked for Mark near lunch time and was told by the receptionist that he had already left: a clear indication that he was still irritated. At the restaurant where they had chosen to meet, Mark was already waiting and Nathan Shadburn was just arriving. Mark tried to ignore Harry, who made a conscious effort to pass close enough to say hello.

"I'll get right to the point," Shadburn said as they ordered coffee. "I was very skeptical of you two the last time I was here. I thought you were just trying to hold out for more money. Now I realize that you're really serious about this ethics thing.

"I guess I'm getting too callous by working around so many unethical people, whose only god is money. I apologize, and I still would like to handle your equipment." Then, looking at Harry, he quickly added, "I mean, at your standard prices, plus a little for government paperwork. One thing about it: Nobody will be able to undercut us for a long time at these prices."

The look on Mark's face told the entire story as he turned a bright red from embarrassment. Harry just smiled and said a silent prayer of thanks to the Lord, because he knew that his decision might have caused the ruin of their company. In fact, he had just been pondering how they were going to make payroll that month.

"I also know that you guys are having some cash-flow problems with your other distributors, which makes your decision not to allow me to sell a marked-up version even more impressive. I'm willing to prepay for the first $500,000 worth of equipment for delivery to the government. I'd also like a chance to invest in your company if you'll allow me to. It's not often I meet honest men, and I believe what Harry said about God blessing you. I'd really like to be in on that."

Nathan Shadburn ultimately invested over $2 million in Mark and Harry's business, as well as building them a new manufacturing plant and leasing it back at below market cost. Two years after the first meeting, Harry prayed with Nathan to receive Christ. He became their most faithful and active board member and helped to arrange several large sales that built the company into a multimillion-dollar-a-year business.

"Much wealth is in the house of the righteous, but trouble is in the income of the wicked" (Proverbs 15:6).

Part 3

YOUR BUSINESS AND YOUR LIFE

18

Corporations and Partnerships

Any Christian who runs a business is faced with critical decisions on a daily basis. In reality, though, the decisions begin even before the business gets off the ground and questions have to be answered: Should I have a partner? Who should be in control? Should I incorporate? Am I liable if the business fails? Who will take over if I die? Each of these questions can be answered with help from God's Word. If you're already in the middle of an operating business, you may need to reassess some earlier assumptions.

IS IT LEGITIMATE TO INCORPORATE?

Today the use of the corporate shield to avoid personal liability for business losses is accepted as legitimate. But is it really? When businesspeople with decision authority order equipment or materials from another person, does the fact that they were representing a corporation remove their personal responsibility? I believe in great part it depends on the circumstances, just as it would if they were negotiating on their own behalf.

I have observed instances in which the use of the corporate shield was a blatant attempt to defraud others, but I also have seen instances when the presence of the corporate shield was legitimately used to limit the liability of an innocent party. We'll take a brief look at two examples of corporate liability.

Quincy was a tool designer, operating out of his home, where he maintained a small office. He had grown up in the tool-and-die business in his father's small machine shop and had worked at his trade for nearly 16 years before he finally saved up enough money to start a small tool-making company of his own. He was good enough that, soon, larger companies were sending design work to his shop, because he could design much of the equipment they needed for a fraction of what it would cost in their own plants.

Once Quincy's reputation was established, he received many offers to consult with other companies. Eventually his design work exceeded his shop's capacity, so he shut it down and went into full-time consulting. He was offered a lucrative consulting contract with a company that was started by a former automotive executive, who was developing a new car company. The contract was so large that it required Quincy to stop all the other projects he was working on. He was promised an interest in the new company. Plus, he would get a sizable bonus, if he could complete the project in one year.

To design the tools and set up the equipment to do the specialized fabrication, he worked 12-hour days for nearly nine months. Little did he know that the head of the new company was using Quincy's efforts to convince bankers and investors to risk large amounts of money in the new venture. Most of the money was diverted through a variety of other subsidiary companies. Quincy was given a small stipend and large promises to keep him on the job.

Just as the project was nearing completion, he came to the plant one day to find the doors locked and bolted. The owner had shut down the operation and filed for bankruptcy protection. He had never intended to produce cars—only raise money. Not only was Quincy out the profit he never made but also tens of thousands of dollars in other work he could have done.

During this period he had borrowed against his own business to finance his efforts, because the would-be entrepreneur had told him he was having difficulty raising all the capital. This would-be car maker was able to avoid all personal liability, because all the contracts had been executed in the company's name. The corporate shield was used more like a club in this case, a practice which, unfortunately, is not all that unusual today.

In the second example, Dominic Russo operated a small import/export business that specialized in office decorations. He used products from many of the developing countries that were highly promoted by the U.S. government, including window coverings, such as drapes and blinds. The products he marketed were of high quality and were handled through official import/export agencies of the other countries' governments.

Dom made a particularly large sale of window blinds to a national company that required a fireproofing guarantee to meet the local fire codes for office buildings. He contacted his supplier's representatives and gave them the specifications he had been given. Within a week the certification came back, along with the report from the foreign-based testing laboratory.

Based on the data, the company purchased nearly $150,000 worth of window coverings, netting Dom a $45,000 profit—his largest single profit ever.

A few months later one of the office buildings sustained a fire, during which the window coverings flashed and spread the flames. Several people were injured and, consequently, filed lawsuits for several million dollars against the company that owned the building. The company had some of the window coverings tested and found that, not only did they fail the fireproofing requirements, they put off toxic fumes when they flamed. Consequently, the company filed suit against Dom for its losses.

In court, Dom showed evidence that he had relied on the data supplied by the foreign government agency representing the manufacturer, just as the office building owner had. The official response from the government agency was that the company was no longer in business and that it refused all responsibility.

Dominic Russo lost the lawsuit and was assigned damages of more than $15 million. His liability insurance paid the $500,000 it was liable for, and the remainder was assessed against Dom's company, which was forced into involuntary bankruptcy because it had virtually no assets. But he was spared the burden of this debt, because the corporate shield prevented him from being sued personally. In this case the corporate shield provided the function for which it was originally designed: to protect an innocent party.

ARE PARTNERSHIPS SCRIPTURAL?

The next major issue is whether to go into a partnership. If so, what are the scriptural guidelines?

The question, "What is a partnership?" can be answered best by examining the definition of a yoke, which was used as an illustration by the apostle Paul in 2 Corinthians 6:14, when he instructed believers not to be yoked (bound) together with nonbelievers. The word Paul chose to describe a partnership is the Greek word *zugo*, meaning a yoke used to bind two animals together, commonly oxen, for the purpose of pulling a burden.

In Paul's generation this yoke was the perfect example of an equal partnership, such as a marriage. The animals had to be selected with great care because of the burden they would share. If one animal were larger than the other, the heavy yoke would press down on the smaller animal, eventually causing it to collapse under the unequal load.

Also, the animals had to be balanced in temperament. There could be only one lead animal, but there had to be at least one. If both oxen tended toward being the lead animal, they would struggle against the other's dominance and quickly wear themselves out. If neither wanted to lead, they would stop unexpectedly and wander off the track.

Thus the principle of being equally yoked meant exactly that: equal and balanced.

The verse I referred to previously says, *"Do not be bound together with unbelievers; for what partnership have righteousness and law-lessness, or what fellowship has light with darkness?"* (2 Corinthians 6:14). This has been interpreted many ways, but the most straightforward interpretation is "bound together in a common task." The most common biblical example of such a relationship is marriage; in a marriage two people are bound to each other for the common purpose of raising a family.

In the business environment, the most common example is that of an equal partnership. In this arrangement each of the partners is obligated by whatever agreements the other partner(s) arranges. So if one partner commits to a contract in the name of the partnership, all partners are jointly and severally committed.

The obvious logic behind the apostle's admonition not to be bound with nonbelievers in such a relationship is the potential of conflicting values. In a marriage in which one person is a committed believer and the other is not, the potential for conflict and compromise is nearly 100 percent. Since I was an unsaved husband whose wife became a Christian several years before I did, I understand this principle well. I was not an atheist, because I believed there was a God who created the universe, but my relationship to the Creator was one of passive indifference. I logically assumed God could kill me if He really wanted to, so I didn't do anything to rile Him if I could help it.

But when my wife wanted to tithe to her church, I put my foot down on such foolishness. When she wanted our children to go to a Christian kindergarten, I agreed. I figured a little religion never hurt anyone, but I balked when she suggested a Christian school for the boys; after all, there were perfectly good public schools that cost nothing. Our marriage went on like this for the better part of three years. I loved my wife, but I could not see that the things she suggested would do anything other than cost me money and warp our children.

If I hadn't become a Christian, I honestly don't know what the ultimate outcome would have been. In that three-year period of being a non-Christian husband living with a Christian wife, I learned something that I've found to be true in virtually every partnership between a Christian and a non-Christian: If the partnership survives, it is because the Christian has learned to compromise, and it doesn't matter whether it's a marriage or a business partnership.

THE BURDEN OF AN UNEQUAL YOKE

Few knowledgeable Christians would marry a nonbeliever (although some foolishly do). Yet many Christians will enter partnerships with nonbelievers, thinking they can make them work. If they succeed, it is generally because they aren't committed to applying God's principles to their business. Usually these partnerships are rationalized on the basis of economic necessity — not biblical principle.

Please don't misunderstand. It has been my experience that, in general, most people who call themselves Christians are no more ethical or honest in their business dealings than most non-Christians (though they should be). Certainly God did not issue orders that the Jews should not commingle with the nations around them because the Jews were more faithful or ethical! The reason God wanted them to remain separate was because He did not want them to be corrupted by idol worship.

In our society, Christians have been assimilated into the mainstream so thoroughly they often aren't detectable. For the committed believer the decision becomes, "Do I serve God or man?"

Dale was a physician who had just finished his residency in obstetrics and gynecology in the Navy. He was entering private life and had several offers from OB clinics where he wanted to locate — to his knowledge, none of them Christian. He was careful to question each of the managing partners about abortions and other practices he opposed.

He also made his Christian beliefs known and asked if they had any objections.

The list of available clinics dwindled to three, and he made his choice based on the one that was the best and most respected by the OB nurses at the local hospital. He went to work in the practice with real vigor and a commitment to good medicine.

Dale had no immediate difficulties with any of the other physicians regarding the quality and care of mutual patients. (It's not unusual in a medical partnership for one physician to see another's patients. This is particularly true in an obstetrics practice; the "on call" doctors often deliver the babies that arrive during their shifts.) But after Dale had been in the partnership nearly a year, word of a growing problem began to filter through the office. Often he would use the opportunity of the delivery process to share Christ with the patients and, in fact, several had prayed to receive Christ with him.

One of the other doctors confronted Dale directly and demanded that he quit "preaching" to his patients. It seemed that a Jewish patient had taken great exception to his evangelizing.

"I'm really sorry she was offended, Fred," Dale said when his partner confronted him. "But I didn't do anything that would have compromised her childbirth in any way."

"Well, she said that she felt like if she didn't respond the way you expected you might decide not to treat her baby properly," the other physician said with obvious irritation. "Why can't you just leave the evangelizing to Billy Graham and concentrate on your medicine?"

"That's not fair, and you know it," Dale responded defensively. "I do my part and more in this practice. I would never let my Christianity affect my professional attitude toward a patient."

"Listen, I personally don't want any psalm-singing evangelist coming to my door, so I know how the patients feel when you try to corner them during one of the most intense times of their lives. Just don't evangelize my patients anymore! Okay?"

Dale tried his best to limit his evangelism to his own patients, but when he could see an obvious need in a patient's life he would share what he knew to be the answer: Jesus Christ. The final straw came when he was called into a general meeting of the partners over an incident that had occurred the previous day. The meeting was chaired by the senior partner, Gavin Andrews.

"Dale, did you tell Mrs. Kinner that her fetus was a living person and that terminating her pregnancy because of an abnormal reading in the amniotic fluids would be a sin?"

"Yes, I did," Dale responded. "I thought the position of this partnership was to avoid abortions."

"In general that is true," Dr. Andrews replied as he looked at the chart of records before him. "But the amniocentesis shows a high degree of brain damage in the fetus."

"Correction, Doctor," Dale replied. "The test shows a high degree of suspected brain damage. As you know, those tests are not totally accurate."

"Duly noted, Doctor," the older physician agreed. "But the probability of mental retardation is very high. If we recommend that the mother carry the baby to term and it is severely retarded, we stand the risk of being sued."

"But even if the baby is retarded, are we the judge and jury that decide who gets to live?" Dale could see by the faces of his colleagues that their concept of life-and-death decisions was different from his.

Before he could respond further, Fred Rider spoke up, "Is this another one of your religious philosophies, Doctor?"

"Why, yes, it is," Dale replied, thinking about it even as he spoke. "All life is precious in God's eyes, even the retarded among us. Who is to say that the child in question might not become another Mozart? But even if he doesn't, we don't have the right to decide that his or her quality of life is any less precious."

"You see, I told you that eventually his wild-eyed religious ideas would end up costing all of us," Dr. Rider spat out. "We don't need a resident preacher on staff. If he stays, I'm going."

"Calm down, Fred," Gavin Andrews said as he closed the file. "I'm sure we can work this out. Right, Dale?"

"No, I really don't think so, Gavin," Dale replied as he glanced at the men around the table.

"You're all good physicians, and I know you want to do what is best for your patients, but I believe their greatest need is for salvation. To me, medicine is a skill to help open the door to share Jesus Christ. Now I can see that we'll always be working at odds over that goal. Fred is right when he says that my attitude will ultimately reflect on the partnership. If we were in accord, that wouldn't be a problem. But since we're not, it will be."

Dale handed in his resignation and began to shift his workload to the other partners. He could have stayed on with the partnership indefinitely and enjoyed lifetime financial security, but the cost would have been to compromise what he knew to be God's will for this life.

WHAT ABOUT EXISTING PARTNERSHIPS?

Often I am asked about already-existing partnerships between a Christian and unsaved family members. The principles in God's Word don't differentiate between unsaved family members and unsaved friends when it comes to partnerships. If I interpret correctly what the apostle Paul said in 1 Corinthians 7:10–15, if an unsaved partner desires to stay, the Christian should agree, but if the unsaved partner wants to leave the Christian should release him or her. In existing partnerships Christians should seek to remain as they are unless the relationship forces them to compromise their spiritual convictions.

If the unsaved partner is a father or mother, however, I believe there are higher principles governing that relationship. *"God said, 'Honor your father and mother,' and, 'He who speaks evil of father or mother, let him be put to death'"* (Matthew 15:4). Thus the principle of honoring our fathers and mothers is a command that must ultimately supersede that of being unequally yoked. Obviously a Christian should not allow even a parent to force him or her to sin. But assuming that is not an issue, do not kick your father out of your business.

GUIDELINES FOR ASSESSING A PARTNERSHIP

There are two fundamental questions that any Christian thinking about joining a partnership should ask: "Who is in charge?" and "Do we agree on fundamental values?"

1. Who Is in Charge?

Often this question is not asked in the formative stages of a partnership because one Christian doesn't want to embarrass another. Usually if the business just breaks even there is no particular problem. But if the business either succeeds greatly or fails, this issue will become the central one.

The power that comes through controlling a successful enterprise will test the commitment of the strongest Christian. If the issue of who is in charge is not settled up front, it can easily create a rift in the partnership.

Conversely, if the business (or investment) gets into financial difficulty, strong, decisive leadership will be required to pull it out. Saving a business that is in trouble may well mean laying off family members involved in the enterprise and restricting the outflow of money. For one partner to tell another that he or she has to go out and get a job because the business can't support two (or more) people is impossible, unless the issue of control is settled from the outset.

Richard was half-owner in an electronics manufacturing firm. His partner, Gene, was a brilliant engineer who had developed several patented products, which their company manufactured and sold to other companies. The business was divided into two basic areas: research and development, under Gene's supervision; and sales, under Richard's authority. The idea was to have equal but separate responsibilities—a great concept that rarely, if ever, works.

For nearly three years the business just barely got by financially. Richard ran the business side of things, and Gene ran the engineering side. Then one of the products became very successful and the company was launched in a big way. For the first time they had the capital to move into a facility that would provide adequate office and manufacturing space. But suddenly Richard found himself in frequent arguments with his partner over equipping offices versus buying additional test equipment.

He apparently doesn't understand that we need an office environment that will be more comfortable for the employees, Richard thought as he walked away from their meeting. In his mind he went back over the conversation they had just had.

"Listen, Richard," Gene had said. "I don't see why it's necessary to spend 20 grand on office furniture and carpets. I need all the capital we can get our hands on right now to develop the new computerized version of our equipment."

"But we've hardly scratched the surface for the sales of the last unit," Richard had argued. "If we come out with another model right now, we'll kill the sales for the existing units. I suggest that we hold off on the development of the computerized version for a while. Besides, most of our customers don't really need the computerized model. They don't have the volume to justify the additional cost."

"I want to start work on the new model," Gene had said with a final emphasis in his voice. "This business has been built on my designs so far, and now I finally have the funds to do some real research."

"That's great for DuPont or GE," Richard countered. "They have the product base to support their research. But we don't. We need to sell what we have and concentrate on repackaging it for use in smaller companies."

"I'm not going to spend my time redesigning hardware, Richard. I need to be working on new ideas. I know you'll find a market for them; don't worry about it. Maybe we'll redo the offices next year, after we've completed the design on this new line."

Richard realized that he was considered the lesser partner because of his lack of technical expertise. But he also realized that the best product in the world was worthless if it didn't sell. And Gene was intent on pursuing his own interests, regardless of the need.

Looking back, Richard realized that they had avoided discussing any details of their partnership. Since they were both Christians, they had assumed they would be able to work out any difficulties as they came up. Now he was seeing another side of his partner. The business was simply a means for Gene to pursue his interests: design and development of new equipment. Richard was there to sell Gene's products to allow Gene to develop more.

Richard decided that he had three basic choices: (1) quit the partnership, (2) fight for his rights as an equal partner, or (3) allow his partner to control the business. After praying about his decision and discussing it with his wife, Richard came to the conclusion that he should give a portion of his stock in the business to Gene, thus securing his partner's position as majority owner.

The next day when Gene came into his office he found an envelope with one share of stock enclosed on his desk. He was confused. He had assumed that Richard would fight him for control of the business. In fact, he and his wife had discussed the situation and decided that, if necessary, they would go to court to maintain control. Staring at the stock certificate, he realized that Richard had done voluntarily what no court would have imposed upon him. He walked over to his new junior partner's office.

"Richard, why did you do this?" he asked in a subdued tone as he held the certificate in his hand.

"Well, I prayed about it, and Donna and I decided that either we believe what the Bible says or we don't. The apostle Paul wrote in

Philippians 2:3, *'Do nothing from selfishness or empty conceit, but with humility of mind let each of you regard one another as more important than himself.'* Since we know there can't be two heads of a business, I figured this would settle the issue. So you just tell me what you want me to do, Boss, and I'll do it."

Gene just stood there, not saying anything. He knew that God had just taught him a lesson in humility through his partner. He replied, "I guess I would like for you to pray with me, Richard. As you know, I've always had a problem with my pride. I never could've done what you just did—not even under a court order. I feel a little like a giant coming out in his battle attire, only to be met by a kid with a slingshot."

Richard and Gene spent the next half-hour on their knees in prayer together. This became their routine for the next three years they were in business together. From that day on, Gene never attempted to mandate a decision on Richard. Instead he would present his ideas and then ask for his partner's perspective. Without exception he followed Richard's leading in all business decisions, including the research and development budget. The business was eventually purchased by a larger company that made Richard the director of the marketing group and Gene the head of research and development. It just proves that *"The reward of humility and the fear of the Lord are riches, honor and life"* (Proverbs 22:4).

2. What Are Your Absolute Values?

One of the best exercises in preparation for any potential partnership is for everyone involved to spend some time praying about what his or her absolutes are. By absolute values, I mean the principles by which you operate and will not compromise for anyone. You won't be totally aware of all of them the first time you attempt to make your list, but the more you do this exercise the more will surface.

I rather suspect the men and women in politics or ministry who have gotten caught up in their sins never took the time to solidify their absolutes. Later they realized that they had compromised what they believed, but by then it was too late.

If you are to be in partnership with someone, both of you should know from the outset what the other stands for. Partnerships between believers are not prohibited scripturally, but as the apostle Paul said, *"All things are lawful, but not all things are profitable. All things are lawful, but not all things edify"* (1 Corinthians 10:23). In other words, you may be allowed to enter a partnership with another believer, but such an alliance will not necessarily be profitable. Be very sure that anyone with whom you will share a partnership also shares your personal values and convictions.

There are values and convictions that should be discussed with any potential partners.

a. Are we committed to giving to the Lord's work and to charity from the business? If so, how much and to whom?
b. Will we sue to collect debts?
c. Will we hire family members in the business?
d. Will we use non-Christian managers or employees?
e. How many hours per week will we commit to the business?
f. How much travel time away from home will we spend?
g. Will we evangelize through the business?
h. Will we sell the business at some future date?
i. How will the death of a partner affect the distribution of assets?
j. Are we willing to be accountable to each other and to an outside group?

LAYING THE GROUNDWORK FOR A SUCCESSFUL PARTNERSHIP

I can honestly say that I have seen some very successful partnerships, but I have seen many more fail than succeed. Usually the deciding factors were the willingness of each party to be totally honest from the outset and the partners' mutual commitment to the principles described in God's Word.

The best counsel I can give anyone about partnerships is to approach them with a high degree of caution. Unraveling a partnership is usually as heart-wrenching as a divorce. It would be better to hurt someone's feelings up front by declining a proposed partnership than to devastate that person when the partnership fails.

If you can reach a mutually satisfactory agreement on a partnership, I recommend that every single detail be written down. It has been said that most of us will retain only 10 percent of what we hear a month after we hear it. Combine that with the fact that one person will often misunderstand what another says, and it is easy to see why so many business partners have difficulty sorting out the agreements later.

The simplest way to resolve this problem is to draw up a written agreement and have all the parties sign it. Even this will not resolve all misunderstandings, but at least it will help, and you'll be in better shape than the average Christian partnership. If a prospective partner is offended by the fact that you want to write out the total agreement, it is better to know that partner's attitude in advance.

ARE LIMITED PARTNERSHIPS REALLY PARTNERSHIPS?

During the seventies and eighties a new legal entity called a limited partnership came into common use in the United States. Its purpose was to allow individuals to invest in a business venture and acquire the tax benefits of a partnership without the liabilities of a full partnership.

In such a business relationship, the individual investors are limited both in their liability and in their authority. The managing partner, called the general partner, retains total management authority within the confines of the existing laws. The general partner also assumes all liability for the operation of the partnership. The limited partners are liable only to the extent of their capital contribution or assignment.

Without a doubt many, if not most, of these limited partnerships are bad investments, and many people have lost a great deal of money in worthless investment schemes. Because of this some Christian financial teachers have labeled limited partnerships unscriptural, saying they are unequal yokes.

I agree that most Christians should avoid bad investments and that Christians who risk their money with unbelievers may be opening themselves up to compromise in terms of the types of investments they acquire. But I don't believe that a limited partnership constitutes a yoke. If the legal entity involved had been labeled a "limited liability investment," most Christian teachers would have no difficulty with it. Since its title carries the word *partnership*, it raises immediate controversy.

Without a doubt I would counsel Christians to avoid most limited partnerships on the basis of good stewardship. They may be bad deals, but they aren't yokes.

EMPLOYEE-EMPLOYER RELATIONSHIP

Many Christians are unduly concerned about working for unbelievers or having unbelievers working for them because of being unequally yoked. Such a relationship is not a yoke or partnership; it is an authority relationship, in which one person is clearly the authority and the other the subordinate. Unless the Christian employee is being forced to compromise his or her Christian principles, there is no scriptural admonition against this type of authority relationship.

IS STOCK OWNERSHIP A YOKE?

To determine if owning stock in a company constitutes a yoke is not as simple as it would first appear. Obviously if someone buys a few shares in IBM or GE, that person is not yoked together with those companies; he or she is purchasing only the right to an equitable distribution of dividends and a minority vote in company policies.

But what about a corporation owned by two people, with each holding equal shares? Is that a yoke? If the intent is to create an equal sharing arrangement, it is a partnership, just as certainly as if the term *partnership* were used.

The simple solution to an "unequal yoke" in such an arrangement is to do what Richard did: go to the other partner(s) and ask if he or she (they) would be willing to accept some of your stock so that the line of authority would be clearly defined. I would imagine that such a move could be the first step in many unsaved partners coming to the Lord. Even if they don't, such a move could be the first step for many Christians in accepting God's Word as their absolute authority.

|| 19 ||

Business Tithing

The principle of tithing from a business is not dramatically different from tithing from personal income. Actually, most of the Old Testament Scriptures on giving deal with business-generated income, since few people were actually employees in the sense they are today. The vast majority of people in Old Testament times were self-employed in agriculture, as were most Americans prior to the twentieth century.

I have discussed the principle of tithing in other books, but I would like to answer once again the questions that are most often asked by businesspeople.

IS THE PRINCIPLE OF TITHING APPLICABLE TO CHRISTIANS?

Some Christian teachers today believe that the tithe is not applicable to Christians because it is an Old Testament law pertaining only to Jews. I believe this teaching is in error, as is the opposing view that tithing is an absolute commandment for all God's people. I do not believe that tithing is a commandment for God's people; nor is it any kind of qualification for admission into Christianity. But, having said that, I must add that I also don't believe you offset one extreme by adopting the other.

The tithe was never a law. Although tithing is mentioned 15 times in the books of the Law, there is never a punishment prescribed for failing to tithe. If you examine the laws given by God to man, you will find many very severe punishments, including execution, for failure to observe the laws. However, one Jew was never allowed to punish another for failing to tithe.

It is true that there was a consequence associated with failing to tithe: *"You are cursed with a curse, for you are robbing Me, the whole nation of you!"* (Malachi 3:9). Clearly the tithe was always intended to be a voluntary contribution to God's work, as the apostle Paul so clearly stated: *"Let each one do just as he has purposed in his heart; not grudgingly or under compulsion; for God loves a cheerful giver"* (2 Corinthians 9:7).

Whenever the Lord or one of His apostles discussed a biblical issue, any changes they made to the Old Testament law were stated very clearly. Examples of this would be the issues of divorce, sacrifices, retribution, and the Sabbath. If the issue of tithing had been a question for the Christians of Paul's day, I'm sure he would have clearly outlined the changes in the Old Testament teaching to make it conform to the Lord's will for Christians.

In other words, the principle of the tithe is as applicable to a twentieth-century Christian as it was to Abraham, who gave the first tithe many years before the law was given to man by Moses (see Genesis 14:20). It is an acknowledgment of God's sovereignty over everything we have, both the spiritual and the material.

I agree with what J. Oswald Sanders said in his book, *Enjoying Intimacy with God*: "Will a Christian who is experiencing intimacy with his Lord wish to take advantage of grace so that he can give less to God's work than the less privileged Jew who knew nothing of Calvary's sacrifice?" I think not.

SHOULD I TITHE FROM MY NET OR MY GROSS?

Steven was a new Christian attending a Bible study with a group of other Christians. He had come out of an agnostic background and knew little about Christ's teachings, except what he had heard as a boy in Sunday school. One thing that had stuck in his mind was the need to tithe to God from his "first fruits." So Steven asked the group: "Does God want me to tithe from my net or my gross?"

The answer from most of the men was, "You should always tithe from your gross."

"Do all of you tithe from the gross income of your businesses?" he asked with the innocent honesty displayed by most new Christians.

The group was totally silent. Todd Grey, another businessman in the group, spoke up, "Well, you can't tithe from your gross income in business. It's not possible. So you tithe from your net."

"But why should I tithe from my personal gross income but not from the business?" Steven asked. "Is there a different principle for a business?"

"You have to be practical about this," still another member of the group said, reversing his original position. "You can't tithe from your gross sales because most businesses don't make a 10-percent gross profit."

Steven left that meeting confused and dissatisfied with the answers he had heard. He could not accept the idea that God's Word would deal with personal income in one fashion and corporate income in another. So he called me to ask if he could come by to discuss this issue. I agreed, saying I had been wrestling with the same issue and believed I had found some answers.

Steven asked the big question as soon as he came in: "Larry, should I tithe my net or my gross?"

"Let me ask you something," I replied. "Are you asking because you really want to know, or are you looking for a loophole in God's Word that will allow you to give less?"

He was a little surprised by the question and somewhat offended as he answered, "I'd like to do what God's Word says. I just can't discern exactly what to do, since it doesn't look possible."

"The reason I asked that question, Steven, is that I believe giving is always a voluntary act on the part of God's people. If people are reluctant to give, I always encourage them not to."

"Why would you say that? I thought God's Word commands us to give," Steven said.

"Absolutely not!" I said. "God loves a cheerful giver, as the apostle Paul said in 2 Corinthians 9:7, and that really hasn't changed since Abraham gave the first tithe many years before the law was given to men through Moses. You can read about it in Genesis 14:20."

"But what about the requirement to give a tithe in Malachi?" Steven asked.

"God had Malachi challenge the people of Israel because they were robbing God: *'Will a man rob God? Yet you are robbing Me! But you say, "How have we robbed Thee?" In tithes and offerings'* (Malachi 3:8). But He never commanded a punishment for not tithing. There is always a consequence of disobedience, and Malachi states this in verse 9: *'You are cursed with a curse.'* But God does not want grudging gifts. After all, the purpose of giving is to show respect and thankfulness for God's authority over our lives, isn't it?"

"I guess so. I just never thought about it in that way," Steven answered, still confused. "But how can I give a tenth of my gross income from my business when I don't make that much profit? If I give 10 percent of my gross revenues, I won't be able to pay my bills."

"About how much do you pay in taxes a year?" I asked.

"Golly, I don't know exactly, but it's probably about 20 percent or so," Steven answered.

"How are you able to pay 20 percent of your income in taxes?"

"Well, the government requires that I do it," Steven answered as he began to see the connection.

"And what about interest, Steven? What percent of your income is dedicated to paying your creditors for the loan of their money?"

"I don't really know, but it's probably 6 to 8 percent average," he replied.

"Then you already know where God's tithe is going. It's going to fund the government that now provides many of the services that God ordained His people to provide. And the rest is going to pay interest to the devourer. Borrowing is a consequence of ignoring God's statutes and commandments, according to what the Lord said in Deuteronomy."

I pulled out my Bible and read, "*'The alien who is among you shall rise above you higher and higher, but you shall go down lower and lower. He shall lend to you, but you shall not lend to him; he shall be the head, and you shall be the tail. So all these curses shall come on you and pursue you and overtake you until you are destroyed, because you would not obey the Lord your God by keeping His commandments and His statutes which He commanded you'* (Deuteronomy 28: 43–45)."

"So you're saying that because God's people have chosen to ignore His principles and go their own way, He has allowed the government and the lenders to come in and take His portion away?" Steven asked as he considered this "revelation."

"I believe that is essentially true. We have allowed ourselves to become so attuned to the world around us that we are now following its principles rather than God's. The lack of giving is a sign of our disobedience—not the cause of it."

"But what can I do to break out of this snare now that I'm in it?" Steven asked. "I really want to honor the Lord with my life and my finances."

"It would appear that we can't do very much about the cost of government right now," I answered, "so I guess the best we can do is to get ourselves out of debt and give that portion to the Lord."

"But that may take me several years," Steven argued. "What can I do in the meantime?"

"Just do what you can. If you can't give a full tithe and still pay your creditors what has been promised, then give what you can. But have a goal to get totally debt-free and then use the interest you were paying for the Lord's work."

Steven began by giving a small percentage from his business income, while maintaining his own personal giving from his salary. It took him almost seven years to become totally debt-free. In the process he passed by some good business opportunities that he could have participated in if he had been willing to go further into debt.

Most of his Christian friends thought he had gone off the deep end when he heeded my counsel. The standard argument is almost always the same: "You can make a lot more money to be able to give more later." But my experience has been that somehow most people never seem to get around to giving more later.

Steven is now essentially debt-free and gives a tithe from the adjusted gross income of his company. He may never be listed among the billionaires of our society, but he is probably high on a much more important list.

The Bible says, *"Honor the Lord from your wealth, and from the first of all your produce"* (Proverbs 3:9). The first from all your produce can also be accurately restated as "your harvest." When a farmer brings in a crop, he has expenses associated with it. These include the wages of his laborers and his payments to suppliers and creditors.

In our generation the average farmer could not tithe even a fraction of his harvest because his costs are high and his profits low. Yet I know several farmers who are able to tithe and still maintain excellent lifestyles. The single common denominator among them is that they are all debt-free. They don't borrow to plant their crops, and they don't borrow to pay their bills. They borrow only to expand their operations, and they never use their existing property as collateral to buy more land.

Many Christians in our generation think that giving a tithe from their companies' incomes is virtually impossible. And it is, as long as a Christian continues to operate by the world's rules. But isn't it interesting how one person's impossible task becomes another's primary testimony?

Perhaps the two men most noted for their giving in the twentieth century are R. G. LeTourneau and Stanley Tamm. I never had the privilege of meeting Mr. LeTourneau, since he died before I became a Christian, but I have met Stanley Tamm several times. He is a good businessman who has developed a very successful company (U.S. Plastics) and dedicated the majority of the proceeds from it to the Lord's work.

The issue of tithing from the gross or net was not at question to these men. As LeTourneau said in his book, *Movers of Men and Mountains*, "I shovel the money out, and God shovels it back in — and God has a larger shovel than I do." A common characteristic of great givers is that they keep their businesses debt-free and thus are free to give the creditors' portion to the Lord's work. That may seem a little radical in our generation, but if it were easy anyone could do it. I'm convinced that God's Word will work in this generation as well.

HOW CAN I GIVE NONCASH ASSETS?

I am frequently asked, "How can I give out of the increase if most of it is noncash assets?"

A good example of this can be seen in farming. A farmer may say, "I hardly made anything this year," when, in fact, he added a combine, a new tractor, and another barn. The return was there, but it was in non-cash assets. So how can you give in such a situation?

The answer for many Christians is to give a partial ownership in the business. That way, as the business prospers, so does the Lord's portion. This is exactly what Stanley Tamm did with his business. He deeded a portion of his company stock to a foundation established to do the Lord's work. If a dividend was declared, the foundation got its share. If the company is ever sold, the foundation will get its equitable portion.

Another example of God-sized giving can be found in Paul Meyers, founder of Success Motivation Institute (SMI) and several dozen other companies. Mr. Meyers said he was greatly influenced by the testimony of R. G. LeTourneau, who as a young man committed that one day he would give away 90 percent of his income, which he did. Then at age 65, LeTourneau committed to giving 100 percent! He has given countless millions to the Lord's work, resulting in tens of thousands of souls being saved. Our society could use a lot more Stanley Tamms, R. G. LeTourneaus, and Paul J. Meyerses.

Many Christian business owners give their products, as well as money, to the Lord's work. When we were refurbishing our ministry offices, for example, a Christian who owned a window-blind company donated the blinds for our windows. Other Christians have donated trucks, airplanes, food, and office equipment to various ministries. All of these gifts represent costs that the recipient ministries did not have to incur. This may well be the best form of gift, in fact. I know that every time I look up and see the blinds in my office, I thank the Lord for the businessman who gave of his time and talent to further our work. I also remember to pray for his business regularly.

The gift of stock in a company can be a double benefit to both the ministry and the businessperson. Since existing tax laws allow the value of a noncash gift to be claimed at its fair market value, the donor can receive a tax deduction above the actual cost. For instance, if a donor has a cost basis in his or her company's stock of $10 per share, but the current market value is $100 per share, the tax-deductible gift value of the stock is $100. Since the stock wasn't actually sold by the donor, there is no capital gains tax due, so the entire gift value is a deduction.

If the stock had been sold and the proceeds donated, the donor would have to include the sale in his or her income for tax purposes and then deduct the gift. Donating the stock prior to sale, therefore, represents a significant savings. If the ministry is a nonprofit organization, the stock can then be sold without incurring the capital gains tax.

One interesting side note is that many business owners have used the gift of company stock to avoid some significant transfer (gift) taxes when they give stock in a closely held corporation to their heirs. Knowing that the IRS tends to undervalue the stock of closely held corporations when it is donated to nonprofit organizations, they give the stock and then ask the IRS to establish the value of the gift. Once they receive the estimate (for donation purposes), they then give stock to their families and use the lower estimate provided by the IRS to establish that value as well. It's hard for the government to object, since they made the valuation!

WHAT ABOUT AFTER-DEATH BEQUESTS?

Much has been said in Christian circles about making bequests to the Lord's work after one's death. For those expecting to die prematurely I believe this is a good idea. But it is far better to "Do your givin' while you're livin', so you're knowin' where it's goin'," as a good friend of mine once put it.

Ministries come and go, and usually as the leaders come and go. A ministry that might be entirely sound and viable during your career years may go sour as the founder(s) passes on. I believe it is far better to give what you can to help such a ministry in its growth years than to wait until your death. Nevertheless, to have a plan in the event of your untimely death is both logical and biblical.

It is my personal conviction, based on my observations, that a Christian should not endow ministries beyond his or her lifetime. All too often a well-endowed organization becomes complacent, and complacency breeds liberality. A look at any of the well-heeled universities in the Northeast will verify this observation. A look at most denominations that have been around 100 years or more will also confirm this tendency. I suspect a great many saints of past years would choke at how their endowments are now being used to promote every anti-Christian idea from abortion to homosexuality.

Obviously, there are exceptions, such as the Moody Bible Institute, the Navigators, and many others. So if you plan to endow an organization, you need to pray and seek God's wisdom, as God's Word suggests: *"If any of you lacks wisdom, let him ask of God, who gives to all men generously and without reproach, and it will be given to him"* (James 1:5).

Remember, only God is wise enough to see the future. Do your giving while you are still around to see how it is used. *"The generous man will be prosperous, and he who waters will himself be watered"* (Proverbs 11:25).

20

Retirement Decisions

"A little sleep, a little slumber, a little folding of the hands to rest" (Proverbs 6:10).

I wonder how many American Christians associate that verse and the several dozen similar Scriptures with retirement? Not very many, I would suspect, and yet the sentiment expressed in that verse is the retirement philosophy of the majority of Americans (Christians included). Their desire is to work just enough to be able to retire and do what they want. Generally it's because many people are trapped in fruitless careers and are trying to escape through retirement. That's a waste of a lot of good years.

We have been sold a lie about retirement, especially Christian business owners. I would challenge any Christian, on the basis of God's Word, to justify the millions of dollars being hoarded for what we call retirement.

IS RETIREMENT SCRIPTURAL?

It is interesting to note that the only reference to retirement in all the Bible is found in Numbers 8:25: *"But at the age of fifty years they shall retire from service in the work and not work any more."* That's not much of a foundation to go on when building a multibillion-dollar retirement system like we have today, particularly since the temple priests referred to then took on other priestly duties. Any thinking Christian would have to conclude that our system of retirement is not biblical and, therefore, is a passing fad. One argument I've heard in favor of our retirement system is that people live longer than they used to, and so they need to retire because they are no longer productive. That is true to some extent.

However, when you compare the life span of an average American today with that of the first several generations of people in the book of Genesis, our oldest person would be a youngster by comparison. It seems they stayed productive and useful for quite a few more decades back then.

I believe there are some principles taught in Proverbs that can be applied to retirement, but only in relation to slowing down as we get older—not stopping. *"Go to the ant, O sluggard, observe her ways and be wise, which, having no chief, officer or ruler, prepares her food in the summer, and gathers her provision in the harvest"* (Proverbs 6:6–8).

Statistics tell us that the "harvest" years for most of us are between the ages of 25 and 60. Therefore, it would be entirely prudent to lay aside some of the surplus for the latter phase of our lives, when our income abilities decline, so that we don't become burdens to our children.

But, it is important to balance this reasoning with the instruction the Lord gave us in the parable of the so-called rich fool. *"The land of a certain rich man was very productive. And he began reasoning to himself, saying, 'What shall I do, since I have no place to store my crops?' And he said, 'This is what I will do: I will tear down my barns and build larger ones, and there I will store all my grain and my goods. And I will say to my soul, "Soul, you have many goods laid up for many years to come; take your ease, eat, drink, and be merry."' But God said to him, 'You fool! This very night your soul is required of you; and now who will own what you have prepared?' So is the man who lays up treasure for himself, and is not rich toward God"* (Luke 12:16–21).

At what point does good planning become hoarding? When what you lay aside is sufficient to meet your needs for 100 years and your wants for another 50 (that's my personal definition).

Consider the example of the apostle Paul. He had certainly served his time in the service of the Lord even before he began his third missionary journey. No one would have faulted him if he had elected to retire at Corinth or Ephesus and write his memoirs. He might even have returned to his Mediterranean home near the city of Tarsus and lived out the latter part of his life in peace.

Instead, Acts 21 depicts his last travels after he told the elders of the church at Ephesus that he was headed back to Jerusalem and they would never see him again. Paul was probably in his late 60s—old even by today's standards. By the standards of his generation, he was ancient. It was reported that Paul required a constant traveling companion to assist him because of his failing eyesight. Even so, he gave no thought about retirement as long as he was able to perform the duties God assigned him. If retirement is a biblical principle, God apparently forgot to mention it to Paul.

I recall what R. G. LeTourneau said to his long-time friend Dr. Robert Barnhouse about retirement: "Maybe I will retire someday, but I'm just too busy right now." He was about 80 years old at the time.

In the last year of his life LeTourneau was traveling across the U.S. and into South America, sharing the Gospel and helping teach third-world Christians the skills they needed to feed themselves. Obviously he felt he would have plenty of time to relax when he reached eternity. That is a perspective many Christians could benefit from today.

Remember the words of our Lord: *"For this reason you be ready too; for the Son of Man is coming at an hour when you do not think He will. Who then is the faithful and sensible slave whom his master put in charge of his household to give them their food at the proper time? Blessed is that slave whom his master finds so doing when he comes"* (Matthew 24:44–46). If you really think His work is better done in retirement, have at it. But if not, then reconsider your goals.

A recent study done by Harvard University supports this scriptural perspective. (No doubt it has been a long time since anything from Harvard has supported the Scriptures.) The study involved two groups of Harvard graduates between the ages of 65 and 75. One group of 100 men retired at 65 and the other group of 100 continued to work to age 75. (In an effort to narrow down the variables, the study excluded those men who had suffered any major health problems prior to 65.)

In the first group, those who had retired at 65, seven out of eight were dead by age 75. In the second group, men who continued to work, only one in seven had died. The conclusion drawn by this study was that retiring too early in life significantly reduces one's probability of surviving that additional 10 years (or more) by a factor of six!

It is possible that this study would not be representative of our society as a whole, since so many people are employed at work they dislike. As far as stress goes, therefore, it probably doesn't matter whether they quit or continue. (But that's a subject for an entire book itself.)

SHOULD YOU SELL YOUR BUSINESS?

One of the logical questions of any business owner approaching retirement is, "Should I sell out?" Often when a business is sold it goes to the highest bidder. That's great for the owner(s) and major stockholders. But what about the others who have labored long and hard to make the business successful? And what about those who have never had the opportunity to work in a Christian environment and perhaps never will? If the highest bidder is a non-Christian, that business will be lost as a tool for God.

I would like to present a radically different perspective on this issue. As a Christian in charge of a company that has been dedicated to the Lord, you do not have a right to sell out to non-Christians just because it's more profitable. Either you believe (there's that word again) that God is the owner or you don't.

If this concept irritates you a little, then you need to take a good hard look at your attitude about stewardship. Stewards never own the assets with which they have been entrusted; they merely manage them for another. If you accept the premise that God owns everything, then it's hard to justify selling God's company to unbelievers. I have known many Christians who outwardly professed to turn everything over to the Lord but whose total surrender broke down when they had a chance to sell out at a significant profit.

Obviously, if the company is publicly held or you are not the majority owner, the decision may not be yours. Remember that God only holds you responsible for what you can do, not what you can't do.

It seems totally contradictory to me that a Christian would labor to instill Christian principles in his or her business, only to sell out to non-Christians who will dismantle virtually everything that has been done in the Lord's name. The negative witness this action brings to the employees is clear: "You say one thing but do another." You would be like the workman the Lord described in Luke 14:28 who began the construction of a tower without having considered the entire costs.

Cliff had helped to start a chemical company that had grown to several million dollars a year in sales. A few years earlier he had bought out his partner when he decided to retire, so for the past 10 years Cliff had been the lord and master of his company—literally. He made virtually every decision and ruled the company with an iron hand. He was known as a dictator and tyrant—but one who paid very well. He had to, his employees said, or no one would work for him.

Then, at nearly 50 years of age, Cliff lost his wife to cancer and found himself questioning his whole value system. He began to attend church and through the influence of a business associate made a profession of Jesus Christ as his Savior. For the next several months he attended virtually every Bible study he could find and began to grow and mature spiritually. As he did, his attitudes toward people changed; his employees actually saw him smile at them as they passed in the halls. Then at one of the Bible studies he heard of a seminar on how to operate a business for the Lord and decided to attend.

At that "Business by the Book" seminar Cliff heard from Christian businesspeople he knew to be extremely successful, and yet who had chosen to dedicate their businesses to Jesus Christ. He made a vow then and there to do the same with his business.

For the next several years Cliff worked at sharing Christ with his employees, customers, and associates. To show his employees that he cared for them, he implemented many changes in his business, including a daily devotional time, free seminars, and a tape library. Over the years many of his employees came to know the Lord, including most of his managers. Many others left because they couldn't agree with his actions. Within a period of about five years, virtually all of Cliff's managers were Christians.

Unfortunately, Cliff became increasingly discouraged with the level of spiritual growth on the part of his employees. In spite of the time and money he had invested, most continued in the same old track they had been in when he began. So he began to direct more and more of his personal efforts outside the company, sharing with peers and other Christians who were intent on serving the Lord. (In other words, he decided to do his fishing in a stocked pond.) The rewards of this were immediate and effective as he found hundreds of like-minded Christian businesspeople who were willing to listen.

Within a few months Cliff found himself discouraged with the business and felt called to minister to other groups. When the opportunity arose to sell the company, he jumped at it. The group that bought the business was a non-Christian conglomerate that was seeking to expand its business in his industry. Their decision to buy was based purely on the potential profits that could be reaped in the chemical business.

Within a month of taking control of the business, the conglomerate had erased every vestige of Christianity within the company and replaced most of the previous managers with its own. Cliff's 10-year effort to develop a Christian-run enterprise was completely dismantled in a matter of days. Many of those who had shared Cliff's vision found themselves out of a job.

Cliff fared well because his interest in the company netted him several millions of dollars with which to serve the Lord. I sincerely doubt that the next employer will have any luck getting any of Cliff's previous managers to believe his personal testimony. As James said, *"But prove yourselves doers of the word, and not merely hearers who delude themselves"* (James 1:22).

No one can dispute an owner's legal right to sell his or her business to whomever he or she chooses. But the attitude of ownership conflicts with the principle of stewardship. Consider what the apostle Paul wrote: *"Do not merely look out for your own personal interests, but also for the interests of others. Have this attitude in yourselves which was also in Christ Jesus"* (Philippians 2:4–5).

EMPLOYEE RETIREMENT BENEFITS

If, as an employer, you set aside funds for the purpose of retirement or even supplemental income for your latter years, then an equivalent amount of money should be made available to those who are under your watch care. In fact, most employees probably have a greater need for supplemental funds in their older years because they don't have as much income-earning ability as their employers in their earlier years.

It would be easy to adopt the traditional attitude: "To the victor belong the spoils." In other words, "I built it; I deserve it." Each of us can be very thankful, however, that God has not adopted that same mentality. After all, He owns it all and has an absolute right to keep it for Himself, doesn't He?

It's a bad witness that in our generation the secular world has taken up the rights of the average worker, rather than the Christian business leaders in America. In past generations the argument could be made that we lacked the resources to provide for everyone adequately. That is no longer a valid argument. Just look at the "barns" of business leaders today! Perhaps limited resources will be a valid argument again if our economy, which is based on shifting sand, collapses. But in the meantime most successful business owners can provide for their employees' needs, both current and deferred.

You must make your decisions based on the principles provided in God's Word, not on the visible image of the church and its ministries today. I can think of few businesses that operate as unbiblically as some ministries I have observed. Their leaders build great edifices to their fund-raising abilities, while forcing many of their staff to exist on subsistence-level incomes (or less).

Perhaps the classic example of this is the situation in Christian schools throughout our country. Those to whom we have entrusted the future generation are forced to live at or below poverty level! What kind of example does this provide the students, who come to see Christianity as a "loser's" religion?

Many full-time vocational Christians approach the latter years of their lives with concern because they have no cash reserves or retirement funds. Look around and see if there isn't someone in full-time service whom you can help. As Luke wrote, *"And the congregation of those who believed were of one heart and soul; and not one of them claimed that anything belonging to him was his own; but all things were common property to them"* (Acts 4:32).

These principles are just as applicable today as they were in the first century. It's all a matter of application, as Leonard Rolls, a physician friend of mine, discovered. He was a member of a large professional association (P.A.) with over 20 employees. His income was nearly $200,000 a year, so he was consistently in the highest tax bracket. To partially offset the taxes, he joined the P.A.'s pension/profit sharing plan and invested several thousand dollars a year.

Then the tax laws on retirement plans changed, requiring the association to begin a retirement plan for the nonprofessional employees as well as the professionals. The group hired the best pension attorneys in town to find any loopholes in the new laws.

"I think the attorney has come up with a novel way to reduce what we'll have to provide for the employees," Dr. Rolls said to the other partners in the group at their weekly meeting. "He recommends that we pay into the plan based on our Social Security withholding ratio."

"Great idea," Dr. Benz said enthusiastically. "That means the lower-paid employees won't be eligible for much, and our portion will be the largest, since we pay the most to Social Security."

"Yes, that's what the attorneys said too. They're sure this method will stand the test of the IRS, since we're using the government's own system of allocating compensation."

"I love it," said Dr. Avalon, the oldest partner. "I never have liked the idea of taking the money we earn and giving it to the grunts."

Leonard didn't say anything at first because he was the junior member of the group, but he wasn't at all sure he agreed with his partners' philosophies. Finally, he spoke up. "Are we sure this is fair?" he asked of his partners.

The doctors looked at him as if he had just told them he had leprosy. It was Dr. Avalon who answered him. "Leonard, you're new to the group so you don't know how it is. If you give the grunts an inch, they'll take a mile, so to speak. We pay them and they work. That's all the benefits they're due."

"But if the law requires that we provide a retirement plan for them and we have the money, isn't it wrong not to do it?"

"Are you kidding?" Dr. Avalon replied. "Listen, if those bleeding hearts in Washington thought they could get away with it, they would take every nickel we have and give it to people who want to sit home and collect welfare while we work. We have to obey the law, but we don't have to be stupid."

Leonard went home that evening discouraged with himself. He had a bad feeling about the group's decision to hold the employees' contributions to the absolute minimum. He knew he had caved in to peer pressure and voted for a plan that he didn't fully agree with.

Time passed, and as with most things the guilt and conviction faded until Leonard had virtually forgotten the incident. A little over a year later, the company where his father had worked for nearly 30 years was sold to a large conglomerate. Almost immediately the new management began to replace the older management personnel with members of their own team.

Leonard's father, who was in his sixties, was eventually pressured to retire from the company. Over the years that he had worked for the previous employer he had contributed to the retirement plan, which was based on a ratio of earnings. His total retirement income, including Social Security, was less than $800 a month. He was faced with an income reduction of nearly 50 percent in a matter of a few months and was forced to seek other employment because he could not make such a drastic adjustment in so short a time.

In a graphic way, Leonard came face to face with a situation that closely paralleled the choice he had supported within his medical practice, and this one involved his own family. His father held no bitterness, but Leonard felt a lot of guilt over his earlier decision about the P.A.'s retirement plan.

Within two years the retirement laws were revised again to reduce the inequities created by groups like Leonard's medical association. Unfortunately, the group elected to dissolve their group retirement plan and go to individual plans rather than include the employees in equitable sharing. Leonard left the group and formed one of his own design, which included a fair ratio of profits going to every member of the organization.

21

Implementing God's Plan

There is an old cliché: "Information without application leads to frustration." At this point you have a large amount of new information to sift through and evaluate. Now you must decide what God wants you to do with it. I believe that the responses to the information presented can be divided into three general groups.

One group will conclude that what I have presented is illogical, impossible, or inapplicable. They will put down this book and be unchanged; and, except for a periodic twinge of conscience when they fire someone or lie to get a sale, they will continue to be unchanged.

The second group will accept the principles at face value and will have an earnest desire to apply God's Word to their lives in every area, including business. But as the Lord said, *"The deceitfulness of riches choke the word, and it becomes unfruitful"* (Matthew 13:22). Actually this group will be the most frustrated, because to know the truth and not do it is usually worse than totally ignoring it (at least in this lifetime).

It seems easy enough to apply God's Word in the confines of your office or study. After all, it is a good thing to decide to tithe from your business or to make a commitment to include your spouse in business decisions. But it is quite another thing entirely to allow Christ to govern your thoughts and actions on a day-in and day-out basis.

It is the third group that keeps me going. These are the doers of God's Word. If you are among this group, you have already concluded that God wants you to do something, and you have determined to do it. The remainder of this book is written exclusively to you, because it contains some practical ideas for implementing God's plan in your business.

But, first, to those who will put down this or any other book on biblical principles and remain unchanged, let me share one parting word.

You at least need to accept at face value the words of Jesus in Matthew 16:24–26: *"If anyone wishes to come after Me, let him deny himself, and take up his cross, and follow Me. For whoever wishes to save his life shall lose it; but whoever loses his life for My sake shall find it. For what will a man be profited, if he gains the whole world, and forfeits his soul? Or what will a man give in exchange for his soul?"*

He continued this instruction in chapter 19 in response to a young man who had kept all the religious laws, yet still felt something lacking in his life: *"If you wish to be complete, go and sell your possessions and give to the poor, and you shall have treasure in heaven; and come, follow Me."* But when the young man heard this statement, he went away grieved; for he was one who owned much property. And Jesus said to His disciples, *"Truly I say to you, it is hard for a rich man to enter the kingdom of heaven."*

I once heard a reporter ask Senator Harold Hughes how he could be sure that he was born again. Senator Hughes certainly had been changed by something; that was evident. He responded by saying, "All I can tell you, friend, is, *'Once I was blind, and now I can see.'*"

If you don't have that same assurance in your life, you need to consider what the apostle Paul said in Romans: *"If you confess with your mouth Jesus as Lord, and believe in your heart that God raised Him from the dead, you shall be saved; for with the heart man believes, resulting in righteousness, and with the mouth he confesses, resulting in salvation"* (Romans 10:9–10).

Don't waste your whole life thinking that somehow you can work your way into God's kingdom; you cannot. The only path is the same one trod by every believer since time began: You must surrender your life to the Lord and allow the Holy Spirit to direct and control your life.

YOU CAN'T DO EVERYTHING

Perhaps the easiest way to frustrate yourself and everyone else around you is to try to implement the material from this book in one month. That would be like trying to live the mature Christian life one day after salvation—it just won't happen. We all grow and mature in a progressive manner.

Even the apostle Paul spent his early Christian years in the wilderness, learning about his Lord. The more we listen to God's voice, the easier it is to recognize it when He speaks to us. That's an example of the "assimilation syndrome."

Your mind will grasp the things you are interested in and filter out those you do not care about. The more you attune yourself to God's way, the more He will be able to show you. I suggest that you begin by focusing on one specific area that you see as the key one in your life right now. It may be developing good hiring policies in your business to put people in jobs for which they are well suited. Or it may be a concentrated effort to treat those around you as spiritual equals, even though they may be several management levels below you.

There are some things you can do immediately and some things you cannot do. For example, if you work in a unionized company you will not be able to implement a plan to compensate employees according to their needs, because union rules and contracts prohibit employers from pay discrimination within the same job classifications.

Rather than fighting that system, start where you can. Set up a benevolence fund, using your own money and perhaps employee funds too. Then begin to educate your people with the fact that you sincerely care about their needs and would like to help wherever possible. Can you imagine a union trying to convince its members that this is not a good idea?

If you don't have good communications with your spouse, I wouldn't recommend starting with a detailed discussion of business problems. Instead, start with attending a good conference on communications, such as a marriage encounter weekend offered by Campus Crusade for Christ. The point is to start where you are, not where you would like to be in a year or two. But if you never start, you'll be in exactly the same condition a year from now.

START WITH YOUR OWN LIFE

The one thing the union, an unsaved spouse, an uncooperative management, or a lack of available resources cannot prohibit you from doing is applying biblical principles to your own life. Decide that you're going to love the people around you, even those you don't particularly like — or, perhaps especially those you don't like.

If you have the tendency to lock yourself away in an ivory tower and look down on the masses of workers below, perhaps you need to consider swapping offices with the janitor so you can mingle with those masses. A move like that will certainly convince those around you that something unusual has happened in your life! They may think it's a midlife crisis, but if you don't show up wearing a black leather jacket and riding a motorcycle, they probably will realize something else is going on!

START A DEVOTION TIME IN YOUR BUSINESS

Almost any business owner can implement a periodic time for devotions. As of this writing that's still legal, as long as it is optional. Those who wish to continue working during that time should be free to do so. I would recommend bringing in speakers from outside the company to address critical subjects, such as drugs, child rearing, husband-wife communications, or budgeting.

Topics like those touch virtually everyone, and if you select your speakers from those with proven track records in their fields, you'll be helping your employees. Those who are helped will share with others around them, and the Lord's blessings will increase.

BE A WITNESS

You may want to start witnessing to your employees, creditors, and customers. But until you are sure that you treat employees with love, pay your creditors on time, and provide a good product to your customers, I recommend that your witness be limited to changes in your own life. Once you demonstrate that Christianity works in your own life, then you may want to consider trying some of the more overt ways of sharing that others have found effective. Not every idea for witnessing will fit any one person or business, but at least one will.

Stanley Tamm of U.S. Plastics in Lima, Ohio, whom I mentioned in an earlier chapter, once painted a sign on the side of his building facing the interstate that says: "God Loves You and We Do Too." When I first heard about this as a young Christian in business I thought, *That's okay for him, but what will it accomplish? I mean, after all, how many people get saved by reading the side of your building?* Then I heard Stanley share the dozens of testimonies of men who saw the sign, stopped in, and found the Lord. I decided, if it works, it works!

The Edwards Baking Company in Atlanta stamps Bible verses into the aluminum pie pans holding its delicious products. I met a businessman who was saved after reading one such pie pan in his kitchen one evening. His wife, who was a Christian, had just died after a long illness. The day of her passing she had ordered an Edwards pie and left it in the refrigerator for her husband. Just before she died she told him, "I left a surprise for you in the refrigerator, Honey. Read it carefully."

The verse stamped into the pie pan was Romans 8:28: *"And we know that God causes all things to work together for good to those who love God, to those who are called according to His purpose."*

A chemical company in Birmingham, Alabama, puts a Bible tract in every box of materials it ships. The president of the company questioned how effective this practice was, since he rarely heard from anyone who had read the material. So he instructed his shipping department to stop. Within a month he received more than a dozen letters asking if the company had been sold. Several people gave glowing testimonies of how the tracts had been used to lead fellow employees to the Lord and saying what a testimony it was to others that a successful businessman would take such a stand for the Lord.

The owner of a chain of convenience stores in the South decided to remove all cigarettes and alcohol from his stores after he became a Christian. In defiance of all the national statistics that show convenience stores cannot survive without the sale of liquor and cigarettes, his stores continue to prosper. His witness is visible even to the kids who live in the neighborhoods near his stores.

As I said before, no one can apply all the techniques that others have used in taking their stand for Jesus Christ. Find the plan that God has for your life and your business and it will work. There are approximately 250,000 businesses in America that are either owned or managed by Christians. If even 10 percent of these companies were used as tools to expand the gospel of our Lord, we would make an impact on the society around us.

To take such a stand requires a total surrender of self and a willingness to accept ridicule from those who hate the things of God. But that's really no different from the way it has always been. It's just that Christians in America today have so much more to lose.

In order to be used by God we must first be willing to die for Him. As the apostle Paul says, *"But whatever things were gain to me, those things I have counted as loss for the sake of Christ. More than that, I count all things to be loss in view of the surpassing value of knowing Christ Jesus my Lord, for whom I have suffered the loss of all things, and count them but rubbish in order that I may gain Christ"* (Philippians 3:7–8).

The real question I would ask in closing is: Do you believe that? Or do you just *say* you believe it?

Study Guide

PART 1: BUSINESS BY THE BOOK

CHAPTER 1: A RADICAL APPROACH TO BUSINESS MANAGEMENT

Summary Statement—The Bible, God's Word, gives principles of business management that lead to long-term success and stability.

Read the story on pages 3–4.

Do you think it was good "business sense" for Will to help John, his competitor?

What would you have done?

BUSINESS THEN AND NOW (PAGES 4–6)

Please complete these statements.

1. In nineteenth-century America, most businesses were privately owned _____ _____.
2. Prior to the twentieth century, business schools and courses were based on _____ _____.
3. After the Civil War, _____ assumed a stronger position in the private sector.
4. Industries such as railroads and steel began to form large _____.
5. Congress and the courts protected big business and controlled the growing organized _____ _____.
6. After World War I, the U.S. emerged as a global _____ _____.
7. Because of growing animosity between labor and management, the government assumed the role of _____.

8. After World War II, business became _____-funded rather than _____-funded.

THE BIBLICAL PERSPECTIVE ON GETTING AND SPENDING (PAGES 6–8)

Larry Burkett points out that when God's Word doesn't match our own logic, we tend to go with our logic. However, God intends that we take Scripture literally. How did Larry's car dealer friend discover that truth?

Between 1950 and 1970, what three factors combined to sound the death knell for many U.S. industries?
1.
2.
3.

What form of government allows businesses to be "privately owned but centrally controlled"?

What country continues to operate on business principles from the Bible (albeit without acknowledging the Lord)?

Look up Matthew 7:24–25. What does Jesus promise?

THE OUTLOOK TODAY (PAGES 8–9)

The Christian businessman or businesswoman faces a very unfavorable economic environment today. What is the catalyst behind most of our nation's current debt?

In what way can this economic cycle be reversed?

FOR FURTHER DISCUSSION

Can you recall making a decision that was perceived as "against the norm" but that you knew was right?

Do you tend to separate your business activities from your personal witness and ministry?

CHAPTER 2: Basic Biblical Minimums

***Summary Statement*—** As Christian businessmen and businesswomen apply basic biblical "minimums" to their business practices, they are distinguished from others in the business world.

SIX BASIC BUSINESS MINIMUMS

1. REFLECT CHRIST IN YOUR BUSINESS PRACTICES (PAGES 10–11)

Read Proverbs 3:32 and 4:24. Is it realistic to follow these admonitions today? Why or why not?

In the story of Sam and his health-care organization, Sam could have chosen *not* to repay Medicare for the unauthorized services. Yet he refused to compromise his integrity. Can you think of a similar situation that faced you? Was there a cost attached to resolving it with integrity?

Reread Luke 16:10. What are "accepted" business practices that conflict with the scriptural principle? How do you handle them?

Name as many Bible characters as you can recall who refused to sell out their integrity.

2. BE ACCOUNTABLE (PAGES 11–16)

How could surrounding yourself with those who always support your decisions become a liability?

What king drifted off course because he listened to his "advisors"? What was the result?

Read Genesis 2:24. Is the husband-wife relationship limited to non-business situations?

How can your spouse offer counsel when he or she knows little or nothing about the business?

What lessons can be learned from the story about Jackie and her husband?

How can an accountability group help? What is the alternative?

3. PROVIDE A QUALITY PRODUCT AT A FAIR PRICE (PAGES 16–17)

Value can be defined as _____.

If you accept the Bible's standards for service and products, what will the end result be?

As examples of how customers perceive value, Larry cites the doctor who switched from a fixed fee structure and the Chick-fil-A™ company, which provides a quality product. Their success shows that the best advertisement is _____ _____.

When you truly _____ others more than yourself, you want them to get the _____ _____ _____.

4. HONOR YOUR CREDITORS (PAGES 17–19)

Explain in your own words Larry's view toward businesses that delay paying suppliers. How do you feel about that issue?

_____ is a rare commodity today, especially where other people's money is concerned.

5. TREAT YOUR EMPLOYEES FAIRLY (PAGES 19–21)

The principle of fairness not only involves pay and benefits, but also _____ and _____.

How can you give the same honor and regard to all employees, regardless of their rank or station?

6. TREAT YOUR CUSTOMERS FAIRLY (PAGES 21–22)

Customers take you seriously when you give them a good _____ at a fair _____ and stand behind your _____.

Why do you think Larry's customer sought his counsel years after the sale was made?

Can you think of similar situations you have encountered that opened the door for ministry? Are there some you know you have missed?

Read Philippians 2:3. Name several ways today's business practices run opposite to Paul's admonition.

FOR FURTHER DISCUSSION

How can you justify risking a loss in profit by taking a biblical stand when you have employees depending on the success of your business?

Do you find it difficult to honor employees who seem never to be satisfied with their salaries or benefits?

CHAPTER 3: BUSINESS BONDAGE

Summary Statement—Bondage to one's business can manifest itself in many ways, but it always diminishes one's effectiveness for the Lord.

Business bondage can best be described as _____
_____.

On pages 23 and 24, Larry describes a television commercial featuring a father and his son. What symptoms of business bondage did the father display?

The resolve of many Christians to serve God breaks down when they sense that God wants them to do something that will _____ more than they are prepared to _____.

Read Luke 9:57–62. What was the young man's response when Jesus said, "Follow Me"?

What did the man mean by that?

What was Jesus' reply?

Jesus laid out a simple choice to the young man. What was it? Decide
_____
_____.

SYMPTOMS OF BUSINESS BONDAGE

SYMPTOM 1: AN AIR OF SUPERIORITY (PAGES 25–28)

What is the fallacy in the term *a self-made businessperson*?

In the stories about the businessman's outreach dinner and the man who organized the teaching conference, what surfaced as the underlying motive?

SYMPTOM 2: OVERWORK (PAGES 28–31)

Larry states that no one can maintain the correct balance between work, family, and God if he or she is regularly working more than _____ hours per week.

Read Psalm 127:2. What are the three things the psalmist says are vain to do?
   1.
   2.
   3.

What was the drastic plan Larry's pastor friend implemented to help him keep proper priorities?

In the story of the workaholic pastor, what was the church's reaction?

SYMPTOM 3: EXCESSIVE USE OF CREDIT (PAGES 31–35)

What lesson from the Great Depression have we failed to learn?

What was the commonsense principle from Proverbs 22:7 that the land syndicators and the builder ignored?

SYMPTOM 4: DISORGANIZATION (PAGES 35–37)

The Bible describes disorganization as _____.

A smart entrepreneur learns that although _____ start businesses, _____ makes them successful.

What important ingredient was lacking from Bob Gray's business as it began to grow?

SYMPTOM 5: A GET-RICH-QUICK MENTALITY (PAGES 37–39)

At what point does success in business become unscriptural?

All get-rich-quick schemes are based on _____, which has _____ _____ at its core.

Read Proverbs 28:20. How does the story of Alex's franchise business illustrate this verse?

Name the three basic errors caused by a get-rich-quick mentality.
    1.
    2.
    3.

FOR FURTHER DISCUSSION

Would you be able to sustain your business during an extended economic downturn?

Have you or a business associate ever been stung by a get-rich-quick "opportunity"?

CHAPTER 4: PERSONAL LIFESTYLE GOALS

Summary Statement—Being a good steward in business starts with personal stewardship and goal setting.

Read Luke 12:22, Hebrews 11:1, and Luke 14:28. Describe how we are to maintain a balance between faith and the need to plan.

The majority of Scripture leans heavily toward retaining _____ surpluses because of the dangers associated with _____.

Too much planning can lead to _____, and too little can lead to an unnecessary _____.

PERSONAL GOALS

1. SET UP AND MAINTAIN A PERSONAL BUDGET (PAGES 42–43).

Read Luke 16:10. It's true that the way people handle their _____ finances is usually the way they will handle their _____ finances.

Is this true in your case?

Personal budgeting is the responsibility of both _____ and _____.

2. ESTABLISH SOME SHORT-RANGE AND LONG-RANGE PERSONAL GOALS (PAGES 43–45).

Establishing personal goals involves weighing _____ as well as setting _____.

Read Matthew 23:12.

Larry says that our position in the Lord's kingdom will be _____ proportional to how we _____ ourselves in this lifetime.

The _____ believe that to follow Jesus a Christian must sell everything and become a pauper.

We find in God's Word that we are merely _____ of God's resources.

Indulgence can be defined as buying things that have little or no _____ to us.

Your goals must grow from your understanding of _____

_____ _____ _____

_____.

DEBT (PAGE 45)

Every Christian should have the goal of becoming totally

_____ _____.

LIFESTYLE (PAGES 45–46)

Describe Larry's "radical idea" from God's Word.

When asked "How much is enough?" Bernard Baruch replied, "Just a little more." What is your response?

AUTOMOBILES (PAGES 46–47)

Read Luke 12:34. If you compared the quality of your car with the quality of your giving to the Lord's work, where would you say your treasure (and therefore your heart) is?

When God answered Judy's specific prayer for a car with electrically adjusted seats, what lesson did Larry learn?

A PERSPECTIVE FOR SETTING LIFESTYLE GOALS (PAGES 47–49)

Christianity is in dire need of some affluent Christians who know how to exercise _____.

Read Matthew 6:19–21, 33. How do you lay up treasures in heaven?

What does it mean to you to seek God's kingdom in your life?

Read Matthew 7:26 and 16:26. What type of person hears the Lord's words but does not obey them?

Read Matthew 19:29–30 and 23:11–12. What does God promise to do for those who humble themselves?

FOR FURTHER DISCUSSION

Have you and your spouse set a workable budget?

In what ways does a borrower become the lender's "slave"?

CHAPTER 5: BIBLICAL BUSINESS GOALS

Summary Statement—Establishing long- and short-term goals keeps your business in line with its primary purpose.

LONG-TERM GOALS FOR A CHRISTIAN IN BUSINESS

1. FUND THE GOSPEL (PAGE 52)

Larry says the purpose of a business is to glorify God. What is the important function he mentions?

How can a Christian business practically apply Proverbs 3:9?

2. MEET NEEDS (PAGE 52)

Read 1 Timothy 5:8 and James 5:4. What is it that God requires of a Christian employer?

3. BE A DISCIPLE (PAGES 52–54)

Alfred found the secret of winning his employees to Christ. What was it?

Employees have a tendency to believe what they _____ rather than what they _____.

How did the employees help Alfred?

4. MAKE A PROFIT (PAGES 54–55)

Is there a biblical admonition against making a profit?

Do you agree or disagree with Larry's comments about profit sharing? Why or why not?

SHORT-TERM OPERATIONAL GOALS FOR A CHRISTIAN BUSINESS

SET PRIORITIES FOR THE USE OF MONEY (PAGES 56–58)

Pam's story illustrates how important it is for a company to have a viable _____ _____.

If someone is a true disciple of Jesus Christ, the evidence will be found in that person's _____ _____.

FINANCIAL PRIORITIES (PAGES 58–61)

List in order who should be paid first when things get tight:
   1.
   2.
   3.

SET PRIORITIES FOR USE OF TIME (PAGES 61–62)

Does Scripture indicate that a six-day work week is excessive?

What is your perspective of the work week? 40 hours? 60 hours? More?

Those who require employees to work long hours at high pay find that money is only a _____ _____.

SET ETHICAL PRIORITIES (PAGES 62–70)

Taxes. Read Matthew 22:21. Was Jesus' exhortation to "render to Caesar" an endorsement of Rome's sinful practices?

Fraud. Proverbs 10:9 illustrates that nothing short of _____ _____ is the minimum acceptable standard for a Christian.

Misuse of company property. Many business owners have the tendency to treat company property as their own. Name three areas in which they are tempted to misuse company property.

    1.

    2.

    3.

Confession and restitution. How did the businessman who owned the packaging company justify his dishonesty?

Where did his financial problems really begin?

FOR FURTHER DISCUSSION

What are some major long-term goals that you have for your business?

Why do you think it is easier to lie or steal than to confess and make restitution?

CHAPTER 6: KEEPING VOWS

Summary Statement—Once a vow is made, God expects you to fulfill it.

What is a vow?

A FAITHLESS SOCIETY (PAGES 72–75)

Two of the strongest vows that are being discarded today are _____ and _____.

Even God's people have lost the concept of _____ when it comes to keeping our word.

In the story about the NFL players' strike, why do you think it was so difficult for the player who called Larry to decide what his obligations were?

WHAT IS YOUR WORD WORTH? (PAGE 75)

Some of the most successful attorneys are those who can weave the most _____ _____ into a contract.

What did Larry's father do when he found out he had underbid?

A PROMISE IS A PROMISE (PAGES 75–78)

Roy was willing to lose over $200,000 rather than go back on his word. What did he learn from Proverbs 11:3?

Was Roy obligated to give the lady the $100,000?

Why do you think he did it?

GUIDELINES FOR MAKING VOWS YOU CAN KEEP (PAGES 78–81)

List the five rules that will help you avoid making commitments you may later regret.

1.
2.
3.
4.
5.

FOR FURTHER DISCUSSION

What has contributed to our society's "vow-breaking" mind-set?

Read 2 Chronicles 16:9. Can you give testimony to God's strong support?

CHAPTER 7: THE BENEFITS OF COUNSEL

Summary Statement—It is important to seek godly counsel with a right motive.

Read Proverbs 15:22. Christians should weigh all counsel against
_____ _____.

CONSIDERATIONS IN ASKING ADVICE

1. AM I LOOKING FOR SOMEONE ELSE TO MAKE MY DECISIONS FOR ME? (PAGES 82–84)

The role of a counselor is to act as an _____
_____.

When Cal came to Larry for advice about the sale of his company, did Larry tell him what to do?

What did Larry do?

Who had given Cal the correct advice all along?

In what ways does Colossians 3:17 help a Christian maintain a right perspective in decision making?

2. AM I JUST SHOPPING FOR RATIONALIZATIONS? (PAGES 84–85)

What is the fallacy in thinking that our giving obligates God to prosper us?

3. AM I LOOKING FOR A MIRACLE OR A HANDOUT? (PAGES 85–87)

Have you known of similar situations to those Larry describes with the woman in the trucking business and the son-in-law's business venture? What was the outcome?

4. DO I GENUINELY WANT HONEST COUNSEL BEFORE MAKING A DECISION? (PAGES 87–89)

On page 88 Larry tells about giving a car to a needy couple. Why was this gift a mistake in this case?

USE OF PROFESSIONAL COUNSEL (PAGES 89–90)

What is the reason some Christians seek the advice of secular counselors?

Does Larry say never to use non-Christian advisors?

FOR FURTHER DISCUSSION

Cite one or two instances in which you received good counsel that helped you make an important decision.

How important do you think it is for a counselor to have a biblical frame of reference?

CHAPTER 8: YOUR BUSINESS AND YOUR SPOUSE

Summary Statement—Good husband-wife communication is essential for good decision making.

While Gordon's idea for an integrated service was readily accepted by his customers, what was its basic flaw?

Although Gordon's wife might have failed to see this flaw also, why was it still important that he consult her?

THE NEED FOR ACCOUNTABILITY (PAGES 93–97)

Name two excuses some spouses give for not wanting to be involved in business decisions.

    1.
    2.

Why does a husband-wife team make better decisions?

Why is it that entrepreneurs tend to avoid seeking counsel?

The unwillingness of individuals to be accountable to their spouses makes them vulnerable to their _____.

Read 1 Peter 3:7. What does "fellow heir" mean in the context of a marriage?

In the story of Dave and Michelle, Larry ignored Judy's hesitation about this couple. What should Larry have done initially?

Name two ingredients essential to husband-wife accountability.
    1.
    2.

SET ASIDE TIME TO TALK (PAGES 97–98)

When is a good time to discuss daily business events with your spouse?

How does Matthew 6:21 apply to time spent with your spouse?

WORKING TOGETHER IN BUSINESS (PAGES 98–100)

When spouses work together in the same business, clearly defining _____ is difficult but absolutely essential.

In the story of Carlton and Paula, what steps could they have taken to make their business relationship function more smoothly?

FOR FURTHER DISCUSSION

In what practical ways can you include your spouse in decision making?

If you were to die suddenly, would your spouse know enough about your business to make wise decisions concerning it?

PART 2: CRITICAL POLICY DECISIONS

CHAPTER 9: LEADERSHIP: THE FOUNDATION FOR ALL YOUR DECISIONS

Summary Statement—A leader's attitudes and out-look—toward self, other people, and God—will affect every policy decision.

KNOW YOUR PERSONAL(ITY) ASSETS AND LIABILITIES (PAGES 103–105)

At this point what do you consider your leadership strengths?

At this point what do you consider your leadership weaknesses?

PROMOTE RESPECT AND DEVELOP TRUST (PAGES 105–106)

One way to ensure a good working environment and even improve the bottom line is to display and encourage _____ for others.

Identify some ways that you personally show respect for others.

Name ways that your organization enhances teamwork and acknowledges that personality differences are assets.

COMMUNICATE, COMMUNICATE, COMMUNICATE (PAGES 107–108)

When was the last time your company reviewed how policies are coordinated among various departments?

Can you think of ways to improve the policies (or to implement some if they have been overlooked)?

Are you aware of how you handle bad news from employees?

Do you have an informal means of getting feedback? What is it?

INVEST IN TRAINING (PAGES 108–109)
Does your company currently invest in training?

List three ways your company can better train employees.
 1.
 2.
 3.

HAVE A CLEAR VISION FOR YOUR BUSINESS (PAGES 109–110)
Summarize your company's mission statement.

If you don't have a mission statement, identify key elements that need to be included in one.

Has there been a major shift in your vision? What were the results?

Read Matthew 5:16. How can you let your light shine a bit brighter?

FOR FURTHER DISCUSSION
Think of ways that you can minimize your weaknesses and maximize your strengths.

If your company has a limited budget at present for training, what are some creative means of low-cost (or no-cost) training that can be implemented?

CHAPTER 10: HIRING DECISIONS

Summary Statement—Establishing a reasonable hiring policy helps you match the right people to the right job.

STEPS IN HIRING EMPLOYEES

1. DEFINE THE JOB CLEARLY (PAGES 112–113)

Every job is a combination of _____ _____ that must be done on a regular basis. In order to hire the right person for a job, it is necessary that the job be _____ _____.

2. HIRE THE BEST PERSON FOR THE JOB (PAGE 113)

Read Proverbs 22:29. What is the result of hiring the best person for the job?

3. MATCH THE PERSON TO THE JOB (PAGES 113–117)

Name the four sets of personality types discussed:

     a. _____ versus _____
     b. _____ versus _____
     c. _____ versus _____
     d. _____ versus _____

Knowing how various _____ interact is essential to organizing a productive and efficient company.

4. MAKE HIRING POLICY DECISIONS (PAGES 117–120)

Explain how the principle of "unequally yoked" (2 Corinthians 6:14) does not apply to the employer-employee relationship.

Read Proverbs 31. Describe some of the woman's activities that go beyond normal household duties.

Does Titus 2:4–5 prohibit women from working outside the home? What was Paul saying?

5. ESTABLISH A TRIAL PERIOD (PAGES 120–121)

Larry encourages the establishment of a _____-day trial period for new employees.

FOR FURTHER DISCUSSION

Have you ever held a position for which you really were not suited?

What other factors besides personality and skill level should be considered in hiring?

What does Larry say is a key part of any human resources program?

CHAPTER 11: FIRING DECISIONS

Summary Statement—Established guidelines tempered with compassion make the employee dismissal process clear and fair.

Read Luke 11:42. Malcolm's manager, Stu, hit the nail on the head when he described Malcolm's brand of Christianity, saying it was based on _____, not _____.

In the end, Malcolm learned an important lesson: _____ are more important than profits.

BIBLICAL PRINCIPLES FOR FIRING (PAGES 128–129)

Name the prerequisites a Christian owner or manager must meet before even considering dismissing an employee.

1.
2.

3.
4.
5.

THE NEED TO COMMUNICATE (PAGES 129–132)

It is important that an employer not allow _____ to build up until they become intolerable.

Which of the five prerequisites listed did Peter fail to meet when he hired Brad as his field supervisor?

Give two references from Proverbs that provide a balance when you need to confront a problem.

FOR FURTHER DISCUSSION

Have you ever had to fire an employee? What did you learn from that experience?

Which prerequisites needed more emphasis?

CHAPTER 12: JUSTIFICATION FOR DISMISSAL

Summary Statement— Allowing problem employees to continue uncorrected encourages others to follow their example.

REASONS FOR DISMISSAL (PAGE 133–142)

List four biblically justifiable reasons for dismissing an employee.
1.
2.
3.
4.

Read Matthew 9:13. The Lord tells us that we should always lean more toward _____ than toward seeking _____.

Name three basic principles that comprise a Christian work ethic.
    1.
    2.
    3.

Before dismissing an employee for incompetence, first attempt to determine if he or she is _____.

STEPS TO DISMISSAL (PAGES 142–143)

List three essential steps to take prior to dismissing any employee.
    1.
    2.
    3.

REASONS TO ABORT A DISMISSAL ACTION (PAGES 143–146)

List four reasons why it may be necessary to reverse a decision to dismiss an employee.
    1.
    2.
    3.
    4.

FOR FURTHER DISCUSSION

Have you discovered a method for dealing with "subtle" disobedience?

What are possible "outside factors" that a Christian employer should consider before firing an employee?

CHAPTER 13: Management Selection Decisions

Summary Statement—Determining basic standards for managers makes the hiring of new managers or promotion of employees to management positions easier.

SHOULD ALL MANAGERS BE CHRISTIANS? (PAGE 149)

How does Larry answer this question about the need for all managers to be Christians?

LIFESTYLE CRITERIA FOR MANAGERS (PAGES 149–153)

In what ways can you apply 1 Timothy 3:1–3 to managers in a business?

List three important lifestyle traits to look for in a manager.
1.
2.
3.

What is the primary lesson you learned from the story of Pat and the loss of Victor's printing business?

Like Janet, have you ever been confronted with a manager who was not respectable? How did the situation work out for you?

WHAT TO DO WHEN A MANAGER REBELS (PAGES 153–155)

Should you handle a rebellious manager any differently from any other rebellious employee?

In the case of "Rebellious Reggie," what might have been the outcome if Andy had backed down and allowed Reggie to dress as he pleased?

HIRING WOMEN AS MANAGERS (PAGES 155–157)

Name a situation in which discrimination on the basis of sex would be legitimate.

In Larry's opinion, does the role of women in the church (1 Corinthians 14:34–35) apply to women as business managers?

FOR FURTHER DISCUSSION

How can you uphold biblical criteria when interviewing a prospective manager?

How can you structure your hiring or promoting process to avoid *de facto* discrimination?

CHAPTER 14: EMPLOYEE PAY DECISIONS

Summary Statement—The Bible speaks clearly to the issue of employee wages, but the Christian employer must seek God's wisdom to apply God's plan fairly and consistently.

What does the story of Ron and Jennifer say to the employer who says, "I know they need more, but my hands are tied by rules and regulations"?

BIBLICAL PRINCIPLES FOR PAYING EMPLOYEES (PAGES 159–160)

Read James 5:4. How does it apply to your business?

Summarize the four conclusions that the Bible teaches about paying employees.

    1.

    2.

    3.

    4.

WHAT ARE MINIMUM NEEDS? (PAGES 160–162)

Describe a simple method of determining people's minimum needs.

SITUATIONAL ECONOMICS (PAGES 162–166)

Give two reasons why a company might be tempted to replace older, long-term employees.

    1.

    2.

Larry says that in the ethics of a Christian, _____ and _____ play predominant roles.

THE POWER OF REWARD (PAGES 166–167)

Most people in authority are "High D" personalities who are quick to _____ but slow to _____ the work of their subordinates.

What characteristics made Mr. Rhone a good boss?

REWARDING DIFFERENT ABILITIES (PAGES 167–170)

What does *The Peter Principle* state?

How did Adam Yates apply the principle "Pay well for a quality job"?

REWARD LOYALTY (PAGES 170–172)

What is loyalty?

Name characters in the Bible who were rewarded by God for their loyalty.

FOR FURTHER DISCUSSION

What is your system for determining an employee's salary?

How do you think your secretary (or assistant) would rate you on a scale of 1 to 10, with 1 meaning "never praises" and 10 meaning "always praises"?

CHAPTER 15: BORROWING DECISIONS

Summary Statement—While not prohibiting borrowing, Scripture gives warnings about its dangers.

Name two ways the government borrows money that aren't reflected in the category of "national debt."

1.
2.

IS BORROWING UNSCRIPTURAL? (PAGES 174–176)

List several inherent dangers caused by borrowing.

What Scripture reference is cited by "absolutists" who believe all borrowing is wrong?

What might be a literal interpretation of the verse (in context)?

SCRIPTURAL PRINCIPLES FOR BORROWING (PAGES 176–184)

Is the practice of borrowing ever encouraged in the Bible?

List the three fundamental scriptural principles related to borrowing.
1.
2.
3.

Define *surety*.

What principle did Edgar ignore in building his land development business?

THE BOTTOM LINE COMMANDMENT

REPAY WHAT YOU OWE (PAGES 184–187)

What does Psalm 37:21 say about the person who does not repay his debts?

The lender has an implied right to _____ the faithless borrower.

THE PERILS OF CREDIT (PAGES 187–191)

List the three potential perils that the use of credit brings.
1.
2.
3.

FOR FURTHER DISCUSSION

How is it possible to borrow money yet not go surety?

Larry states that in most cases borrowing is a symptom rather than a problem. A symptom of what?

CHAPTER 16: LENDING DECISIONS

Summary Statement — Almost any business is a lender, and lending and collecting practices should follow biblical guidelines.

TO WHOM DO YOU EXTEND CREDIT? (PAGES 192–193)

Is it wrong for you to extend credit if you yourself don't practice borrowing?

Regarding the use of credit cards, what is the merchant's responsibility?

WHAT HAPPENS WHEN PEOPLE DON'T PAY? (PAGES 193–195)

State the one important rule to follow when extending credit.

Why is the ability of a Christian lender to collect a delinquent debt greatly curtailed?

COLLECTION CONSIDERATIONS (PAGES 195–199)

Name three considerations you must make when collecting a debt.
1.
2.
3.

Before turning a delinquent account over to a collection agency, what does Larry suggest doing?

SUING TO COLLECT (PAGES 199–201)

When does Scripture allow an individual Christian to sue another Christian for payment?
Explain why a Christian can sue a "Christian" corporation.

SETTLE OUT OF COURT, IF POSSIBLE (PAGES 201–208)

What is a better way to settle disputes than going to court with another believer?

Read the sections listed below and then complete the statement that follows.

> **What About When You Are Sued? (pages 202–204)**
> **Handling Lawsuits Against You (pages 204–205)**
> **Defense in Court (pages 205–208)**

Any Christian who is faced with a lawsuit has a _____ and
_____ right to bring the truth to light.

FOR FURTHER DISCUSSION

If you were to employ a collection agency to handle your delinquent accounts, what guidelines would you give it to follow?

What is your personal view on lawsuits and countersuits?

CHAPTER 17: DISCOUNTING DECISIONS

Summary Statement—All discounting decisions revolve around the biblical standard of "Do unto others as you would have them do unto you."

Read Proverbs 11:1. Explain how Chuck the car salesman used "differing weights" in his sales negotiations.

ARE PRICE DIFFERENCES HONEST? (PAGES 210–212)

Name at least one practice that Mexican street merchants and American merchants have in common.

How can Matthew 22:39 be practically applied to price negotiations?

WHAT PRICE DIFFERENCES ARE LEGITIMATE? (PAGES 212–213)

List three ethical reasons why a merchant might charge differing prices for the same item.

1.
2.
3.

A FAIR PRICE STANDARD (PAGES 213–216)

What was J. C. Penney's pricing policy?

Read Proverbs 15:6. How does that apply in the story of Harry and Mark's electronics business?

FOR FURTHER DISCUSSION

Does your business have a clear and consistent discounting policy?

What might have been some of Mark's rationale for wanting to accept Mr. Shadburn's initial offer?

PART 3: YOUR BUSINESS AND YOUR LIFE

CHAPTER 18: CORPORATIONS AND PARTNERSHIPS

Summary Statement—Proper motives and obedience to God's Word are essential when structuring your business.

IS IT LEGITIMATE TO INCORPORATE? (PAGES 219–221)

When is the use of the corporate shield legitimate?

ARE PARTNERSHIPS SCRIPTURAL? (PAGES 221–223)

Read 2 Corinthians 6:14. Explain the idea of being bound together ("yoked").

THE BURDEN OF AN UNEQUAL YOKE (PAGES 223–226)

What would constitute an "unequal yoke"?

Should Dale have even considered joining the OB-GYN practice?

WHAT ABOUT EXISTING PARTNERSHIPS? (PAGE 226)

In light of 1 Corinthians 7:10–15, Christians should seek to _____ in a partnership unless the relationship forces them to _____ their spiritual convictions.

Why should you view a partnership differently if the unsaved partner is your father or mother?

GUIDELINES FOR ASSESSING A PARTNERSHIP (PAGES 226–230)

Name the two fundamental questions that any Christian who is considering joining a partnership should ask.

1.
2.

The story of Gene and Richard points out that there should be only _____ person in charge.

Although partnerships between believers are permitted, are such partnerships necessarily profitable?

LAYING THE GROUNDWORK FOR A SUCCESSFUL PARTNERSHIP (PAGES 230–231)

Larry counsels anyone to approach a potential partnership with a high degree of _____.

What else does he advise?

ARE LIMITED PARTNERSHIPS REALLY PARTNERSHIPS? (PAGE 231)

Does a limited partnership constitute a "yoke"?

What caution does Larry give regarding limited partnerships?

EMPLOYEE-EMPLOYER RELATIONSHIP (PAGES 231–232)

Explain why working for an unsaved employer does not cause the employee to be "unequally yoked."

IS STOCK OWNERSHIP A YOKE? (PAGE 232)

How might a share-holding arrangement comprise a yoke?

FOR FURTHER DISCUSSION

In the story of Quincy the tool designer, if the owner had not filed for bankruptcy, would Quincy have a scriptural basis for suing the company for his losses?

Why is it important that a business have one ultimate authority?

CHAPTER 19: BUSINESS TITHING

Summary Statement—The principle of tithing can be applied to businesses as well as individuals.

Most Old Testament Scriptures about giving deal with _____ income.

IS THE PRINCIPLE OF TITHING APPLICABLE TO CHRISTIANS? (PAGES 233–234)

What is wrong with the argument that the tithe is part of the Old Testament law?

SHOULD I TITHE FROM MY NET OR MY GROSS? (PAGES 234–238)

Read Proverbs 3:9. What does "the first" of all your produce mean?

How is it possible for a business to tithe from its gross income in our day?

HOW CAN I GIVE NONCASH ASSETS? (PAGES 238–239)

Name two ways to give when your "increase" is mostly noncash assets.

    1.

    2.

WHAT ABOUT AFTER-DEATH BEQUESTS? (PAGE 240)

Why does Larry recommend giving during one's lifetime rather than making after-death bequests?

FOR FURTHER DISCUSSION

Could giving to worthy secular causes be included in your business "tithe"?

Read Proverbs 11:25. How would you apply that to your own business practices?

CHAPTER 20: RETIREMENT DECISIONS

Summary Statement—Biblical "retirement" may mean a change in work load, not a cessation from work and ministry.

IS RETIREMENT SCRIPTURAL? (PAGES 241–243)

How many references to retirement are found in the Bible?

Read Proverbs 6:6–8. What are the "harvest years" for most individuals?

It is entirely _____ to lay aside some of the surplus for our later years.

According to Larry, at what point does good planning become hoarding?

What did the Harvard study reveal about retirement and life span?

SHOULD YOU SELL YOUR BUSINESS? (PAGES 244–246)

Explain why a Christian business owner does not necessarily have the right to sell out to non-Christians.

What was the bottom-line result of Cliff's selling his company?

EMPLOYEE RETIREMENT BENEFITS (PAGES 246–249)

How would you apply Philippians 2:3 to the issue of employee retirement benefits?

FOR FURTHER DISCUSSION

What are your plans for your "retirement years"?

Are you satisfied that you are doing all you can for your employees' retirement needs?

CHAPTER 21: IMPLEMENTING GOD'S PLAN

Summary Statement—When making changes in your business practices, begin with yourself and then move on to other aspects of your business.

Larry concedes that his readers will probably be in one of three groups. In which group do you find yourself?

YOU CAN'T DO EVERYTHING (PAGES 251–252)

Of all the information presented in this book, how does Larry suggest you begin applying it?

START WITH YOUR OWN LIFE (PAGES 252–253)

If you find yourself isolated in an "ivory tower," what radical step does Larry suggest you take?

START A DEVOTION TIME IN YOUR BUSINESS (PAGE 253)

What are some topics you could cover in optional devotional times?

BE A WITNESS (PAGES 253–254)

List ways you could witness overtly through your particular line of business.

FOR FURTHER DISCUSSION

Read Philippians 3:7–8. Do you believe it, or do you just *say* you believe it?

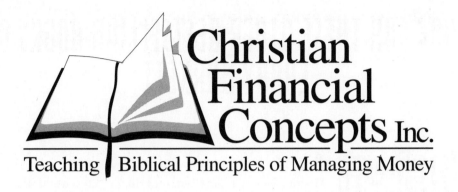

Christian Financial Concepts Inc.

Teaching | Biblical Principles of Managing Money

Larry Burkett, founder and president of Christian Financial Concepts, is the best-selling author of more than 50 books on business and personal finances. He also hosts two of CFC's four radio programs broadcast on hundreds of stations worldwide.

Larry earned B.S. degrees in marketing and in finance, and recently an Honorary Doctorate in Economics was conferred by Southwest Baptist University. For several years Larry served as a manager in the space program at Cape Canaveral, Florida. He also was vice president of an electronics manufacturing firm and marketing manager in the aerospace industry. His business experience and solid understanding of God's Word enable Larry to give practical financial advice to families, churches, and businesses.

Founded in 1976, Christian Financial Concepts is a nonprofit, nondenominational ministry dedicated to helping God's people gain a clear understanding of how to manage their money according to scriptural principles. Although practical assistance is provided on many levels, the purpose of CFC is simply to bring glory to God by freeing His people from financial bondage so they may serve Him to their utmost.

Larry and his wife, Judy, reside in Gainesville, Georgia. They have four children and seven grandchildren.

Visit CFC's Internet site at **www. cfcministry.org** or write to the address below for further information.

Christian Financial Concepts, Inc.
PO Box 2377
Gainesville, GA 30503-2377

LOOK FOR THESE OTHER BESTSELLING BOOKS BY LARRY BURKETT

The Illuminati
A Novel

Financial analyst Larry Burkett brings to life a world whose imminent economic collapse creates the ideal circumstances for a deadly secret organization called the Illuminati to come to power.

0-7852-7529-0 • Mass Market Paperback • 384 pages

The THOR Conspiracy
The Seventy-Hour Countdown to Disaster

This number one bestseller revolves around an EPA executive who, after discovering that the United States government itself blasted the hole in the ozone layer during rogue testing in the 1960s, ends up running for his life. He then must find the one man who can corroborate his information and become an international hero. If he fails, he may end up dead, allowing America's tyrannical government to continue its path to global destruction.

0-7852-7200-3 • Trade Paperback • 336 pages
0-8407-7801-5 • Hardcover